BRUCE

FLASHING METAL WITH IRON MAIDEN AND FLYING SOLO

DICKINSON

JOE SHOOMAN

Published in 2007 by
INDEPENDENT MUSIC PRESS
Independent Music Press is an imprint of I.M. P. Publishing Limited
This Work is Copyright © I. M. P. Publishing Ltd 2006

Bruce Dickinson: Flashing Metal With Iron Maiden And Flying Solo
by Joe Shooman

British Library Cataloguing-in-Publication Data.
A catalogue for this book is available from The British Library.
ISBN: 0-9552822-4-1 and 978-0-9552822-4-9

Cover Design by Fresh Lemon.
Edited by Martin Roach.

Printed in the UK.

Independent Music Press
P.O. Box 69,
Church Stretton, Shropshire
SY6 6WZ
Visit us on the web at: www.impbooks.com
and www.myspace.com/independentmusicpress
For a free catalogue, e-mail us at: info@impbooks.com
Fax: 01694 720049

Bruce Dickinson

Flashing Metal With Iron Maiden

And Flying Solo

by Joe Shooman

Independent Music Press

contents

acknowledgements

My thanks to everybody who agreed to share their thoughts on Bruce for this book, and certain people who declined to be credited but know who they are. Thanks massively, that was well beyond any reasonable call of duty and I am extraordinarily grateful.

Massive thanks also to interviewees, in alphabetical order: Chris Dale; Alex Elena; Jack Endino; Rob Grain (and the estate of Paul Samson); Robin Guy; Jennie Halsall; Steve Jones; Dean Karr; Neal Kay; Bill Liesegang; John McCoy; Tony Newton; Keith Olsen; Tom Parker; Tony Platt; Dave Pybus; Stuart Smith; Thunderstick; Bernie Torme; Chris Tsangarides; John Tucker; Joakim Stabel.

A huge thank you also to the venerable Spencer Leigh of the BBC and the legendary Henrik Johansson and Matthias Reinholdsson of www.bookofhours.net for making their archives available for this project. Sherry and cake all round, chaps. Thanks also to Kenn Taylor, for his work on the discography and transcriptions, and to Jon Hall for the transcriptions and the whisky. That I bought him.

There are several people who pointed me in the right direction and were happy to chew the fat on many occasions, thank you for the support to Tank Ernst; Dave Ling; Joel McIver; Raziq Rauf; Karen Toftera and, as ever, the Independent Music Press team and all Shoomans past, present and future.

Special thanks to Tony Coates.

Joe Shooman, March 12, 2007.

introduction

There are many words to describe Bruce Dickinson – and some of them are, happily, printable.[1] What is beyond doubt, however, is that to have a thirty year career at the top of the music industry takes a character of certain qualities; in an unpredictable business, a massive amount of self-belief, passion, hard work, good decision-making and good luck, is necessary to not only consolidate but *thrive*.

His trademark operatic vocals are as much a part of British culture as is making a cup of tea in the advertisement breaks of *Coronation Street*, and as the singer in multi-million-selling heavy metal heroes, Iron Maiden, Dickinson has toured the world countless times, performing to many generations of rampant and roaring metal fans.

But Bruce Dickinson is far, far more than just a spandex-panted screamer, hammering at the skies with those remarkable vocal chords; his interests and constant aversion to any form of standing still – physically, and mentally – has seen him don many different guises. He's been a competition foil fencer to European standard; a best-selling fiction author; a radio DJ; he's had a more than acceptable solo career in music; been both a television presenter and actor; he has a commercial pilot's licence; and Dickinson also stands alone amongst the metal fraternity as the only individual to have piloted British nationals home from a rather dodgy international conflict. Indulging in flights of fancy and of mercy at equal turn, this history graduate is constantly on the move, changing heads as the situation demands from one moment to another – like some sort of heavy metal Worzel Gummidge.

Iron Maiden's immense success is, of course, undeniable, and without Maiden this book would not exist. But Maiden have existed, if not thrived, without Bruce, and Bruce has clearly existed, and certainly thrived, without Maiden. That the two go together like nitro and glycerine is merely a happy quirk of fate.

This is not the story of Iron Maiden, then, but a look at the activities of an artist whose words and deeds span three decades of flux. As is customary in these situations, there's only one place to start, and that is at the beginning.

chapter one:
History

1958 was a year where the world was realigning itself somewhat after the ravages of the Second World War. Over in America, President Dwight D. Eisenhower – in response to the previous year's launch of the Sputnik satellite by the Soviet Union – approved the launch of his country's first earth orbiting satellite, *Explorer One*. Subsequently, there was established the National Aeronautics and Space Administration (NASA) with a brief to both protect the United States and to explore space. Gripped in the midst of a Cold War of mistrust between former allies, both sides were mutually awed by the literally world-shattering power each country's nuclear arsenal possessed, and so the battle was being held in other arenas – the space race was well and truly on between the two conflicting ideologies.

The Americans were, with some trepidation, slowly moving away from the strongest aspects of the McCarthyist persecution of 'disloyal' citizens suspected of having communist tendencies by the late 1950s; 1958 also saw a landmark legal decision where the Supreme Court ruled that denying the artist Rockwell Kent his passport after he refused to sign an anti-communist document was unconstitutional. During the same year, a law graduate and rebel named Fidel Castro began first mobilising then leading an ultimately successful revolution against the Cuban regime of General Fulgenico Batista, whilst in China, Chairman Mao instigated the Great Leap Forward – a programme of accelerated, communal reforms to increase production and therefore attempt to technologise that huge country. It was, politically, twelve months that had great resonance, and many of its ripples are still being felt to this day.

Buddies of the Yanks, over in the good old UK, the Brits were not to be left out of all the sabre-rattling going on – but it was rather more mundane – and quintessentially British in tone. In response to Iceland expanding its fishing waters to twelve nautical miles from its coast, the UK decreed that its trawlers would fish said waters under the protection of its warships. After some minor skirmishes, the Brits yielded to the Viking descendants, although there were some grumbles, and gruntles being dissed, no doubt, amongst the queues at fish and chip[2] shops throughout the Sceptred Isle. The UK-US Mutual Defence Agreement was signed the same year by Tory Prime Minister Harold Macmillan, enabling the sharing of classified information between the two countries on nuclear activities and weapons development. Over in the middle east, the Iraqi monarchy was overthrown and the country declared a republic, prompting great fears of instability in the region.

Sports-wise, the football World Cup of that year was held in Sweden, yet to come into its own as the flat-packed heaven for cavernous furniture megastores that sell tables and cupboards called things like George, Bungle and Zippy. England's team of the time, managed by Walter Winterbottom, were drawn in a tough group alongside Austria, Russia and eventual winners Brazil.[3] It was the first time that the awesome talent of a seventeen year old genius called Pelé was introduced to the world, scoring, let's face it, a downright fluky winner against a tremendous Wales side in the quarter finals – his first World Cup goal.

This was the first time that the tournament had been televised worldwide, a measure of both the sport's popularity and the growing financial post-war recovery that enabled more households than ever to own consumer goods such as black and white televisions. 1958 was the year that the final vestiges of rationing were repealed in the United Kingdom; in July, the restrictions on the purchase of coal were removed, and a generation was growing up with a wider freedom of choice than the previous twenty years had offered.

It wasn't easy street, however, by any means imaginable. It was only through immense hard work that a reasonable level of stability was possible for young couples starting out in life; none more so than in the heart of Robin Hood country, Nottinghamshire. Specifically, the Anglo-Saxon town of Worksop, situated right at the edge of Sherwood Forest, and a town bursting with history (it was mentioned for the first time in the Domesday book of 1086, although the area had been settled for many years before that). Worksop was granted Royal Charter in 1296 by the bloodthirsty Plantagenet King Edward I, the subjugator of Wales and a king who revelled in the very heavy-metal title 'The Hammer Of The Scots' for his defeat of William Wallace. The Midlands town, however, subsequently had rather a quiet existence for several hundred years, relying on its agriculture and surrounding rich landscape to supply it with the raw materials for its markets and expertise in timber-working, millinery and production of malt. The market-town remained relatively unchanged until the days of the Industrial Revolution, during which the Chesterfield Canal and the Manchester, Sheffield And Lincolnshire railways were both completed, linking the settlement with its larger and more illustrious neighbours. The factories in the bigger towns and cities, bolstered by new technology, required huge amounts of fuel to increase production – none more so than Sheffield's massive cutlery businesses. To that end, Worksop's surrounding areas began to be explored for raw materials and several coal mines opened up to feed the ever-rapacious maw of industry. With mining quickly taking over as the expanding industry of the area, the town's population grew fourfold during the course of the 19th Century.[4] Population stabilised at around 16,000 throughout the first half of the Twentieth Century, and following the decimation of the two world wars, by the end of the 1950s Worksop's recovery, borne on the need for fuel for industry and home use, was beginning to kick into action. Though the Marshall Plan, a series of economic policies implemented by the USA in the immediate post-war years, had helped to stabilise Europe a touch, times still nevertheless decreed that for a young couple starting out in life, scraping by was difficult enough without the addition of a sprog to the mix.

Therefore, when Paul Bruce Dickinson gave his first public performance ('Scream For Me, Midwife!') on August 7, 1958,[5] it was a tricky situation to reconcile for his young parents. Finances pretty much dictated that the young trio (his mother was 17, his father only a year older) moved into a house with Bruce's grandparents, a coal-face worker and a housewife/hairdresser respectively. Bruce's mother, Sonia was a talented dancer who had won a scholarship to the Royal College Of Ballet prior to falling pregnant with Bruce, which effectively ended her career; Bruce Dickinson Snr was a mechanic in the army while his wife worked part-time in a shoe shop. Thus were the first six years of Bruce's life spent, before his parents moved to the larger city of Sheffield to find better paid work, necessarily leaving him in the care of his grandparents, a time he was later to refer to as 'extremely happy'.[6]

The young Bruce was also lucky enough to be growing up during one of the most exciting times for British pop music. Following the rock 'n' roll explosion of '56, Elvis Presley had gone into the army a rebel two years later, only to come out of the experience the archetypal all-American boy and subsequently embarking on a series of ever-more emasculating dead-eyed cash-in dung-movies. Despite his own career descending into mediocrity during the early 1960s, Presley and his compatriots had already lit unquenchable fires of self-belief and rebellion amongst a generation that were truly finding their own way through life. The rock 'n' rollers had introduced black rhythm 'n' blues artists to the world, and none more so than to ported cities such as Liverpool, where the influx of American soldiers and workers brought with them vinyl gems with exotic monikers such as Muddy Waters, Howlin' Wolf and Chuck Berry. For any teenager remotely interested in music, a new record was a new event, something to be shared and played over and over again in wide-eyed wonder. Skiffle groups began to spring up all over the place, bound together by the twelve bar and the harmonica, playing covers of these exciting new sounds, and wearing slick bikers' jackets inspired by Marlon Brando's 1953 film, *The Wild One*. One of these skiffle groups was even named after the gang of that film (albeit with one differing vowel)[7] – scouse moptops The Beatles. Dickinson was later to remark that his first musical memories were dancing to 'The Twist' – Chubby Checker's version – and badgering his grandfather (then still only in his forties) to buy him The Beatles' breakthrough 1963 smash, 'She Loves You'. In an interview with Beatles expert, author and broadcaster Spencer Leigh, Dickinson would later comment that his "favourite Beatles track by a million miles is 'Let It Be'. I find it so amazingly uplifting; it's like a hymn, and I like some hymns." It would be impossible for anyone excited by music to have ignored the growing impact of the early Beatles, whose nascent career wrapped up the lip-curling, raw, sexual aggression of the rockers – honed to perfection in Beatle-land by their gruelling stints as house band in dodgy clubs in Hamburg's Reeperbahn – with a stunning, natural pop sensibility and a growing edge of innovation encouraged and developed by legendary producer George Martin. The fact that the technology on which to play their records was becoming more affordable, allied to the emergence of pirate radio stations including Radio Luxembourg, meant that the musical life of kids growing up in the 1960s was to be richer than ever before.

For Bruce – newly landed in Sheffield to move back in with his parents, and his sister Helen, born in 1963 – this musical education was bolstered by regularly watching TV show *Jukebox Jury,* and bashing away on an elderly, nigh-unplayable acoustic guitar he'd discovered; as it turned out, it had belonged to Pops Dickinson, who in a previous incarnation, according to Bruce, had appeared with his wife as a duo in a 'performing dog act'. Still, the music bug had struck; a very useful diversion on which to draw during the relative instability of changing schools from the notoriously rough Manor Top Primary, where the new kid was, as often happens, the subject of ridicule and occasional physical digs here and there, to the posher private school, Sharrow Vale. Bruce's grandfather had, however, taught him to stick up for himself, to be proud of who he was, and not to take stick from anybody: lessons that were to prove useful – and occasionally problematic – not only through his school life, but in the crazy years to follow.

During 1971, by which time Bruce had turned thirteen, his folks had, with much industry and knuckle-whitening work, begun to put themselves on a stable financial keel; a series of wrecked houses were bought cheaply by the Dickinsons before being refurbished and then sold on at a profit (ironically, particularly given events much, much later, they were so successful that they'd probably warrant their own *Property Ladder*-style TV reality show). As there was enough cash to be able to offer their lad what used to be called a 'classical education', they packed 'number one son' off to the exclusive Northamptonshire private boarding school, Oundle.

Again, it is something of an irony that Oundle by then had become as firmly an establishment experience as Eton, having been founded in 1556 by then Lord Mayor of London, Sir William Laxton. H.G. Wells even wrote a biography of one of the school's headmasters, Fredrick William Sanderson, which was published in 1924.[8] Sanderson was something of a free-thinker in his time, whose openness to individual development and firm belief in intellectual freedom was both unique and somewhat anti-establishment during his tenure that spanned the cusp of the 19th and 20th centuries.[9]

Built on tradition, discipline and traditional methods of learning, the English private school system was based on the learning of Latin, Greek, Classical history and a large and regular slice of often harsh physical exercise. And though Oundle School had a history of comparative innovation and left-field approach – and whilst the teenage Bruce welcomed the chance to be independent from his parents – he was later to admit that, within the forbidding walls of the beautiful school complex near Peterborough, bullying was rife. Once more, he didn't quite fit in – his rather itinerant school life and consequent self-reliant nature up until then saw to that – and his sharp tongue and refusal to knuckle under to the established and entirely irrational pecking order of schoolboys often meant that he was involved in several incidents where older boys from Bruce's school house, Sidney House, would use their greater physical strength for negative force. However, even during the worst beatings, Bruce's self-sufficient spirit remained unsullied, telling himself that despite the fact that he may be smaller in size and he may be copping a nasty kicking, his tormentors, however, could "beat the shit out of me, but [they were] not superior."[10]

Later, Bruce was to describe the Oundle experience as being a situation where parents sent their children to take advantage of opportunities denied to themselves, and though he enjoyed the amateur dramatics, debating and fizz of activity of the school, the place itself was "the most illiberal place on the planet. Whacko! Mass floggings over minor practical jokes."[11] As for the students, Bruce "didn't get on well with the others who, to me, were just greedy opportunists."[12]

There are many ways in life to plot revenge strategies, and it is not always the obvious and immediate kick back against the antagonists that is the most advisable, or even the most practical. So, even whilst he was picking raw egg from his bedsheets, or drying out clothes that had been sodden with water whilst he was elsewhere, the cogs and gears of the young buck's sharp brain would work overtime in designing suitably wicked comebacks, fuelled somewhat by his growing interest in the military. Dickinson was active both in the establishment of Oundle's first war-games society, and rose to a high rank in his school's cadet force. He would get his own back on the tormentors in many ways, such as setting off smoke bombs on a night-time, camping trip rampage through the schoolmasters' tents, or arranging for a significant amount of horse manure to be delivered to his housemaster. Most of the time, he got away with his pranks.

Musically, Dickinson had discovered acts like Deep Purple, whose track 'Child In Time' he had first heard blasting out from the study of a fellow pupil. Purple became his main fixation, particularly their stunning 1970 LP, *In Rock*, which was the first album he ever bought. As activities outside the confines of Oundle were restricted, and therefore the access to the local record shops was intermittent at best, music would become a powerful and magical force within the student community. Live bands also made occasional appearances at Oundle, with Van Der Graaf Generator, Wild Turkey and The Crazy World Of Arthur Brown all causing a stir amongst the school's population. Arthur Brown, along with Purple's Ian Gillan, would become a massive influence. The more music Bruce heard, the more he felt an affinity with these heroes who stood outside the establishment, touring the world living on their instruments and their wits. By 1973, Bruce had taken his first tentative steps onto the stage himself, joining Oundle's amateur dramatic society and immediately feeling at home deciphering and delivering the works of Shakespeare, including *Macbeth*. The sense of theatricality, allied to his growing, burning love for music, would inevitably mean that Bruce would be drawn to performing as a musician. Originally, it was the drums to which he was attracted – mostly because of his Purple fixation; he would later muse that his ambition was to be "Ian Paice's Left Foot", but as he couldn't afford a drum kit, the young pretender had to be content with watching the rehearsals of school bands with richer (i.e. owning a kit) but less talented (i.e. they couldn't play – and punk was still a good three years away) members. Liberating a set of bongos from Oundle's music department, Bruce began to sit in on the sessions of one particular set-up that also featured guitarist Nick Bertram and vocalist Mike Jordan. It was during a particularly horrendous run-through of The Beatles' 'Let It Be' where, hearing Jordan struggle on the high notes, Bruce joined in to bolster his bass-register bandmate's vocals. It was a moment of revelation; the soaring vocal chords of Dickinson meant that he soon abandoned the bongos in favour of fronting what can only be described as a 'band' in the loosest sense.

"So, in the back of my head I thought, 'Maybe I can do this?'" Bruce subsequently recalled, "I've done a lot of amateur dramatics as a kid, both in and out of the classroom, and I loved being onstage, although I can never be an actor because it took everything far too seriously. The problem with acting is they always have to make such a big thing out of it ... I could never hang out with these people! So the ideal thing of being a rock 'n' roll singer is combining the two elements."[13]

In subsequent rehearsals, the nascent musicians were soon rolling along nicely, covering BB King and other blues classics, as well as the mighty 'Smoke On The Water', before one of Bruce's most famous pranks finally got discovered, with rather final results.

"I wee-d in the headmaster's dinner," he shrugged in an interview with Spencer Leigh. "We did it without him knowing; two of us. They were having a dinner party to celebrate that they had built the extension to this house that we used to live in, and they'd run out of cooking [oil]. The school prefects were all scoffing away in there, so it was our statement."

14

Remembering his biology lessons well, he would have known that a small amount of boiled urine was harmless to ingest (the pair had 'topped up' the cooking oil they had lent to the prefects responsible for cooking the meal), but this time the joke was a step too far. Enjoying a drink in the sixth form bar, the two reprobates couldn't help themselves letting their compadres in on the reason for their paroxysms of mirth as they watched everyone tucking into their added-value meal. Within the confines of a boarding school it was inevitable that the tale would spread like wildfire. And before long, the culprits were identified.

"We got grassed up," continued the singer in the same interview, "and I got thrown out. The kid that did it with me didn't, because he was a candidate for Oxford or Cambridge. They thought they'd suspend him for three months and then bring him back so that he could add to the school's statistics. It's the way they work."

The resentment at being singled out was obvious, the rustication of his academically-gifted co-conspirator inevitable; but in many ways being expelled from Oundle was the best thing that happened to the unconventional pupil. His parents were surprisingly quiet about the incident, and in 1976 Bruce began to complete his 'A' levels at a Catholic school back in the relative normality of Sheffield – a comprehensive which was mixed-gender, rather than the rather odd tradition of a single-sex public school that had been a major part of his formative years. During his first week at the new school, Bruce also ran into four guys with whom he would hook up on a musical level. Suddenly, getting caught short seemed like it was opening up a whole new world of possibilities, and in many ways the real history starts here.

chapter two:
In Which Our Gallant Hero Joins Lots Of Bands That Begin With The Letter 'S'

1976 was a massive year for British Music; not only did Brotherhood Of Man win the Eurovision Song Contest with their gory deathcore classic, 'Save All Your Kisses For Me', but around the UK musicians were galvanising themselves into groups following whispers emanating from London about a four-piece of passion, anti-grown-up sneer and a celebration of youth – the Sex Pistols. Whilst punk was close to exploding into the nation's consciousness and shattering the music industry's smug ivory towers,[14] rock bands had been playing in pubs wherever a stage could be stuck; pub rock was in many ways a forerunner to both punk and the galvanisation of the UK's heavy metal acts for its energy and relatively liberal attitude to any musician who had the nous to form a band.

For Bruce Dickinson, 1976 saw a pivotal meeting; sitting in class in his new school, he eavesdropped on a conversation between two of his fellow pupils, Paul Widdicombe and Robert Hodgson. The latter pair were somewhat vexed that the vocalist in their nascent group had quit, and were wondering aloud whether to go ahead with a rehearsal that they'd had planned for the same evening. Ears pricking up, and with the 'triumph' of his pre-pissy-beans blues-rock knockabouts at Oundle still fresh in his mind, Bruce decided to pipe up that he had the ability to fill the vacancy. The pair invited Dickinson to rehearsals, where Bruce was surprised to find that the drummer, Paul Bray, had in fact gone to his old school. Playing a set comprised mostly of covers – including Wishbone Ash's entire *Argus* album – the band were hardly professionals; usually the rehearsals would take place in guitarist Hodgson's bedroom on his acoustic guitar, with Widdicome's bass barely ever plugged in. Still, it was a step up from what had come before, and Dickinson even went to the lengths of heading into Sheffield City Centre to purchase his very own microphone and amplifier; necessary because his group was to *actually play live*.

"They didn't even have a proper microphone," recalled Bruce. "They had this cassette player mic that was taped to a jack plug – it was useless – nothing came out of it at all except this awful feedback! But they said to me, 'Wow, you're the best singer we ever had – you're in the band.' And I said,

'Great! When do we start gigging?' And they said, 'Gigging? We don't do gigs, we just rehearse in the garage once a week.' And I said, 'You mean you don't write your own material?' And they said, 'God, no!' So, I ended up being the driving force of the band, and we actually did do some gigs."[15]

The city itself was something of a mixed bag of individuals at the time. "Saturday night out was Northern Soul night," he recalled. "There were clubs where you went and bought a pint and they gave you a knife with it."[16] Getting the band up to performance speed in Hodgson's dad's garage, the group put in many hours trying to knock off some of the rough edges. All very fine so far, aside from the name: Paradox. Bruce for one hated it, and drew – possibly for the first time in his musical career, but certainly not the last – on an element of his classical education to suggest a replacement moniker: Styx.

In Greek mythology, Styx is the river that forms the boundary between Earth and Hades; to drink from the river Styx was also to attain immortality. Two very good, and very cool, reasons to name your band thus. Who wouldn't want to listen to the music of a group who straddle the Underworld, whose music would surely make you live forever? The reasoning is sound, at least. In practice, however, when Styx finally played a gig at Sheffield's Broad Fall Tavern in the summer of 1976, their din was such a racket that they actually woke up a sleeping steelworker, who had been on the night shift. Said chap proceeded to invade the Broad Fall Tavern's stage, such as it was, and in his ire both bottle Hodgson and proceed to smash up Paul Bray's kit. Bruce himself was later to claim that he 'attacked [the steelworker] with a chair.'[17] The incident even made the local paper, giving Styx a profile that belied the ramshackle nature of the group, who, in the best traditions of the punk rock attitude, promptly split up. Just as well; there was also the matter of a rather enormous American proggish-rock band of the same name, who had been releasing records with rather silly pictures of dragons and buxom maidens with swords on the covers since the dawn of the decade. Crisis unwittingly averted (not least because the Sheffield version were blissfully unaware of their US counterparts, although with Bruce's growing musical knowledge, this seems more of an oversight than anything else), the world breathed a collective sigh of relief. The experience of performing live, however, had left a big imprint on the seventeen-year-old singer – who now, of course, owned the essential bits of equipment too.

Having successfully completed his 'A' levels in June 1976, Bruce was undecided as to what to do next. Finally leaving school is a daunting prospect: even the patchy educational career that Dickinson had had, always offered another term to look forward to, new explosives to invent in physics and chemistry classes, new pranks to pull. And now all that had gone, and in common with many eighteen-year-olds, the would-be sticksman and newbie ex-Styxman was at something of a loose end. His interest in the military, combined with suggestions from his father, meant that there was only one place for it – the army.

Or, to be more specific, the Territorial Army, or TA. The TAs are, essentially, a part-time reserve force for the UK's regular army, often referred to rather disparagingly as the 'Weekend Warriors', a reference to the fact that during the week the TA members might be working in banks, as postmen, bakers, or even rabidly unsuccessful music journalists – but come Saturday they don their uniforms to go out on manoeuvres and train in the various army skills. But if Dickinson was looking for a safe haven away from the less savoury individuals of the city centre, he was sadly mistaken. Although he enjoyed the camaraderie of the set-up, the reality was far removed from what he had expected or hoped for on joining; there was a serious culture of booze-n-pulling the likes of which the would-be singer had never previously encountered. Not that the youngster was averse to the odd bout of drinking himself, but he very quickly found that a certain section of his compatriots took the carousing to another level entirely. In 2005, Bruce recalled that he "saw quite a few loose women while I was there, but they were never loose enough to do anything with me."[18] "Considering my education, I was supposed to take the exam to become an officer. But I strongly disliked officers and army men in general."[19] Realising that army life was not for him, he decided very quickly to apply for university, and was accepted to read history at the London college, Queen Mary's, a decision that somewhat bemused his parents, not least because their son had never previously visited the capital in his life.

Queen Mary College provided many opportunities to develop and grow, and a relatively safe springboard between adolescence and adulthood. If you were an aspirant rock singer, you could take advantage of the fact that you were in England's capital city and further your musical education alongside your book-smarts. So Bruce set about getting involved with the college's Entertainments department – who were responsible for booking groups to play at the college. And there was nowhere better to be than in London during such a vibrant period at the dawn of the punk era; the Sex Pistols played some secret shows at the facility, and Dickinson soon found himself helping to set up the stage for the likes of mod-punks The Jam, Ian Dury And The Blockheads and even space-rockers Hawkwind. It was here also that Dickinson met one Paul 'Noddy' White, a multi-instrumentalist who went one step further than just owning an amp and a microphone, but was also in proud possession of a full P.A. system. Needless to say, Bruce immediately enthused with his new compadre about the possibilities there must be for forming a band. Rehearsing on a regular basis, the pair decided to name their project *Speed*, a reference, apparently, not to the amphetamine-based drug that was massively prevalent during the punk era, but rather to the accelerated pace of the tracks they were playing. Eventually, Speed became a five piece outfit, with Bruce on vocals and rhythm guitar, pounding out the chords that White had taught him, one Martin Freshwater on lead guitar, Paul White playing either keyboards or guitar, Adam Hayand as bassist, and the half-Welsh Steve Jones on drums. The latter was, in many ways, one of the most experienced amongst the performers.

"Prior to joining Speed," Jones told me, "[which was] through an advert seen by a friend at Queen Mary College, I was in a band called Lucifer – which changed its name to Angel Witch after my departure." More of those chaps a little later. At the time, Jones was gainfully employed by the Post Office as an engineering apprentice, and he first met "Bruce, along with Noddy, Martin and Adam at an audition at their Halls Of Residence."

"Firstly," continues the erstwhile drummer, who is now an elected member of the National Executive of the Communication Workers Union, "none of the lads really fitted the image of a rock band. In some ways, at the time, Bruce less so than the others. In fact, his full beard made him appear more [like the] Goodie, Bill Oddie, than a rocker. It has to be said that [I joined the band] despite my disappointment with the apparent lack of image, a little short-sighted I know. It was Bruce's truly outstanding vocal range and control that grabbed me. It was also the original songs with a rock and [punk edge] that made me join."

Speed's sound was a blend of breakneck hard rock/hefty Judas Priest-style metal and swirling, with added neo-classical keyboard action, much in the vein of another bunch of pub rockers caught up within the growing punk scene by accident and/or design, The Stranglers.

"Paul wrote most of the music," recalls Jones. "While I believe Bruce was the lyricist. There was usually a twist or message to the lyrics which I always liked, a far cry from Iron Maiden. Songs about 'Snoopy' – a hermaphrodite who never sinned; or a degenerate 'Tax Payer'; another was called 'FBI', which also referred to the CIA and the KGB; there was also a song called 'Dental Decay', which was every bit [reminiscent of the band] Status Quo. We always threatened to dump this but the audience seemed to love it. I recall a gig at Queen Mary where the audience shouted their appreciation, to which Bruce's response was to say, 'Strange!' – we never liked it that much, [it was] more something to fill the set with. We also had a song called 'In the Moonlight' which started off with Noddy on the Hammond organ with – you've guessed it – the 'Moonlight Senator'. Probably the only song not played at breakneck speed."

Hence the band's moniker, perhaps. But even as the world elsewhere was being turned upside down by snotty lads and lasses with ripped clothes and attitude, not everybody was on the punk vibe at the time, as Jones points out.

"As far as other bands [around in that period were concerned, it was] all a bit odd really as the music scene at the time was a bit strange, particularly for people like me who were brought up on Zeppelin and Purple but were

19

perhaps more comfortable playing Lizzy and the Stones. Punk threw a real spanner in the works for me."

"I believe Bruce was the President of the Students Union when Speed was on the go. I always sensed he was quite headstrong and focused even in the early days. Frankly, I think Bruce could have succeeded at anything he set his mind to."

Being involved with the Entertainments Department had other perks; Speed grabbed and ran with the (Sheffield) Styx baton in terms of actually playing live on a regular basis; many concerts took place at the Green Man pub in nearby Plumstead, and in order to get the band's equipment there, Bruce and the boys would borrow the college minibus, making room for the gear by unbolting most of the seats in their make-shift tour-bus. The vocalist was really beginning to cut his teeth in the live arena, and during the latter months of 1977 through to June 1978, Speed began to pick up a mini-following amongst gig-goers of the East End of London.

"The main venues we played were Queen Mary College in Mile End," notes Jones, "as well as the Halls Of Residence, The Green Man and a boozer in Basildon. I don't think we played with anyone of any 'fame'. [The audience reaction was] pretty good but I don't think we were really together long enough to have tested it properly. Bruce was always a fairly confident frontman. Took him a while to sort his image, but he got there in the end – I think!"

As for the bearded Bruce, he was throwing himself into the student lifestyle. So much so, that he'd put on almost two stone by the end of his first year in college. Not that it was just ale that was on offer at the time. "I tried out all sorts," he recalled. "[Many things] coming my way [were] interesting to me, and I'd get into it!"[20] However, Bruce realized he needed to calm himself down a little, and subsequently went on the wagon for several months, not even touching a drop of beer. No mean feat for a student with a major fixation on rock 'n' roll, living in the middle of punk-era London! But he was also gradually feeling his way through to the music that truly floated his boat as a performer.

"I recall playing Bruce a tape of Lucifer – who went on to become Angel Witch," says Jones. "And he 'jokingly' said they were in need of a good vocalist. There was a much heavier edge to Lucifer which clearly appealed to Bruce. I was conscious that if Bruce went anywhere near Angel Witch he could have been lost to Speed. Should that have happened, who knows how things would have turned out. In the early days it was touch and go as to which of these bands was going to hit the big time. I seriously think that Bruce was the defining factor. It was evident that whilst Speed worked, it wasn't what Bruce wanted; perhaps in the same way the Angel Witch sound wasn't for me."

As is often the case in college-based bands (Jones excepted), a combination of workload, searching for a satisfying personal sound, and other assorted use-your-imagination-type interests was bound to throw up a stumbling block – and Speed duly disbanded in the summer of 1978. Later, some recordings that Noddy White and Bruce had put together for an unrelated college project subsequently surfaced on the single 'Man On The Street'/'On The Road', a 7" that was released independently in 1980. 'Man On The Street' is a punk-influenced piece of fairly basic garage-band British rock, sounding a little like the Pink Fairies, with an enduring keyboard solo courtesy of one Gary Edwards, guitars courtesy of another mate, Steve Adams, and Jeff Moody providing the backbeat along with Noddy White himself on bass; 'On The Road', meanwhile, is a basic knockabout 12-bar blues offering with a grotty-sounding Motorhead-esque guitar solo as the track winds up in pace and density, playing fast and loose with tempo throughout, before fading out in some bemusement. A curio, of course, by virtue of its singer, who offers some rather accomplished rock screams and whoops – which is probably why the single is so very sought-after amongst collectors and regularly fetches upwards of £300 in online auctions; mostly worth it, one feels, for the moustachioed photo of an otherwise exceedingly fresh-faced Bruce that adorns its black and white cover. It's important to note that although it was released under the Speed moniker, the actual line-up on vinyl is significantly different to the gigging unit, Speed had, to all intents and purposes, broken up prior to the recording sessions. It should be taken for what it was: a chunk of White's compositions recorded, basically, for the fun of it. The best way to describe the 7" is probably, 'interesting'.

Bruce, however, had had a taste of fronting a band, and he wasn't done with rock 'n' roll quite yet. Twiddling his thumbs one day leafing through *Melody Maker* magazine, his gaze fell on a rather intriguing advertisement calling for a vocalist needed to put the finishing touches to a recording session. Intrigued, Dickinson proceeded to put together an audition tape that says much about his sense of humour. Rather than sending in a cassette of the usual sing-over-classic-track type, he set the tape recorder running in the corner of his room and made as many rock-style whoops and noises as he possibly could for half an hour; on the other side of the tape was a classic comedy set from John Cleese, Bruce wrote a note to the effect that if his would-be bandmates weren't enamoured by his vocals, perhaps they would care for the jokes on the B-side. Of course, even in such a rough and ready format, Dickinson's developing voice was still arresting enough to warrant a call-back from the chaps that had placed the advertisement, Phil and Doug Siviter. During the subsequent recording session – which spawned a track called 'Dracula' – the Brothers Siviter were astonished at the singer's prowess. Despite his relative lack of real experience, Bruce took on, and mastered, complex multi-tracked harmony lines with aplomb. Even at some thirty years' distance, the track retains an atmospheric edge, its swirling backing and jerky guitar lines sweeping into a rock-ska verse and rather silly lyrics about waiting for the midnight hour on top. Still, it's clear that musically and vocally Dickinson had progressed considerably even in the course of the few months between Speed and this new band, called Shots. The line-up for the live gigs was Bruce on vocals, backed by guitarist Tony Lee, Arthur Young on bass and drummer Phil Adolphia. Bruce's involvement with the Entertainments Department came in handy once more; he was able to book his new band support slots with a series of groups visiting Queen Mary's, including, notably, Mannfred Mann's Earth Band. The Shots were firmly a gigging band, and played in many of the venues that were beginning to buzz with excitement at the new rock revolution as 1978 went by. One of the key venues in the rising tide of hard rock was The Prince Of Wales in Gravesend, as Rob Grain – later to become road manager for the band Samson – recalls.

"The Prince Of Wales pub was a mile from my house," he told me. "At the time, it was a few beers and a band but you didn't pay that much attention because there was a group on every night. I was working there as a stagehand, taking the money on the door. I wasn't employed at the time, so if the guv'nor had a band on of an evening, I used to go down and help him put the P.A. up and all that, which is where I learnt my job! It sorta crept up, it wasn't the case that all of a sudden there was this 'thing' going on. Because you were there all the time, it crept up on you without you knowing and you suddenly noticed bands coming in from out of the area."

It wasn't exactly situated in the most salubrious of areas, however.

"It was on the edge of quite a big rough council estate," recalls Grain. "The guys from the estate, I used to go to school with – they were fine with me and used to buy me beers. Quite a lot of people used to say, 'I'm not going to the Prince Of Wales, it's full of pikeys' – but as soon as the bands would start, they'd go round to the other bar anyway. But there was never any trouble. What you used to find was, then and now, all through life, wherever you find a pub with live music you don't find trouble, fights, stabbings and people getting glasses shoved in their faces – because people are there for the music. The sort of people who are going to cause trouble and to start fights don't go to those pubs 'cause they can't stand the music."

The bands, however, loved it; during 1977 and 1978 some of the major groups on the scene descended on the venue, which was getting quite a name for itself amongst the blossoming rock and metal movement.

"Paul Samson started playing there," continues Grain. "Right at the start when it was Paul, Chris Aylmer and Clive Burr. Another band on the scene was Hotline, [whose members included] bass player Jerry Scherwin who later joined Sledgehammer, Pete Jupp who later joined Samson, and the guitarist was Bucket, who's now in Bad Company. It was a breeding ground, really. There was a band from Hastings called Die Laughing; The Nicky Moore Band played – and every night of the week there was a band playing in these pubs."

Typically, there was some jostling for position amongst the owners of the venues in the vicinity, as they attempted to corner the rather lucrative market in rock fans, who, let's face it, are known to enjoy a small sherry on occasion. "The Red Lion in Northfleet and the Prince Of Wales were about three or four miles from each other so you used to get a bit of rivalry going. I used to use both pubs and knew the guv'nors, and so they would ask me, 'See you tomorrow?' 'Nah I'm going to the Red Lion to see so-and-so'. 'Well, you tell them from me that if they go and play there, don't bother trying to come back in here again!'"

The crowds, however, were often slightly demanding, although appreciating groups that made the effort, there was still a need to entertain. Not that the bands exactly had a great set-up with which to work. "The Prince Of Wales had no stage, it was just a flat pub," laughs Grain. "There was a corner where the bands would play, and in the corner was the entrance to the toilets. So anyone wanting to go to the toilet while the band were playing had to walk through the band, or down the side of the band."

The Shots, however, had a chap up at the front for whom this basic facility was an opportunity to be grasped rather than a limitation to be endured. "Bruce used to catch people; between songs if someone went to or from the toilet he'd hassle them, start talking to them and stick a mic in their face," laughs Grain. "Just general larking about. I can always remember one instance with this big local biker, nobody messed with him. I knew one of his family in school and they were one of these families that *nobody* messes with, you know. He came out of the toilet as the Shots finished a song, so Bruce said something to him, and stuck the mic in his face. And the bloke just looked at him and went, 'Bollocks!' And so Bruce said something else to him and he went, 'Up Your Kilt!' And then Bruce said something else to him and he just went, 'Don't push it' and walked off! And Bruce just went, 'There you go, if you've got bollocks up your kilt, don't push it.' And that's the sort of thing he did."[21]

The sense of humour and theatre was being developed at an early stage; musically, however, Shots had a lot to offer. "As a band they were great," continues Grain. "The guitar player was really good. The songs were hard rock, as were most of the bands at that sort of time on the circuit. Song-wise there was 'Snoopy',[22] one called 'Middle Class Song', and the covers were 'Bad Motorscooter' by Montrose, 'Under My Wheels' by Alice Cooper and I may be wrong – but also 'Halo Of Flies'. All the bands would do their own material – but they would never get out of the pubs alive if they didn't do a few covers! No matter who they were. Hotline used to do 'I'm Eighteen',[23] and Jeff Beck's 'Lead Boots'."

Shots fitted into the scene nicely, although there was something rather different about their vocalist. "He was a screamer," laughs Grain, "What you did notice was that in actual fact you'd probably look forward to the song in the set that didn't have a scream in it. All the other bands who were on the circuit at the time, you'd find that the singer was good for one scream in the whole set, with him it was three screams a song! He was great with crowds. He could really get them going."

Bill Liesegang was later to join the Shots as a guitarist; he recalls the time well, not least for Dickinson's rather unique sartorial sense in those days. "When I knew Bruce he was at college," Liesegang told me in an interview for this book. "His main thing was that he was into extreme theatrical people like Arthur Brown. With the Shots he was trying to steer the band into that kind of thing with masks and weirdness – Bruce used to wear these really sort of long boxing sort of lace-up boots and this sort of pudding-basin haircut and he looked quite extreme really."

"At the time it wasn't really the thing I suppose, it was sort of post-Genesis and a lot of the other musicians I knew weren't really into that sort of thing, wearing masks and stuff like that. Which is probably why the Shots didn't take off at that point! But Bruce was always singing with that same kind of high, falsetto vocal thing – that was always there right from the start. In fact, in many of the songs that we did you can hear its Bruce, even if you compare it to what he does today, you know it's got his trademark stamped right on it."

Times, as ever, were rather sticky for a young band. Not least financially.

"When nobody had any money, we used to go to rehearsals at Monster Music in Stretham. We used to rent a P.A., but we couldn't afford the mixer in the room so alls we had was that P.A., so I used to plug Bruce into my Coloursound Overdriver which was just sort of a Pre-Amp for the guitar, but it had treble and bass on it so his microphone had some sort of gain going into the P.A. system. I still have that overdriver now and they're actually worth a lot of money but it's probably more famous because Bruce sang through it in the early days."

"I wasn't actually in The Shots for that long," continues Liesegang. "I auditioned for them, I think they'd had another guitarist and he'd disappeared.

So I auditioned for them and Bruce was in the band then and we kind of got quite friendly, did some recordings and rehearsed for like a few months. I don't think we did any gigs as such."

Liesegang subsequently went on to form a band called Xero, who got themselves into rather a sticky situation during 1983, which we shall deal with in due course. Shots, in fact, were attracting a little attention; Bruce's onstage antics as much as his vocal capabilities were to bring him into the orbit of an artist whose career was another step up the ladder, one who in many ways is one of the most under-rated and overlooked forces in hard rock during the 1970s and 1980s.

And his band begins with the letter S as well.

chapter three:
In Which Our Protagonist Gets
Biblical On The World's Ass[24]

Paul Samson, born on June 4, 1953, started his musical career way back in 1969, as vocalist and guitarist for Dartford rock act The Innocence; while the shadows of the Summer of Love, the Woodstock and Monterey festivals still affecting bands the length and breadth of the musical world. It was a time of Hendrix, Led Zeppelin and the Rolling Stones' return to their R&B roots with the previous year's *Beggars Banquet* album. 1969 also saw the Stones – and the 1960s – lurch into deep darkness after the death of founder member Brian Jones, and a free concert at Altamont which was tinged by the sour atmosphere engendered by the heavy-handed and violent nature of that festival's 'security', the local Hell's Angels. The well-documented death of Meredith Hunter is seen widely to be where the hope and hippiness of the 1960s ended; that the Stones had just released an LP entitled *Let It Bleed* was a horrible irony.

Musically, Paul Samson's heroes were those who ploughed the rhythm & blues furrow. "The main one is Hendrix for me," he said. "I was also into Mountain and when I was a kid, Cream. There's also the blues side, cos my dad was a big R'n'B fan."[25] But as the 1970s developed, The Innocence evidently fell by the wayside. Samson's growing maturity as a player made him in demand as a session guitarist; as the decade developed he sat in with Noel Redding – which as a Hendrix acolyte must have been what they used to call "a stooonnee groove, man" – as well as the likes of Slowbone and Atomic Rooster. His next serious band was Kelly, which he originally joined in March 1973. The gigs were mainly centred round the growing pub rock circuit, and although there were tours mooted of South Africa and US Air force bases in Germany during 1974-5, in the end both fell through, somewhat ominously, largely due to behind-the-scenes politics. Paul was by now a vocalist, and though he parted company with the band after they started to go in more of a funk-jazz direction, he was to perform in various line-ups of Kelly, on and off, all the way through to February 1976, when the band finally split (due in part to the drummer, one Roger Hunt, leaving to form an act called Scrapyard along with guitarist Bernie Torme and bass player John McCoy).

It was March 1977. With the spectre of punk rock looming large, Torme left Scrapyard to form his own band, and in one of those curious rock 'n' roll apocryphal-type coincidences. McCoy and Hunt asked Samson if they could borrow his very fine amplifier in order that they may audition a replacement guitarist. Paul wandered down to the rehearsal room to pick said amp up a few days later, only to find a rather disconsolate McCoy and Hunt somewhat disappointed in the lack of quality of applicants for their new project which – keep up at the back – was to be called, simply, *McCoy*. More for fun than anything else, Samson and the pair held a jam session which ended up with the bleedin' obvious smacking them all in the face. And so Paul became a McCoy. The bassist and the guitarist, in fact, got on extremely well as musicians and on a personal level, and wrote a considerable amount of material together during the subsequent months, the first song of which was 'Big Brother'.

"We got Paul in as the guitarist from then," chuckled John when I interviewed him. "We changed the name from McCoy to Samson depending on where we were playing, 'cause if either band had played there the previous month, they didn't want us back! We just changed our name and went anyway, and played the same songs." The gigs would come thick and fast over the next six months or so, as things hotted up for hard rock and heavy metal acts. The three-piece, however, was not to last as a viable unit, and despite having written some seriously decent blues/rock tunes together, McCoy was to leave for pastures new – the band John DuCann beckoned, as did studio work on the other side of the mixing desk. The eternal graph of music-making versus income, so familiar to any musician, was rearing its head.

"It was just a three piece rock band, old style British rock," continues McCoy. " But I got very, very busy; I was doing a lot of production work and sessions. I was *really* busy, and at the time I had a young family and needed to live." Thus shorn of a band, Paul Samson recruited bassist Chris Aylmer who had actually been working behind the Samson band's sound-desk, but also moonlighted as four-string hero in the band Maya; as 1977 developed, Hunt also left this very early Samson line-up, to be replaced by Maya's drummer, one Clive Burr. The trio instantly found a good, locked-in musical relationship and by December of that year were so proficient that they confidently toured USAF bases throughout Italy with a view to using the generated income to fund future recording sessions, the logical next step. This proved to be a lucrative enough tour, and with their growing momentum, the band were able to ramp up the live appearances in and around the London area, rapidly gathering a following. The trio were steady and slick, with Paul developing a singing style that was suitably manageable for the material that comprised the set of the time. This line-up headed into the studio in the spring of 1978, the recording session yielding the subsequent single 'Telephone'/'Leavin' You', a pair of hefty blues-rock bruisers with Paul's guitar to the fore, the 7" being produced by none other than John McCoy and released by the small independent, Lightning Records, in September that year.

Although the three-piece Samson was making great inroads into the rock and metal circuit, and were generally considered to be ahead of a lot of contemporaries including such bands as Bruce's Shots – Paul himself was slightly frustrated with his dual role, feeling that the pressure of being lead vocalist as well as handling the guitar licks alone was to the detriment of his lead playing. And that had a real effect on the band as a whole.

"I know that at the time Paul wanted a singer," confirms Rob Grain. "They'd tried a short period in 1978 with a singer called Mark Newman, who lasted about six gigs, and what you noticed was although Samson worked really well as a three-piece, Paul's playing developed when they had a singer in the band because he wasn't having to worry about both singing and playing. You really noticed the standard of the band go up when they had a frontman – not just visually but musically."

"I actually thought the three piece band was pretty hot," says John McCoy, "and the songs were really written in keys and melodically in a range that Paul was able to handle. It was like, 'This band need a singer', and I could see that, yeah. I could see that they *needed* a singer, but they needed a *good* singer ..." The man himself, Paul Samson, was under no illusions, commenting later that, "as Samson started to play larger venues I knew that I was getting out of my league."[26]

These larger venues were starting to become established; even as the spitting punks were making a mockery of the initial spirited independence of the 1976 movement, the unreported underbelly of bands that were drawn more toward acts like Led Zep, Deep Purple, Black Sabbath and others were finding venues of their own in which to frolic and flail. The most important of these is, quite possibly, The Bandwagon, home to the influential rock disco which was run by the peerlessly entertaining and quite frankly legendary DJ, bon viveur and subversive musical maniac, Mr. Neal Kay.[27] The story of how he came to be one of the most influential people in the rock scene during this period is an insane, intense, interesting and extremely long one, which will be told one day in its entirety, and bloody hilarious it will be too. Suffice to say, having cut his teeth, Beatles-style, in an eighteen month stint at raucous rock clubs in Germany (Berlin in Kay's case) during the early 1970s, he returned to London and through a series of wonderful, serendipitous events, found himself running a rock club in Kingsway's Bandwagon venue; an odd locale for a start, a venue memorably described by *Sounds* magazine journalist Geoff Barton as a 'cheap B-movie set saloon'. It was, without a doubt, *the* gathering place for those souls isolated and marginalized by the punk movement (which Kay described to me as, "the eternal enemy of all-time"). By mid-1978, the venue had begun to attract hairy lunatics from all over the country – and beyond. The growing movement, however, was bereft of supporters in the media, that is, until the aforementioned Barton was finally enticed down to the club, where Kay had been bringing down rock royalty including Ted Nugent, Rainbow, Motorhead and Whitesnake to meet his 'orrible lot.

"In the end, I managed through sheer bloody perseverance and aggression on the phone to dig out old Geoff Barton from *Sounds*, and he came down and was so shocked at what he found he put us as the centre double-page spread. On the front page of *Sounds* that week was, 'A survivor's report, would you believe it – from a Heavy Metal discotheque'. And, oh boy, that did it. It told the whole world we were there. Geoff Barton was the man who put The Bandwagon on the map. That's not even up for debate, he was the man. And after that it was never the same, things started going mad, insane – things I never even dreamed of; it was like I was the unwitting and semi-frightened leader of a mass that was being dragged up the High Road by something bigger than I could even see. And behind me thundered the heavy metal hairy hoardes with The Bandwagon. Suddenly, other journalists start phoning up wanting to come and see what the hell was going on. One of the greatest reviews we got was from my broadcast buddy, Malcolm Dome,[28] who was writing for *Record Mirror*. He declared his article, 'By appointment to HM (Heavy Metal)'. The press were always there – I made sure of it, 'cause this is business. And this is where, really and truly, it starts with the bands because of all this that was going on and the increasingly bizarre behaviour of the punters." There was Rob Loonhouse for one, for a while an honourary member of Iron Maiden, jumping onstage to jam with his cardboard cut-out Flying V guitar (and subsequently forming his own cardboard band, Willy Flasher And The Raincoats, complete with cardboard bass and drumkit and in which he also, according to Kay, was a 'cardboard keyboard virtuoso'); another particular chap revelled in the self-explanatory moniker Superloony, with a penchant for public nudity; the atmosphere was fuelled on a heady mix of bikers and longhairs, and with the heavy metal megastars giving it the seal of approval, it was clear that something major was going down.

"The music press by now were aware, with all these comings and goings and all the mad shit and everything else, that something's happening in Kingsbury," continues Kay. "And they continued to come down; the phone never stopped ringing, 'What are you doing this week then? What's happening, what's next?' and the pressure was huge. Man. It was going worldwide and *Sounds* decided that they would take from me our punters' requested chart that I did every week from the stage. They'd write it down, I'd take it home and compile a top twenty every week and *Sounds* took that and started printing it. And that was it; demo tapes started arriving from everywhere and that was how it all happened. But to make it happen, I first had to make The Bandwagon what it was. It was a business venture; I mean, it was music of my heart and my soul and my spirit, but it had to be properly organised and it was very hard, in all honesty, because I was on my own and had no help."

"So into this electrically charged atmosphere dropped all these demo tapes, and the stories were heartbreaking. They were from all over the world saying the same thing; 'Nobody wants to listen; we're from Norway, we're from Oslo, we're from Germany and nobody wants to listen – please help us.' And I suddenly realised something needed doing and I thought, 'I'm a DJ but I have to do something about this, this is why I've been put here. And now I've got the power and I know the people, it's time.'"

The intent was clear: to publicise this new movement as much as possible. With the tireless work of Kay to add to the mix, the *Sounds* chart and the near-critical mass of artists, fans and hirstute lunatics on board, it was rapidly approaching the point of no return. Bands coming through included Praying Mantis, White Spirit, Iron Maiden – still at this stage of 1978 looking to stabilise and settle into a line-up that truly suited them – and Angel Witch, whose former drummer in their Lucifer days, Steve Jones, had played with Bruce Dickinson in Speed the previous year. Jones remembers the period as being rather a state of flux for those whose music had suddenly become as unfashionable as the flares of the punk era's hated hippies.

"[It was] perhaps a strange time for die hard rock musicians," he muses. "Many of the bands around at the time were in the Thin Lizzy, UFO vein. Some bands that were really pretty good but never quite made the big-time were others such as Magnum, Dirty Tricks, Heavy Metal Kids, Trapeze, Knutz and Paris, etc. Punk-related bands smashing their way onto the scene had a real effect. In particular, bands like The Clash, The Stranglers, Squeeze, Ian Dury, Dr Feelgood etc really shook things up for the traditional rock fan and musician alike. Whilst many of these lasted the course, the punk scene itself soon gave way to 'New Wave' and mainstream rock was quickly back on the agenda, hence the New Wave Of British Heavy Metal.[29] [I remember] bands like Knutz – check 'em out, a seriously good band – changed their name to Rage, and Paris became Grand Prix (both at the insistence of record companies). The lead singer from Grand Prix, Bernie Shaw, [parted company with them] as his image wasn't apparently [right]. The band disappeared and Bernie has been with Uriah Heep for some years now! It's a strange world. Other important DJs of the time were Andy King and the lesser-known Karen Doyle, who used to be known as Karon after some journalist miss-spelt her name. Both Andy and Karen used to DJ mainly at Crackers in Wardour Street, which was a very popular haunt just up from the old Marquee."

By now, Samson were playing five times a week, able to tour everywhere from south Wales to the south of England, and come September 1978 they were also regularly playing at The Bandwagon, where Kay had recently added live shows into the Soundhouse mix. But it wasn't for the faint-hearted; this was an audience who had a deep appreciation for what was put in front of them.

"They loved to laugh, loved to joke," notes the DJ. "But they were the best musical audience of their day. There was all these bloody tapes arriving, bands from all over the place *desperate* to get a gig. And it had to be done, but The Bandwagon was not an easy place to play. I'd made the audience one of the hardest in the country, with an eight thousand watt P.A. to listen to recorded music through. They were not gonna be easily fooled, they'd met Ted Nugent, Whitesnake, Judas Priest *personally* so they were very tough to please and if you were a shit band you never got on. So I never put shit bands on. There was a lower limit which I had to impose because if you weren't good enough you'd get a mauling by the crowd and that was the old Bandwagon Whistle Test."

"Paul Samson came up and gave me a demo, and he used to come up and play at the 'wagon too. I liked him, it was a strange relationship 'cause I suppose we used to do the same illegal substances once in a while, you know? And his wife Jane and my first wife Michelle were really good friends. We used to go down to south London, where he lived, and spend the night listening to music and chewing the fat and stuff. He was also not very extrovert, very quiet, preferring to strum on his Gibson SG. As time went by, there was a kind of a problem that you could only sense at first, and then see. I met John McCoy and he and his wife became good friends as well, we used to go there sometimes with Paul. It was a kinda after hours social club – fuckin' hell, some social club! Many a brew went down and bottles of other things too! Paul used to come up and play at the 'wagon too. I liked him."

The rest of 1978 saw a growing number of quality bands performing in front of one of the hardest-to-please, but ultra-loyal audiences in the country. In the case of Samson, the year drew to a close with recording sessions for their second single, 'Mr Rock & Roll'/'Driving Music', recorded by John McCoy once more, at Ian Gillan's studio during November; McCoy had by now hooked up with the Gillan band as a performer, and subsequently Samson completed 1978 by appearing as special guests of that band on tour. The final gig of an exceedingly busy year – Samson played more than two hundred gigs during 1977 and 1978 – was a New Year's Eve appearance at the Soundhouse, which, as it turned out, was Clive Burr's farewell to the band. In Iron Maiden-land, meanwhile, they used December 31 to ignore the festivities, preferring to get themselves into Skyward studios to record a serious demo for the first time.

In early 1979, Samson had now acquired management courtesy of Ramkup and one Alistair Primrose. Neal Kay was ramping up activities still further, as one of the central movers of the scene the next step was inevitable. "Alistair Primrose bounced this off my head," recalls Neal Kay. "He wanted to put me together with some unsigned acts to do some touring, and his raison d'etre was very simply to promote Samson." As he should; his charges had sold out of two thousand copies of the 'Mr Rock & Roll' single that

31

February, and were shortly to launch their debut album. *Survivors*, which had been recorded by McCoy during April. One Barry Graham Purkis had by now joined Samson to replace Clive Burr, although the former was to have a little fun, donning a featureless canvas face-mask and renaming himself Thunderstick, as Samson's stage show upped the ante in their March/April pre-recording session tour, with a host of pyrotechnics to bolster the blues-based hard rock so beloved of Paul. "The songs that we did were basically the songs that we'd been playing as Samson and McCoy as a three piece out on the road," remembers McCoy. "We recorded that album very, very quickly. Probably in about a week, from beginning to end. It was with Thunderstick, the new drummer, I played bass and Paul did the vocals and guitar. Then Chris Aylmer took over from me. Well, you know, [as a vocalist Paul] had his limitations, but on those particular songs, he handled them well. He'd been singing them for about a year before that, so he should've done. He found his way around them. Singing and playing guitar is a difficult thing at the best of times but he coped pretty well. We had a lot of fun making that album. I can't believe that we actually recorded it as quickly as we did, but it was a good time. It was a question of finance, we just had to do it in the time allotted and just didn't sleep for a week; we actually took it in turns to sleep on the couch in the studio while the others kept on working." At this stage, there was no record label lined up to release the LP, something which the management were to begin working on rectifying."

"We were the first band that had put out an album of the NWOBHM," declared Thunderstick to me. "It hadn't been termed that yet but we were the first to put something on vinyl. That was because Paul had a lot of songs knocking about from the time he was playing with John McCoy. Clive had gone, I came in and we just went straight into the studio. I had about two days rehearsal then we went straight on the road. You don't wanna be hanging around rehearsing for ages, you want to go out there and do it and see how it goes. *Survivors* was a John McCoy album. He produced it, he'd been in on the songwriting, John oversaw the pre-production; everything about it. It was something I had nothing to do with whatsoever."

But even as the band prepared to join Iron Maiden and Angel Witch on Neal Kay and Ramkup's UK tour – now known as the 'Heavy Metal Crusade' – Paul's uncertainty over his ability to perform both frontman and guitar hero jobs was at the back of his mind, as cohort Rob Grain, Gravesend and Northfleet's finest rocker, recalls.

"I used to talk to Paul on the phone a lot at the time. And in the course of the conversation, I'd always tell him which bands were worth catching, because at the time he was busy gigging five nights a week. Occasionally he'd get a day off and want to go out with his missus for a beer, or whatever, and he'd often come down the Prince Of Wales, to have a quietish night out and see – not necessarily the competition, because he was up a level – but see how the other local bands were doing. Paul came from Sidcup, fifteen miles away, and because Gravesend was always a good circuit for him, he'd pop in and let the locals see his face, really. One of the bands I'd told him about a few times was The Shots 'cause they were really good. All of a sudden he turned up one night with this big guy with a mass of reddy-ginger hair and a Kiss jacket on, and Paul said, 'This is my new drummer, Barry.' And The Shots happened to be on. I think Barry – Thunderstick – went to the toilet and Bruce collared him on the way and had a bit of [a laugh] and all that. If it hadn't been for Paul and Barry going into the Prince Of Wales that night who's to say Bruce wouldn't have finished his history degree, become a teacher, and never sung again in all his life ..."

"In late March," said Paul Samson, "I went down to one of our old gigs with Barry one evening for a drink at The Prince Of Wales in Gravesend. There was one band on called The Shots who were very entertaining and theatrical, especially the singer. Even though things hadn't worked out with Mark Newman, my dissatisfaction with being the vocalist and the guitarist hadn't quite gone away. The album sounded fine to me, but half the material had been written in the studio, and I found that I couldn't sing and play some of it live as there was too much to do at the same time. Consequently, I had always had one eye open in the hope that one day I could find someone who could fit in. The guy in The Shots impressed me, and he came over afterwards for a chat and tried to get a support slot with us. We exchanged telephone numbers so we could keep in touch and he told me his name was Bruce. I took Barry down to see him with the Shots a few days later, and again we were quite impressed with his voice and stage antics. He even got me clapping and singing along with the audience, a feat in itself. After seeing him a second time, we were becoming quite interested in asking him to join us."[30]

Barry – Thunderstick – himself explains that it was by accident and design that things came together that fateful night. "We didn't actually know that Bruce was there," he told me. "Paul used to go there quite a lot, not as a local but to go there and hang out and go and see bands; he obviously knew the promoter, Graham. Paul had played there a coupla times as the three piece with Clive and by the time I was in the band it was a case of, 'Look, fancy going out for a drink down there and we'll go out for the evening.'"

"By this time, we'd already been pushed into the idea of finding a vocalist. It was record companies; our management company had CBS come to see us a couple of times when we'd played the Music Machine and done the *Survivors* tour, 'cause it was all about trying to get a major deal at the time. And they said, 'Yeah, it would be a lot better if there was a singer involved.' The reason being that they liked the band, and thought it was great but it definitely needed that centre of attention at the front of the stage. The other candidate for the job was Gary Holton. He was just about to get into acting, hence the reason he wasn't available. But he had always been my idol in the

Heavy Metal Kids because he was totally such a showman, and because at the time we were kinda going down that route, it wasn't a conscious decision to do so but it just happened that we started going down that theatrical route. I'd always been in theatrical bands, I'd loved Kiss, the Tubes, Alice, HM Kids. Any band that put on a show and gave you your money's worth."

"So we went down there and Shots were playing. At that time Bruce, as part of his act, would pick on the audience, a bit like a stand-up comedian as it were. He'd interject the songs with comments aimed at or about someone in the audience. And because I looked fucking mad, I had bright red standy-up type David Bowie-Ziggy Stardust hair at the time and was dressed totally bizarre, he picked on me. I used to just dress in a bizarre way that wasn't of that kind of time. It was kind of weird. In fact, in interviews Bruce has turned round and said in the past that we were all over the place as far as an image was concerned as we didn't have one! I just dressed accordingly to whatever I felt like."

"I've always been quite sizeable as a guy – I'm quite well built, six foot tall, so I suppose I kind of stuck out a bit. He was using the toilet, actually, as a changing room, to go in and do his little bits and pieces; costume changes. And we thought he looked totally mad, 'cause he had this tiny little pencil moustache! And he picked on me [that night]. But there was no intention of going down and finding this guy and asking him if he wanted the job in Samson – it just happened that way. We went down, thought, 'Blimey, he's got a loud voice and is a real showman with it,' and that was it."

"I went into the toilet with Paul afterwards and [Bruce] went white 'cause I think he thought I was going to go in and beat him up! But that was it, we spoke to him after the gig and the rest is history!"

Had Paul Samson not come into Bruce's life, his main career plan may have in fact taken rather a different turn, as he explained to Valerie Potter of *Metal Hammer*. "My plans involved trying to hire a railway arch, putting Portakabins in it, starting a rehearsal studio and living in one of the Portakabins for free."[31]

Bruce's renowned audience heckling was something he credited his college with having fuelled. "Generally, going to school and learning about weird and wonderful Greek legends was of value to me," he said. "If you are observant about the outside world, it's all a help in writing lyrics. You can only write lyrics from your own experience or from observation of things that have happened to other people that you want to comment on."[32] He also said, "I did come away from it with a way of organising my brain, my thought processes and especially dealing with information."[33] And then, presumably, to use that information to take the piss out of people who were only trying to get past your band to have a wazz."

Bruce's humourous schtick, of course, was one of the more compelling parts of The Shots experience; refined through the months, and run through with a dose of sharp intelligence, he could hold his own with anyone who crossed his orbit. But there was another reason why the final-year college student was drawing attention to himself.

"We noticed Bruce 'cause he had this Gillan scream: 'Aiiiii!!'" recalled Paul Samson. "[He] was very theatrical and worked the crowd well. He noticed us, too and obviously knew who we were – 'cos right after the show he came over to get a support slot from us for his band."[34] That support shot was not to be forthcoming; on the contrary, following an invitation to join Samson onstage for an encore of a particular gig at Bishop's Stortford, Bruce had successfully transferred his showmanship and growing confidence to his new friends' act. Paul and Thunderstick were eager for Dickinson to join their act as that elusive fourth member that would enable the guitarist to soar with the freedom he so craved from his beloved instrument, and immediately offered him a job as their full-time frontman.

"He couldn't join there and then because he had to finish his history degree," remembers Thunderstick. "He would come down and do a couple of encores, we used to do 'Rock Me Baby' and he'd come down, do the encore and get the crowd going and what have you. We took that as a kind of audition, thought it worked alright so that was fine."

The rest of Samson raised their collective eyebrows but nevertheless acceded to this puzzling request. After all, they had a Crusade to complete.[35]

Chapter Four:
In Which A Vocalist Acquires
A Double-Barrelled Christian Name,
To The Confusion And Delight Of All

Whilst Paul Bruce Dickinson was delighted with this development in proceedings, there was still the side of him that would not allow himself to throw away the previous years of education so close to attaining a modicum of closure to his university career. "I did my three years at university," he said, "and got the same as everyone else, a 2.2 – which means you did an adequate amount of work and then you do what you are going to do in life afterwards."[36]

And that was to join up with an act with a reputation as a three-piece of hard rock roots; a band who were busy touring the UK, spreading the word far and wide that there was a new force in music, and that was heavy metal. Almost immediately after finishing his exams, Bruce hit Greenwich's Wood Wharf studio with his new bandmates and began learning the *Survivors* tracks; very quickly the band were ready to get out there and hit it live. The music itself was necessarily changing under the new frontman, whose predilection for Purple was grafted atop the influences of the guitarist and founder. "The trio were kind of Hendrix, Rory Gallagher and metal," said Paul Samson, "Except we did these extended jams like Cream and Mountain. When Bruce came in, we became more song orientated with structured solos although we still incorporated some jams."[37]

The Heavy Metal Crusade gigs were still rolling on; the hope was that Bruce would be ready to make his debut with the band for their appearance with Iron Maiden on July 2, 1979. And at that time, it did feel like there was a groundswell of change in music, according to Thunderstick at least.

"It felt like it was a new thing, a new surge," he says. "But you're not aware of it at the time. You're not thinking, 'We're turning the tide.' It was only when we were doing press interviews and the way they angled their interviews you could see that this was something that was beginning to materialise as a body, rather than separate things happening."

"All the bands I loved were suddenly discarded as being dinosaurs; Zeppelin had always been huge, and the likes of Sabbath, Uriah Heep, the list goes on. And then punk came and really kicked that up the arse with this huge great push of energy and there were other bands who thought, 'Well, we need that energy'. Sure, there were other bands who fitted into that niche; bands like Rush that were hard rock; 'Heavy Metal' hadn't even been coined yet. We were a hard rock band. I still insist that we were a hard rock band. We never fell into that heavy metal idiom but unfortunately that's one of the things we got labelled with."

"[At the time booking] agents were no good, the reason being that we were on the tail end of punk and everybody was still booking punk bands all the time: 'What kind of band is it?', 'Well, it's a heavy metal band.' 'No, we're booking The Snot, and The Cum' or whatever, you know. So it was a hard thing. So it did feel like a crusade, we were breaking down barriers within Student Union groups that up until then had been undecided and suddenly there was an audience for it. Gillan were doing the same, they were doing universities and colleges, around that time there was *Rock Goes To College* on television and more and more bands were breaking into that, it was good."

"Ramkup had a lot of good intentions at the time," notes Thunderstick, "and they had money which was the most important criteria because any band cannot survive without money. So they were able to put the band on a retainer wage, they were able to put the gigs on – sometimes at a loss cause even at that time we were burning up sixty or seventy pounds of pyrotechnics every night which in 1979 was expensive! As well as putting the whole thing together and taking it out on the road. So they had a lot of money but they had [limited] knowledge of the music industry and the processes with which you had to work within the music industry."

"At one time, CBS, who later became Sony, were really interested. They had the UK Subs too. That's why, in the end, John McCoy ended up producing one of the Subs' albums. [The management] were members of a place called the Golf Club, which was all Fleet Street journalists, we would go down there and cause havoc. The UK Subs with bright pink hair, Charlie Harper and Samson; there'd be these Fleet Street hacks and people of supposed good standing in society – it was an exclusive club! And we were all going raving mad, and then later on with me wearing the mask in there and doing the full image thing – that was quite amusing."

Contemporaries Iron Maiden had hardly been quiet themselves; by the time the Heavy Metal Crusade dates came about, their 'Skyward' demo had soared to the top of the Soundhouse chart, and their growing excellence in the live arena meant that not only were they building a large and enthusiastic fanbase, they'd also begun to negotiate with a potential manager, one Rodney Smallwood.

"One day Steve came to me and said, 'We've got management, a manager who I'd like you to meet," remembers Kay. "And of course, that was Rod; he and I became friends back then for a while. Rod was a very funny, droll

Yorkshireman who took no nonsense from anybody; he'd already managed Steve Harley and Cockney Rebel, and worked for NEMS so he knew his stuff." And Maiden continued through 1979 developing their stagecraft, sound and aesthetic accordingly, developing activities with growing confidence and the single-mindedness of their founder, Steve Harris. With mercurial vocalist Paul Di'Anno barking, growling and prowling up front, Maiden's stock was ever rising.

As was the stock of the new Samson singer. As things turned out, the very first rehearsals went so well that the group wrote four new songs in just under a week, namely 'Take It Like A Man', 'Too Close To Rock', 'Walking Out On You', and 'Hammerhead', all of which were later set to tape.

"We went back into rehearsal and wrote some more new material including 'Manwatcher' and 'Vice Versa'", said Paul Samson. "The management began to feel that the elusive major deal would only be achieved if we presented the labels with the songs that we had written since Bruce had joined. Def Leppard were reportedly signing to Phonogram for an enormous sum, and Saxon had signed to Carrere, so the release of *Survivors* on an indie label for no advance was not very helpful to our financial situation."[38]

It is also during this intensive rehearsal period that Mr Dickinson was endowed with the rather strange nickname: Bruce Bruce. The popular reading of how this came about is that it is a very specific reference to a Monty Python sketch, entitled, 'Bruces', which was first aired on British TV in Episode 22 of that show on November 24, 1970. In that particular comedy short, four Australians from the Philosophy Department of Walamaloo are sitting around chewing the fat – but as they are all Aussies, their names are all Bruce. (I'm lost too, don't worry). When a new professor, Michael Baldwin, is welcomed on board to teach political science, the other four Bruces ask if they can't just call him Bruce, to avoid 'confusion'. Subsequently, they refer to him as New-Bruce for the rest of the typically surreal sketch, which plays with the idea of crass and raw-mannered salt-of-the-earth type Aussies swilling beer and proclaiming their very macho opinions to the world whilst holding down very intellectually-stimulating jobs and careers, such duality being a familiar Python theme.

So far, so good; where the confusion appears to have arisen is in the re-telling of the story of an exchange between Dickinson and Paul Samson very early in proceedings. Samson enquired as to Dickinson's second name – and hence confusion occurred, as, of course, the singer's full name is Paul Bruce Dickinson. "I'd meant his surname," said Paul Samson, "and he'd thought I'd meant his middle name and I said, 'Wot, Bruce Bruce?' and everybody roared up laughing. Ramkup really liked it though and it stuck so Bruce Bruce he became."[39]

"What probably got mixed up there," according to Rob Grain, at least, "was basically that within the Samson circle, if anybody joined – manager, road crew, soundman – they were referred to as The New Bruce. So when Bruce joined, he was New Bruce *and* his name was Bruce. That's basically how the Bruce Bruce thing came about." Regardless, the joke must have worn a little thin when Paul Bruce Dickinson attempted to cash cheques made out by Ramkup Management in his alter-ego's name.

All in good heart; the new four-piece was more than content with the way things were sounding, although not everyone was as immediately enamoured of the new set-up. "When you saw the band with Bruce it went up a level," recalls Grain. "To be honest with you, the first time I saw them with Bruce I didn't like it. And I said to Paul, 'What have you done?' Because when you get a new person in the band, the music changes, and I felt the music had changed for the worse. I didn't think he sang the original songs so well, but in fairness to Bruce that's probably 'cause I was used to Paul singing them. So my first impression was that it was a wrong move. And I think that was quite a general impression amongst Samson fans. I saw them a couple of weeks later at The Bandwagon, and they didn't die a death – but they didn't go down very well at all. The general vibe around the place was that people preferred them as a three-piece."

By this point, Neal Kay – at the same time as both running the most successful rock disco in London, perhaps the UK, and touring with the Heavy Metal Crusade – had gained a larger venue within which to showcase the live acts that comprised the newly-christened NWOBHM.

"I was offered control one night a week of the Music Machine in Camden Town London," he says. "It was the old BBC Theatre and held around 1500-1800. It had an upstairs as well, a back bar, a stage bar. It was a hell of a place, it was dirty and filthy and we loved it: It was rock 'n' roll. The manager was a guy called Mick Parker, he was a very nice bloke. He asked me if I would like to do my own promotions, he'd pay me and I'd compere the night and present two or three bands."

"And I thought, 'Thank fuck for that, that's it!' Cause we couldn't do it at the 'wagon which was too small. We had six big portable blocks [at The Bandwagon] which we'd put in and the bands would play in front of me, but we really and truly needed something this big to properly present the bands to the industry. Being in Camden, they didn't mind coming. They came to the 'wagon anyway but the stage was better and Mick paid for a sensible P.A. and lights. That happened at the right time. At the same time we're doing the 'wagon and we're on this Heavy Metal Crusade with Alistair Primrose."

For the time being, however, there was recorded material to get out there, and the 'Mr Rock & Roll' single (this time with 'Primrose Shuffle' as its B-side) was re-released in July by Laser Music, who subsequently agreed to release the already-recorded album, *Survivors*, onto the shelves of the UK's record stores, which they duly did in September 1978. The LP's cover, however, rather mischievously airbrushes both Bruce Bruce and Chris

Aylmer into the recent history of the band; but, as John McCoy recalls, their credits – as vocals, harmonica and guitar, and bass respectively – are less to do with what they actually contributed to the album recordings, and more to do with their forthcoming roles in Samson.

"It was a bit of a weird time," recalls Samson producer and long-time collaborator Big John "The whole thing was very strange. There was actually a release on Lightning Records, and that picture was without Bruce, and when Bruce came in, his picture suddenly appears. I've always hated that cover, it's absolutely atrocious. It was difficult for the management; I suppose they wanted it to seem that the band that they managed, and was going out on tour, was the band that recorded the album. So on the back of the album, it didn't actually specify who played what, and when. Bruce wasn't around *at all* when we recorded that but I suppose it made sense to them to have his name on there, and make it seem like he was involved. Paul had a lot of new stuff, but I wasn't able to work on it with him. He wanted to continue our relationship into writing the next album, but I was just so busy at that time, that had to be left by the way. I think it was right that the guys all got involved in the writing. You've got to go out and play it, you've got to feel involved in it."

"When Bruce joined," remembers Rob Grain, "They virtually went straight out on the road on the *Survivors* tour. But what happened was that because they'd started writing new songs it was probably frustrating – they were doing a tour promoting the album that had just come out but they wanted to get on with the new stuff that they were writing, so when they did the *Survivors* tour there were four new songs in the set which eventually went onto the next album, which was [to be] called *Head On*."

Bruce's familiarity with the *Survivors* material was one thing, but the tracks were simply not written for him, some of them even pre-dating the renaming of Samson itself. As McCoy rightly notes, they were written for Paul and as such they didn't really suit Bruce's range, or provide him with a basis from which to really soar. And whilst the band were trying to incorporate new material into a set which was supposed to be linked to the sonic aesthetic of the blues/rock vibe of *Survivors*, there was a collision course waiting to happen. Much like Rob Grain, and the Samson fanbase in general, McCoy wasn't hugely impressed with the Bruce experience at first.

"The management and record company were very keen for them to have a singer," he says. "I think the first time I really saw Bruce, Paul was raving: 'I've found this singer, I've found this singer, he's absolutely brilliant!' blah, blah, blah – and me and Bernie Torme [fresh from supporting Boomtown Rats with his own band, and now employed as guitarist for Ian Gillan'] and someone else from Gillan went to *Crackers*, a club in Wardour Street. It was just a little gig, they did some numbers with Bruce and it was fucking horrible. The whole band was horrible, it was a naff gig." Torme was similarly underwhelmed. "It was the old Vortex club that I'd played in as a punk," says the guitarist. "When NWOBHM began, it kind of changed its colours and became a NWOBHM club. I knew Paul but I hadn't seen him in a while, so John dragged me down because you know the band had changed and our Paul had a singer now."

"To be honest I don't really recall an awful lot about him – I always liked Paul anyway I suppose, what Paul had done up till that point was blues. It was poppier, rockier blues. The main thing I remember about Bruce was that most singers in bands – and this goes continually up to today – are fairly mouthy people and confident and generally fairly aggressive. And Bruce wasn't, he was a fairly quiet, laid back bloke."

"At the time they used to use pyrotechnics and one of the pyros exploded in one of the punters' faces – that's the only thing I can recall basically out of the gig; the most spectacular [thing being] almost blowing up a member of the audience!"

Following the prevailing winds of the time, the initial reaction to the expanded Samson family had been a little hesitant. But it soon began to click into place a little more. They played the following week at the Music Machine," recalls McCoy, "and I went down to that and there was the sort of inkling of the Bruce we now know coming out of his shell there. It was a big gig for him to join that band at that time. He'd done hardly anything [in music prior to joining Samson] and he tried his hardest to fit in the band's sense of humour and just to do his best, but I'm sure he wouldn't mind me saying, he used to look very, very silly. He has leopardskin tights, a lovely moustache – a sort of Peter Wyngarde moustache – and a bowler hat. It's not exactly the image of a heavy rock singer. And he sort of just ran around stage like a demented monkey! But he obviously had an *incredible* range and the couple of new songs that they played that night I remember as being really good and being quite impressed. I talked to Paul about it afterwards and he said, 'We're committing to the guy', and I said, 'Basically he just needs to learn his stagecraft. He needs to know about handling an audience 'cause that's what you've got this guy for – to involve the audience in the gig.'"

Samson may have been growing into their status as a quartet to be reckoned with, but not everybody would rate the music they were doing as progressive. Enter Neal Kay once again. "The problem with Paul is that his heroes were in the past and the kids' heroes were going in the future. Paul's music was very, very Hendrix, Frank Marino, Rush-styled influence. Iron Maiden and Praying Mantis and others represented the future and not the past. Paul was an awesome guitar player, to hear him do 'Talking About A Feeling' live at the 'wagon was an experience. He was, to me, one of the great blues/rock guitar players of NWOBHM. He would say if he was alive today [Paul Samson died from cancer on August 9, 2002] that there was no such thing as the New Wave Of British Heavy Metal – he was around before it but he couldn't understand what all the fuss was about. He couldn't see it. In desperation to try and win the crowd back, he started resorting to these pyrotechnical displays where it was more bloody pyros than music."

The stage show was, nevertheless, attracting attention; from the antics of the gimp-masked Thunderstick to the bundle of nervous energy that was Bruce Bruce, topped off by the free-riffing Paul Samson himself, the only steadying influence was the Ox-like Chris Aylmer, holding the groove down manfully even as the stage was beset by explosives from all angles. And it was time to take the show out on the road, old mates McCoy and Torme helping to secure Samson a coveted support slot during October 1979 with Gillan. For Bruce, this was an unbelievable development; as a major Deep Purple fan, his musical taste and even vocal style owed a massive amount to Ian Gillan; to go on tour with one of his heroes so early in a career was simply astonishing – although his first meeting with his hero didn't go exactly to plan, according to Thunderstick.

"The very first time he met Ian Gillan he was sick," laughs the drummer. "He literally went into the toilet and threw up with nerves. We were in Kingsway, I can't remember if we were recording or if we were just down there for a night off with the rest of the Gillan band 'cause we all kinda mixed together. In came Ian and Bruce disappeared, we didn't know where he'd [gone]. The next thing we knew, Ian came into the control room and said, 'You'd better go and have a look at your singer, he's in the toilet throwing up, he looks really ill.' It was 'cause of the nerves of meeting Ian Gillan, which is quite amusing."

"[Bruce] – he really loved Ian. completely," laughs John McCoy. "He was quite over-awed, you know." As you would be. The tour featured full support from Randy California, and then, as Torme recalls, "The Speedometers and Samson on about half [of the dates] each."

"I mean, to Bruce I think it was even more of a big deal because he idolised Ian. One of the things I also remember is that he tried to keep up with Ian in terms of drinking and this wasn't a clever idea because there wasn't anyone on the planet who could keep up in drinking with Ian. Having come out of Purple who were, you know, a fairly hard-drinking band. I can remember on at least one occasion of Bruce being [very pissed] and Ian not even being slightly drunk!"

"I think he liked him," offers Torme. "He did – all of us did, because Bruce was a nice bloke. There wasn't any second agenda; he was just a nice bloke, basically."

"We rehearsed for the Gillan tour and wrote another new song, 'Hard Times'," wrote Paul Samson in his diaries, excerpts of which are kindly reproduced here, "which featured an *a capella* section with Bruce and myself, and put it into the set. We all did something mad to our hair. I put a tub of red henna on mine, Bruce had his cut by his grandmother, who put a bowl on his head and cut round it, Barry had dyed his bright red and looked like Ronald McDonald, and Chris looked as though his had gone wrong. It started off yellow, then green, blue and red and he looked a right tit! Anyone else would have dyed it brown that night, but he rode the insults until it faded months later."[40]

Touring is a very intense experience: spending hour upon hour on the road, often extremely hung over and/or not entirely 'with it', alongside people with whom you share often extreme moments of emotion, a difficult thing at the best of times. The underside of Dickinson's remarkable vocal talent was that his background was rather different from the more streetwise bandmates with whom he'd landed.

"When Bruce came along, he was as green as grass; he was a college kid and he didn't know shit from breakfast time at the end of the day!" offers Thunderstick. "Paul and I were streetwise south-east Londoners; we'd both been brought up in a similar background and had known each other from schooldays – we didn't go to school together but we'd known each other 'cause we both used to rehearse on a farm. There was one electricity point and boxes of Brussels sprouts all over the place."

"Samson was a strange band in that it was a very 'clannish' band," notes Torme. "The Gillan band was basically a lot of fairly diverse people. I mean, I'd been a punk, Colin Towns had been a Jazzer and whatever else and there wasn't really an ethos of having to fit in as a band, you just had to play – and it was good in that it was fairly grown up in terms of that. We all basically talked about each other behind each others' back, 'Oh shit, look at the clothes he's wearing!' you know. But basically, all of us did it and it sort of worked."

"In Samson there was a awful lot more pressure, I think, to have everyone in the band fit in and at the start off point I think Bruce felt he didn't. I can remember there being some major argument on the coach. They were always up the back of the coach and Bruce was down at the front of the coach, and Paul and Barry and Chris basically had Bruce's case and were taking single items of clothing out and chucking them up the coach at Bruce. And to us this was not acceptable basically, so we turned around and said, 'Look, stop!" and it did. At the time I think there was kind of an element, that they felt that Bruce was a tiny bit of a middle-class kid. When there were temporary arguments it was *extremely* extreme, it was like a gang of kids basically having an argument. To be honest, looking back at it and even at the time, I was always of the opinion that Bruce handled it really well."

"I left the tour bus the day after that and drove myself," laughs McCoy, "because it was starting to get hard work. It was getting a bit stinky and a bit crowded with people that had been met at the previous night's gig. You know, you'd get on the bus and there'd be a body there, and [you'd] think 'Who the hell's this?' Usually female. It was a good, old-fashioned rock 'n' roll tour, pretty bananas. But we had a good time on that tour, it was a lot of fun. It was like being on tour with the Marx Brothers, being on tour with Samson. They were just completely insane, everyday. I think Bruce basically just tried to keep up with them all. It was a really crazy band and a crazy time."

"We were the naughty schoolboys on that tour," laughs Thunderstick. "We went to the joke shop before the tour and bought loads of masks and pea shooters and stink bombs and this, that and the other. Bruce let a fire extinguisher off on the very first night of the tour and we were threatened to be thrown off of it. It was the powder type which didn't go down too well. It went absolutely everywhere. It was at the gig, after we'd played. After Ian had played he was doing an interview with some press and Bruce let this fire extinguisher off and it just went everywhere."

"Not only that but Ian came over to me and asked me if anybody had any cigarettes, 'cause I smoked at the time. Ian was talking to all these record guys, a comparatively small record label, but it was important to Ian. I'd primed all these cigarettes with these smoke pellets and he handed them all out and all these guys were talking away, until all of a sudden all this flaky smoke type dusty stuff's coming off their cigarettes. On the tour coach there was Randy California – from Spirit – Gillan, and us, at the back of the coach like naughty kids in class, firing peashooters at people, just raving mad, we had all these strange masks, stink bombs and all kinds of stuff. It was Bernie and John trying to be as professional as they possibly could, Ian was travelling on his own with his girlfriend in his Roller and these guys from America, Randy and his bassist and drummer thinking, 'What the hell...?' We gave the bass player from Randy California some chewing gum which made his mouth go bright red; he was chewing away and he looked at us and we were pissing ourselves laughing. He looked at us and said, 'What's the matter with you guys? You guys are really into your own personal jokes aren't you?' And we were just absolutely cracking up 'cause his mouth was bright red and foaming and he didn't know it."

"We were serious about what we did musically, but that didn't mean that we had to be really serious people all the time. And we weren't. We were headcases – we were raving mad. You read interviews with Motley Crue and the fans love it that they were raving mad. We didn't take loads of drugs, it was never chemicals with us all the time. It was smoking dope, yeah, but we were just naturally mad as well. There was a lot of pressure on at the time and we were kids, growing up, developing our styles and learning what it was like to be in a professional hard rock band and being out on the road. It came natural to us, we didn't feel we needed to live up to that kind of ideal of throwing televisions out of the window or anything, we were just naturally mad."

Thunderstick is somewhat upset, however, by the occasional portrayal of the Samson gang as a bunch of hooligans. Which they weren't. "It comes over as 'we were never serious' and that's so far from the truth. We were serious about what we did. The way we went about it was probably wrong, in hindsight, but we were always deadly serious. The moment I sat behind a

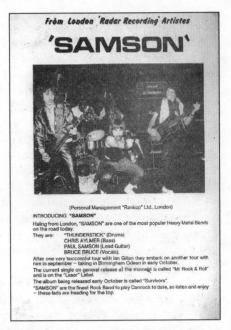

drumkit, or Paul strapped his guitar on, we were serious about what we did and we would always try and push the parameters as much as we probably could, musically." Once the gigs were finished, however, there was plenty of room for pissing about, and why the hell not?"

To all intents and purposes, both Bruce and Samson were feeling their way down a slightly different path than even the previously hard-gigging pre-Dickinson Samson trio had necessarily encountered. It was a time that firmly set the group up as a four-piece band.

"At the beginning I think it was kind of hard for them," recalls Torme, "because our audience was always kind of partisan. It was basically an Ian audience and at the beginning even I got a bit of stick – and I think that the support bands tended to generally get a tiny bit of a hard time. And I think that, coupled with Bruce's lack of experience at the beginning, it was a fairly steep learning curve."

But learn he did; mostly from the side of the stage, watching one of his all-time heroes work the crowd into a frenzy night after night. Being a studious chap, and a very bright chap, Bruce very quickly began to pick up some tips. It was the tour that cemented his place as a performer who could compete at a high level with the best of them.

"It wasn't an enforced thing, but Paul got Bruce to watch Ian Gillan each night and say 'Watch this bit, watch that bit, look what they do here!'" remembers McCoy. "It sounds crass now, but the guy was learning. Ian is a brilliant singer [more so than] in terms of winding an audience up; in fact

Bruce is probably better at that now. But that was my memory of it, I mean, it was interesting to watch the band grow on that tour. By the end of the tour, it seemed like it was a band, and not just Samson plus a singer, they were locked in. And destined for big things. The audience knew the connection between us and them, all the gigs were sold out. It couldn't have been better for them to play big gigs at that time. I do believe if they'd stuck together, they would have been a lot bigger. Because as I say, Bruce slowly came into his own, and by the end of the tour he was like he was in charge. He was running the show, whereas at the start of his involvement with the band, he was just like a guy that was onstage acting silly."

"And he had this bizarre haircut!" Thunderstick recalls. "In actual fact, we went fucking mad at him because his girlfriend (sic) at the time actually cut his hair by doing the archetypal thing of putting a bowl on his head and cutting round the bowl! That first promo picture he has that haircut – we went mad: 'It's a heavy metal band for Chrissake!'"

The eighteen-date tour also featured a day off to record a radio session with the late, legendary DJ, Tommy Vance; meanwhile, the album *Survivors* was gathering four star reviews from the likes of *Sounds* and *Record Mirror* and peaked at Number Three in the Indie album charts, a great fillip for the group. Refusing to rest on their laurels, however, they stayed on the road for the rest of 1979 honing their craft with a headline tour, supported by the brilliant vocalist Nicky Moore and his band and ended it with the double whammy of both headlining their own gig in front of over a thousand souls in Folkestone, but also appearing on the front cover of *Sounds* – complete with a picture of Thunderstick, clad in his now-familiar leather balaclava, with the splendid caption, 'The New Face Of Heavy Metal'.

Samson were not the only ones making progress. Elsewhere, Iron Maiden self-released the 'Spaceward' demos – sans 'Strange World' and retitled *The Soundhouse Tapes* – and promptly sold five thousand copies. Subsequently, the record companies finally, belatedly perhaps, began to take an interest in Maiden, and the combined forces of Smallwood – not a man to be under-estimated lightly – and Neal Kay led to an EMI A&R man coming down to see Maiden in a gig at the Bandwagon. It was packed.

"The A&R guy was about as big as me, about 5 ft 5, if that," laughs Kay. "He was right at the back and he couldn't see a fucking thing, he could not see anything! The legend goes that at the end of the night, he said, 'Well, it sounded good and the people liked it so I guess we'd better 'ave it.' And so they signed." On November 26, 1979 to be exact. There is a lesson in there somewhere kids: if you're after getting a record deal, make sure the A&R scouts can't see anything. Poke their eyes out, if needs be.

Earlier in the year, however, a potential problem which may have delayed matters a little had been caused by what amounted to nothing more than backstage horseplay on the *Crusade* tour.

"There was a falling-out between Samson and Iron Maiden," explains Rob Grain. "Not a person-to-person falling-out, it was just politics really. But what you've gotta bear in mind is that all the bands at the time were trying to headline the same gigs, get the same record deals. So obviously it gets a little bit bitchy, everyone trying to get one jump further up the ladder than anyone else. There was an incident where one of the Music Machine shows had Iron Maiden, and EMI were coming down to see them. So they'd laid on this spread of food in the dressing room. Well, of course, while they were onstage Samson's crew went in and scoffed the lot! So by the time Maiden had finished and invited EMI backstage for the banquet it had all gone. There was lots of that sort of thing going on, inter-band rivalry."[41]

Which could lead to potential problems. Imminently, however, the only blot on the Maiden landscape, in truth, was when they parted ways with their drummer, Doug Sampson. Touring was gruelling, not least due to the fact that in these early days the band were largely still working in day jobs, and often had to sleep in the back of Steve Harris' seven tonne truck, warmly referred to (the only warm thing about it) as *The Green Goddess*. It's not to everyone's taste, kipping in the back of lorries requires a certain kind of character. Doug's eventual replacement was unveiled as none other than ex-Samson kit-clanger Clive Burr, thus completing the drummer swap – Thunderstick had previously been a member of Maiden for around eight months during 1977, and indeed, prior to Burr snagging the job, had actually jammed with his former bandmates once more over the 1979 Christmas period with a view to possibly returning to the fold.

"Prior to joining Iron Maiden [the first time around]," explains the drummer, "I'd been in a professional band in Sicily and I was listening to a lot of prog rock, bands like PFM, Steve Hillage, they were all kind of King Crimson, I loved the time changes and that's what I loved about the early Iron Maiden stuff."

"So I got re-offered the job with Iron Maiden; it was after the Heavy Metal Crusade. I got a phonecall and it ruined my Christmas. They said, 'We've just got rid of Dougie Sampson, are you interested in re-joining?' and I went down and played with them after Christmas. I remember Rod Smallwood saying to me, 'This band's going to be bigger than Led Zeppelin!' and I thought, 'Well, that's really nice you've got that amount of confidence in your own band.' Little did I know! I remember saying at the time, 'The thing really is the Thunderstick character is really taking off.'" So Thunderstick stuck with his gimp-masked alter ego and his current band Samson, rather than go back to the more sedate, controlled Barry Graham drumming persona bashing out the steady beat at the back, which Iron Maiden required.

Maiden's continued existence was – as it for many arguably still is – down to the dogged vision of one man, and that is the band's bassist and driving force, Steve Harris. It is, says Thunderstick, Harris' band, and he is massively responsible for keeping it going and instrumental in all decisions.

"It was always his [band], always. Without a doubt. Even in the early days when I was with them, Steve just had that definition of foresight. There was nothing that was gonna deviate him, he was gonna go for it. In his attitude and his playing. He was living with his grandma at the time, I had my own house in south-east London, in Plumstead, [when I was with Maiden the first time around]. I had one room in my house where the kit was set up and he used to come round and we'd go through bass and drum lines. He was very serious about it and I always thought it was his band. And it was; time has shown it has always been his."

"It was a big deal [to be asked to rejoin]; I was absolutely gobsmacked by it. Can you imagine how gobsmacked I was a few weeks later when we were in Kingsway, recording *Head On* and John McCoy phoned up and said, 'Guess who's just taken a gig with Iron Maiden – Clive Burr!' I thought, 'Oh my God!' So I was playing in Samson with Iron Maiden still written all over my drum cases – and vice versa. Clive was doing the same with Samson all over his drum cases!" The links between Samson and Maiden, like those between the Gillan band and Samson, were very strong in this period – and would soon, of course, be even stronger.

But for the time being, Clive it was for Maiden, and Barry stayed as Thundersticks. It was becoming evident, however, that things were really happening in the New Wave Of British Heavy Metal, and it looked like a definite vanguard was indeed emerging.

All in all, for Bruce Dickinson it had been a rather decent year. He was only twenty one years of age, and had not only fulfilled his ambition of appearing on a major stage, he'd done it alongside one of his major inspirations; the music he loved seemed to be firmly back on the British rock agenda, and with a new decade looming, the only way was surely up.

chapter five:
Head On Collisions ...

The new decade in the UK began with the sharp realisation that the excitement and newness of both the emergent punk and NWOBHM scenes was settling down into something ready to be absorbed by a more mainstream audience. In the case of the metal bands, this meant the inevitable historical marker being put down to set the lid, if you like, on the era. After the triumphs and occasional pain of the Heavy Metal Crusade, the next obvious step was to release a compilation of all the bands concerned on vinyl.[42]

"Metal For Muthas came about 'cause of all the demo tapes I had," says Neal Kay. "A bloke called Ashley Goodhall working junior round table A&R for EMI and myself got together and decided they'd put out this compilation of new bands. I wrote a set of sleevenotes for it, believing EMI was going to put up the money for all these bands to be re-recorded whose tracks I'd picked. Unfortunately, boy, was I wrong, 'cause they *didn't*, which annoyed me, and the artwork was absolutely disgusting. Terrible! Fuckin' tacky! But it's considered by many as a landmark album because it represents a point in time where it was recognised that there was so much happening with small bands in rock at the time."

Metal For Muthas – with its frankly horrendous painting of a purple-cloaked knight wielding her bass guitar (which looks like a Japanese-built Fender Jazz)[43] as a jousting staff atop a mechanical/heavily-armoured fire-breathing horse[44] in some kind of apocalyptic-acid sunset – is an intriguing album. Represented on the disc, which was released on EMI in February 1980, are several of the more familiar Soundhouse/Bandwagon/NWOBHM names – Praying Mantis, Sledgehammer, Angel Witch all holding up manfully with their contributions – alongside the also-rans (hello Ethel The Witch) and some not-yets, including Xero, a group complete with Bruce's old sparring partner in Shots, guitarist Bill Liesegang. For Samson's part, their contribution is a ballad-esque hangover track, a McCoy production and a re-recording of the McCoy/Samson composition which duly appeared on the *Survivors* album. 'Tomorrow Or Yesterday', is a piano-based and very classic workout that owes as much to 1960s soul as it does to anything 'New Wave'; it is, in truth, a timeless piece of music which could have been written at any moment between 1960 and 2007. Paul's solo in the third quarter actually has a tone and aesthetic to it that is, arguably, ten years ahead of its time –

sonically, at least. Samson's offering, however, cannot compete with the dual assault of their contemporaries, compadres, and ultimately competition, Iron Maiden. What turned out to be their second single, 'Sanctuary', not only opened the album with a breathtaking pace, but they are also the only band to appear twice on the LP (the other being the storming 'Wrathchild'). Significantly, Maiden's new management and label were now enabling the band to begin to stand out a little; perhaps demanding respect by their invention, energy and professional approach.

Back in Bruce-land, there was the little matter of another UK tour to contend with, this time with Samson as support to Robin Trower (Maiden were out at this time on the road with the *Metal For Muthas* tour, along with Praying Mantis, Tygers Of Pang Tang and Raven). Although Trower was a legendary English guitarist, whose stint in 1960s heroes Procul Harum is well-documented, and despite his obvious influence on Paul Samson's career, for a group ostensibly keen on being part of the future of the British hard rock scene, Samson's support slot was, possibly, ill-advised, especially if they were seeking to place themselves within the context of being future heroes rather than aligning themselves with the classic musicians of the past.

It was also, inevitably, a series of gigs that were full of incident, as Paul Samson writes in his as-yet unpublished autobiography, *Burning Ambition*. "The tour carried on to Liverpool to Glasgow Apollo where Bruce nearly fell fourteen feet off the front of the stage 'cause we had so little room, then Edinburgh, Birmingham and Hammersmith Odeon. We went down well every night, although we found it harder work in the seated theatres, while Trower's crew did all they could to wind us up. I took to watching Robin's gig each night sat on a flight case at the side of the stage and learnt a lot. He was definitely the master of the understatement and in some of the spacier jams you could hear a pin drop in the gaps though they played loud. Jimmy Dewar the bass and vocalist was always nice to us, but Trower and the drummer barely came near us. I tried several times to have a conversation with Robin, but the most I could get out of him was, 'Alright?' as he shuffled past in his anorak. At Sheffield, things blew up a little bit with the crew when at the soundcheck the monitors were feeding back so much ... in the ensuing fracas, [Bruce's] microphone got broken and we were presented with a bill for £300 for damaging the equipment, and told we would have no monitors for the rest of the tour ... we'd had enough, so we told the tour manager we were going home and pulling off the tour. He went into a panic and said, 'Robin will go mad if you pull off the tour,' and the outcome was that there was no [£300] bill and there were monitors for the rest of the tour. Although God knows what the outfront sound was like."[45]

For Paul, he must have learnt a great deal about guitar playing from Trower, and the band were well-received wherever they played on the tour, which was completed at Newcastle City Hall on February 12, 1980.

"It was an unbelievable mix between the two [audiences]," remembers Thunderstick. "Stoned hippies for Robin Trower, and young kids hanging onto this NWOBHM thing – it was a total mismatch of audience, it was very interesting and we got very laid back toward the end of the tour in soundchecks. It was great, kind of going into these spacey jams and things."

"Yet again, we almost got thrown off the tour on the first night; we used to make it a kind of recurring incident that would happen. The first night would always be the worst night. We did 'Rock Me Baby' as an encore, Robin's guitar tech came back afterwards and said, 'If you do that again, you're off the tour', we said 'What. Do an encore?' and he said, 'No, if you do 'Rock Me Baby' 'cause that's Robin's encore! He does that.' Which we were supposed to know.

I remember Bruce unplugging a wedge, and passing it to the first guy in the audience and saying, 'Can you pass that to the guy who's doing the sound engineering at the back, and tell him that all I'm getting is screaming feedback through it.' And we just watched this wedge make its way back to the control desk at the back! I loved it."

"I was having a whale of time and enjoying myself; we were gathering momentum no matter which tour we were on, we were still getting a large amount of audience turning up to see Samson, which was great."

By now, Bruce had firmly cut his teeth as a frontman, confident in the material the band were offering as well as having won over the previously sceptical fans that had greeted his addition to the Samson line-up with some initial bemusement. And just in time too – Samson almost immediately went out on tour supporting Rainbow, with a series of huge concerts pulling ten thousand people or more; no place for the weak and certainly no place to hide.

"We had a great gig [on the Edinburgh leg of the tour] and the sound onstage was excellent. The crowd were with us all the way and sang their heads off in the participation bits, and Bruce led us well. All too soon our forty minutes were up. The Rainbow tour manager was full of congratulations, and was somewhat surprised at our reception. He said that even Ritchie had enjoyed it. Evidently he watched the set through the one inch gap between my amps and speaker cabinets."[46]

Samson were performing so well during this period, pyrotechnics, and gimp-masked drummers and all, that when the crowd demanded they perform an encore at the Wembley Arena date, the band duly obliged – but unbeknownst to them, this was not a popular decision backstage.

Jennie Halsall was the major freelance PR of the metal scene at the time, and she remembers the incident well. "I was known as the Heavy Metal Queen Of PR, which sounds ridiculous now!" she told me. "I'd worked for EMI then I went off to work with David Geffen and Elliot Roberts in L.A. with The Eagles and Linda Rondstadt and all that lot; I couldn't get a job when I got back so I was a freelance PR again and started my own business which I still have, thirty years on. I looked after Ritchie Blackmore's Rainbow, Cozy Powell, Purple, all those bands. Samson were like the fledgling, new, exciting young band."

After the headliners did not play an encore, "the punters started to break up the place and I never ran so fast from the box office as fast as that! The audience kicked off and started to smash the place up."

Surprised, but undaunted, Samson entered the studio during March 1980 for initial sessions for their new album, and to record the first single to feature Bruce as vocalist – perhaps fuelled by a sense of renewed urgency following Iron Maiden both appearing on *Top Of The Pops* performing their 'Running Free' single, and playing it live on the famous show to boot, unheard of at the time. In Samson's case, the unavailability of McCoy due to other commitments meant that the band would be recording and producing the songs themselves; all new tracks credited to the quartet that now comprised Samson. Initially the intent was to come away from Kingsway Recording Studios with a three track single – 'Vice Versa', 'Hammerhead' and 'Manwatcher' were the tracks initially mooted to be put down to tape – but as it turned out the band were sharp, on a roll, and in fact blasted through enough tracks for an album proper. The previous six months of bedding Bruce Bruce into proceedings had clearly added a vigour and focus to the music which had put a real edge on a band doused in hard rock. And if there's one thing that great hard rock bands can do, it is ramp up the excitement and work quickly. Once the vibe is there and rolling, a band with the technical ability of Paul Samson, the steadiness of Chris Aylmer and the Keith Moon-esque thudding invention of Thunderstick can fly very high very quickly.

Thunderstick maintains that, in his opinion, he produced a lot of that album. "I don't care what anybody says, I know that I was there longer and more hours than anybody else. I was the one who sat there with Chas the engineer and did Bruce's vocals. Paul and Chris went home, night after night, and I spent ages on that. I've actually got tapes here, outtakes of Bruce doing 'Walking Out On You', different tracks."

"I'd always loved production and Paul had always been more about the live aspect and playing; I loved Brian Eno and those kind of people who'd gone into the studio and pushed the parameters a little bit. So all the backwards stuff, and the bits and pieces of percussion and gongs and tubular bells like on 'Take It Like A Man', counter melodies and madness – that was all mine. I pushed really hard for a production credit on it, and all I ended up getting was 'Additonal Ideas By Thunderstick' which was quite a bone of contention. It became a standing joke although it hurt a lot inside because I always felt I should have had a production credit on that."

Thunderstick remembers the actual recording process very clearly, as he told me when I interviewed him for this book. "We put the backing tracks down, bass and drums, the three of us playing live and Paul either playing from the control room or somewhere we wouldn't get overspill on the mics," he says. "As soon as we thought the drums were okay, and there might be some bits and pieces that needed patching, we'd do that. The bass wouldn't be redone, we'd hope to get bass and drums down in the same track. Then we'd put down the overdubs on the guide guitar track we'd recorded. A lot of the time Paul would play in the control room, we'd crank the monitors right up and he'd stand there and just play. We all took part in backing vocals and, as I say, I did the sessions with Bruce on vocals and all the kind of madness was last on the list."

"Alright, it may sound a bit dated [now] but more than anything else, it is a band, the sound of a band finding its feet, and I love it for that, I really do. I'm going absolutely mad all over the place on it, playing-wise. Paul was pushing himself in different directions and using different sounds and techniques; he had the SG he used all the time but then on a couple of tracks he used a Strat … we were just pushing it; *Head On* was our *Sergeant Pepper*."

"It was Bruce's first crack at doing it for real, and we wanted to get the best vocal performance out of him. Some of it came easy. Some of it didn't. 'Walking Out On You' was hard to get. We actually ended up looping one of his choruses because by the end of it … even though we were able to push out the boundaries, we were somewhat limited on time and still gigging between it as well, so we still had to get things done as quickly and efficiently as possible. 'Walking Out On You' is actually the chorus, one take of the chorus that was the best, then we looped it and put it in on each chorus because he'd shot his voice by the end of the night."

Bruce Bruce also had rather an innovative way of warming himself up to get the vocal tracks done, as the producer/drummer remembers. "He used to go and scream at the walls, he'd go and stand in the corner," he laughs. "Bruce used to walk around, he'd get that look in his eyes, walk about and become somewhat distant and removed, and just go to the wall and go 'AAAAAAAAAAAAA' in the corner! I wouldn't say it was hard, but I wouldn't say it was easy either: it was his first 'Big Thing' and he just wanted to make the best vocal performances he could. And also, to become a member of the band, because it took him a while to actually integrate into the three-piece; we had our humour and all that kind of thing, he came in and we had to make it a four-piece. It takes time, you go to a new college, a new school, a new job – it takes you a while to integrate and become part and parcel of what the whole thing represents. And that was his opportunity. That album was his vehicle, 'Alright I'm gonna show you that I am the lead singer of Samson.' And he did. We [eventually] got great reviews for it."

Despite the intent to release a single, 'Vice Versa', on May 9, 1980, negotiations between Samson's management, Ramkup, and the label who were interested, EMI, had stalled. Added to a company-wide pressing plant strike causing further delays, this was a huge blow to Bruce and the boys, who could only sit back and watch as Iron Maiden's stock grew ever larger on the back of their astonishing chart placement of Number 4 for their own full-length eponymous debut, a thrilling and rampant metal album of power; one foot in the Deep Purple camp, and – perhaps due more to the lyrics and vocal delivery of Maiden's cheeky-chap, street-urchin singer, Paul Di'Anno – more than a hint of punk rock about it, in attitude at least. The frustrations were obvious, as Bruce Bruce commented in a *Sounds* interview later that year.

"All kinds of things were apparently going to happen but none of them ever seemed to get off the ground. In the end, there was a gap of several months after we recorded *Head On* when we'd ground to a complete standstill, we were out of the press, out of everywhere. So we missed whatever sort of boat that happened to be sailing around at the time."[47]

It was a touch-and-go decision as to which company the band would sign with. Thunderstick recalls that it was a management decision taken, perhaps, for valid reasons at the time. EMI had promised to do an album deal," he says, "but it became, 'we'll put a couple of singles out and see how they do.' They were in the market for the band and we would have got the spot that Iron Maiden had. And it didn't happen because they wanted to put the singles out, and our management being the way they were, really quite rambunctious about the whole thing and said, 'Well, stuff it, we'll go with Gem 'cause they wanna put an album out immediately, and finance the tour and make the film' so it was all over the music press at the time that we were stolen away from EMI – and part of the deal was this film, *Biceps Of Steel*, 'cause they owned Gem who were a film company and had made things like *Phantasm*, and they got hold of John Roseman and we were given scripts."

So activities resumed on June 6, 1980, with the release of the 'Vice Versa' single, now on Gem – a subsidiary of giants RCA – although there was a growing sense of unease between the band and their management.

"Bruce never signed a contract with Ramkup," notes Thunderstick. "He was the only one that was never, ever actually officially signed. All three of us had put pen to paper and signed." The frustration with the management situation, and the constant flux in which the band found themselves, almost had an incredibly dramatic effect on the group. Bruce himself was on the verge of walking away from it all in early May, 1979.

"He said, 'I've had enough of all this,'" says Thunderstick, "because … we really were losing ground, and we were aware of that. It wasn't for the fact that we weren't very good, nothing to do with the performances or the music, if you'll forgive the pun we were still 'head on' with all that.[48] It was becoming quite obvious that we were losing ground. It was just something that happened, I can't remember the logistics of it but he said, 'Fuck it, I've had enough – I'm going to go, we'll see how The Marquee gigs go.' And of course they were great and so he stayed and that was it.

So Bruce performed with the band during two gigs at The Marquee on May 15 and 16. His change of heart stemmed from the age-old mentality as instilled by his grandfather way back in Manor Top, amounting to advice to *never let the bastards grind you down*. During June they spent three long days recording that aforementioned curious short film at the Rainbow with none other than Julien Temple, director of both the Sex Pistols' *Rock N Roll Swindle* film, and later his own more objective *Filth And The Fury* on the same band.[49] The short movie, *Biceps Of Steel*, was financed by Gem/RCA and is a curious, and often hilarious fifteen-minute piece that is based loosely on the biblical Samson. Basically, the story goes thusly: Samson (*Biceps* version) is a roadie for the band who are busy strutting their stuff onstage. For some reason, the orange-jumpsuited security staff begin to beat up a headbanger. Samson steps in and saves the day to universal acclaim. The baddies, being baddies, don't like it so hatch a plot for a harpie to seduce Samson, which she does so effectively that whilst he is in (presumably) post-coital slumber she cuts off his hair, sapping his strength in the best traditions laid out in the *Book Of Judges*. Cue derision from the security guards in the next gig, upon whom Samson gets his own back by managing to tear down the Marshall stacks by the stage onto everyone's heads. It is, in short, pure nonsense (the tracks used in the film by the band onstage are 'Vice Versa' and 'Hard Times') but from another point of view the *Biceps Of Steel* short is nothing short of a full-narrative video, the likes of which would become commonplace with the advent of MTV, which began broadcasting in 1981 – its running time of fifteen minutes was one longer, in fact, than Micky Jackson's much vaunted *Thriller* piece some two years later, and anyway *Thriller*'s weirdo zombies were much less convincing, and a hell of a lot less scary, than some of the crowd members in *Biceps*. The film was intended to be the preceding short to the Hazel O'Connor movie, *Breaking Glass*, an often difficult tale that follows the career of the main character, Kate, on her journey from nobody to pop star, and the long and painful descent into nervous breakdown. It is a piece of its time that both reflects the aesthetic of the New Wave[50] in terms of music, but also the paranoia and growing sense of helplessness as Margaret Thatcher's Tory government began to make its presence felt in the UK.[51]

One thing that has been lost in time is the fact that the roadie – the Samson character – was played by Thunderstick – Barry Graham Purkis – himself. And he enjoyed the experience immensely.

"It was totally mad! Great for me 'cause I was able to play Thunderstick and then the roadie! With a very dodgy moustache and wig. It was an ideal vehicle for me," he remembers, "because I was Thunderstick anyway so they'd only have to do close-up shots of me doing rolls around the kit or whatever, and the rest of the time I was free to be able to play the roadie. When I'm in shot and there's Thunderstick at the back, the guy playing Thunderstick is my then brother-in-law who later ended up being my bass player in the band, also called Thunderstick. He'd followed my career and he'd been there right from the start of Samson so he was able to dress as Thunderstick and do the appropriate movements in 'Vice Versa'."

The humour of the band was still intact, in their usual streetwise, piss-taking way. "Originally they had Dana Gillespie lined up for the Delilah part, but it didn't happen so this girl came out of nowhere. In the bit where she's feeding me the grapes and what have you," continues The Stick. "You see the band in the background; it was great 'cause they were at the back, she comes and leans all over me and I sit up and look at her and all that kind of thing. And you can hear from the back – 'cause they were playing the music on the stage – you can hear them shouting, 'He's got a hard on! He's got a stalk on him!' It was one, big, mad, few days, because it was kind of before the time of videos so it was an idea of doing a short film and it ended up going out as a B-film for *Breaking Glass*, I wish we'd gone and seen it but we never did."[52] A shame, but it is now available on DVD, so turn the lights down low and enjoy ... stalks an all.

Immediately following *Biceps Of Steel*, Samson swiftly recorded 'Angel With A Machine Gun' – intended to be a B-side – and prepared for the release of the new LP, *Head On*, on June 27. The album, great though it was, needed something of a boost sonically, which was provided by Tony Platt – fresh from engineering AC/DC's legendary album, *Highway To Hell*.

"My managers were Zomba," he recalled when I spoke to him, "and Samson were published by Zomba. [The recorded tracks for *Head On* were sounding reasonably] okay, but hadn't been properly sorted out – I went and remixed the entire album and toughened it up a bit 'cause they hadn't had time to bring out the best in the songs." And he did just that. Bruce's full-length long-playing debut is an album that blends a sense of classic rock whilst launching the unearthly screams of a major talent on to a wider world. Not just as a vocalist – his growing control and delivery was occasionally still prone to veering into Ian Gillanism – but also as a collaborating and solo lyricist.

Take opener, 'Hard Times' for example. Musically, it's as classic melodic hard rock as you can get, albeit with a definite punky edge – think AC/DC meets The Skids – but lyrically, when Bruce Bruce sings of fighting and drinking, he could be referring to those rough old Sheffield pubs of his youth; conversely, the references to going down, being head over heels and wanting to teach a lesson to whomever the song is addressed, have definite sexual overtones. 'Take It Like A Man' details the punishment of an errant lad; again, it would be tempting to read this as both a song about S&M (always comically tempting given Thunderstick's penchant for his leather gimp mask!). The heavily sexual 'Vice Versa' is the most early 1970s-influenced moment on the LP, a mid-paced and taut Purple/Sabs influenced workout that stands strong against anything recorded during this period. Paul Samson contributes a jerky solo here whilst Thunderstick and Aylmer sound like they're having the fun of their lives throughout. 'Manwatcher' is a forgettable, but again, sexually-charged mid-paced rocker. 'Too Close To Rock', meanwhile, with its lyrics referring to college, missing lectures, and music as a career, is obviously resonant as a self-affirmation of Bruce's choice of lifestyle and work. The instrumental, 'Thunderburst' follows, partly-written by Thunderstick, which has a similarity to 'The Ides Of March', which was to appear on Maiden's second LP, *Killers* the following year. It is, hence credited to Samson/Purkis/Aylmer/Bruce/S. Harris.

"I came up with a drum pattern that did that constant rolling," explained Thunderstick. "I would have ideas and Steve [Harris] would then transpose that, because I don't play guitar. It was the same with Samson ... I'm unable to pick a guitar up and show my idea, I have to sit there and go, 'du-du du-du du, no, that's the wrong note' – and we'd go through it like that. So that's how it came about. And I had a drum pattern and I was trying to explain the chords to go down on the drum pattern 'cause the whole thing goes around the drum pattern. I think we played it a couple of times with Iron Maiden as an opening track. Just an intro, it was a throwaway thing, not really a track."[53]

'Hammerhead' is pure Bruce, however, the lyrics dealing with the forging of Thor's hammer, Mjollnir, and referencing ancient Norse tradition. The laid-back, Saxon-esque 'Hunted' – with its rather silly lyrics about nailing brains to trees – follows, before Bruce comes back to the fore with 'Take Me To Your Leader', an inventive, and very punky/psychedelic track which deals with flying saucers, astral plains and mother ships on the surface but is also a call to arms. It happens to feature some of the most astonishing vocal performances of the LP; Bruce's incredible range is shown off to its full effect in the post-choruses, a statement of intent and a real marker for any other vocalists on the scene. It's a real head-banging, silly, busy showcase for every member of the band: one moment Aylmer's romping up and down the neck, then Thunderstick rolls raucously round the kit, the next moment it's Paul's turn for a trademark fluid solo, and then it's Bruce taking the reins, working through the octaves magnificently. It's everything Samson could do at their very best – in one four-minute piece of music. As the album comes to a close with 'Walking Out On You', which veers between Hawkwind-y psychedelic rock, Beach Boys-esque backing harmonies, a tinge of the epic as purveyed by Queen, and AC/DC devilry, it's clear that – on form – this is an act with much to offer.

And the press agreed. The extremely influential *Sounds* eulogised over it, legendary NWOBHM scribe Geoff Barton happy to note within that publication's pages that the "ace musicianship is an outstanding feature" of the album, something that had "hardly been in abundance" over the course of the NWOBHM releases to that date. Impressed as he was with the band's musical qualities, he also conceded that this relatively accomplished, rather than balls-out raucous, approach was possibly one of the reasons that Samson had never "been amongst the trendiest of the new metal bands." Praising the vocals particularly, and comparing Bruce to Free's Paul Rodgers, Barton gave the LP a full five stars, and – perhaps surprisingly given the album's classic rock feel – memorably called it "more metal than the entire fleet of Russian battleships."[54]

Gushing reviews from one of the most influential movers and shakers on the scene may be one thing, but when the chips are down, it takes a lot more than just good press to make a band a viable success. Although the group set out on tour to promote the release, they had largely booked the concerts themselves – Paul and Bruce sharing the workload – and despite the album peaking at a very creditable No 34 in the charts, all was not well between Samson and their management, Ramkup. The group were becoming disillusioned by what they perceived as a lack of support.

Rob Grain feels the management's relative inexperience – compared to someone like the revered Smallwood – exacerbated Samson's slowing momentum: "It was because of that that the other bands started overtaking; Samson were getting much better reviews in the press. They had a huge stageshow with big rigs and loads of pyrotechnics and stuff, and the very first feature in *Sounds* that Geoff Barton did was mostly about Samson's stageshow."

That stageshow was being taken around the country when Samson made the decision to sack their management – on July 4, 1980 – Independence Day, which must surely have appealed to Bruce's sense of irony, if nothing else. Things had begun to unravel very, very quickly just as, musically, Samson was starting to thrive, and in order to get back on track, something had to give. Ramkup were not to be shaken off quite so easily however, taking matters to the high court and obtaining an injunction preventing Samson from working until the law courts' decision had been made. The immediate knock-on effect of this was that the final ten gigs in the *Head On* tour had to be necessarily cancelled; though the band tried to keep it going from their own pockets, it was inevitable that the group themselves would ultimately suffer.

"At the time," says Thunderstick, "we had [another] manager [who had professional freelance connections with the band Gillan] saying that he'd take us on as a manager as long as we got out of the Ramkup deal. He turned round and said, 'Look, if you can get out of the Ramkup deal I'll look after you and I'll make sure you can get to the places that you wanna go to, and start working in Europe.'"

"And because we'd always had this big huge tie-up with Gillan all the time, we were using Kingsway studios, I was doing offshoot stuff with John and

Bernie, gigs at the Music Machine and The Marquee, and there'd always been this inter-band tie-up ... it was a logical thing for us to do."

"This was the tour, where the routing was all over the place. Aberdeen one day and Cornwall the next! It was literally like that, it was unbelievable. At the beginning of the tour [the potential new manager said], 'I can't do anything; it's gotta be down to you guys'. So we wrote an official letter to our management company."

The consequences of this legal disagreement were severe for both the band's profile and – literally – their wallets. "We were all absolutely piss-poor, absolutely skint, we had no money whatsoever. We were doing Radio One interviews with Tommy Vance and the like, and he would say, 'The band's doing really good, it's really progressing' and this, that and the other, and *literally* we didn't have 10p in our pockets. But it was awful; we started the tour with all the accoutrements you take with you and we finished it out of the back of a local hired transit, with a local P.A. somewhere up in Scotland. By that time we were well and truly losing ground, I mean, the fans were promised the big show and the cage and the pyros and all they got was four guys that by this time were feeling rather dejected."

As Rob Grain, Samson's tour manager and confidant, puts it, "whilst all this was going on, all the other bands were still playing, touring, building up a following and Samson, to all effects, were defunct." So, ultimately, there was only one thing for it, as Paul Samson himself acknowledged.

"When it was discovered that it was us who were in breach of contract," he said sadly, "we were all threatened with bankruptcy... we had no option but to go back to Ramkup."[55] When a new Heads of Agreement was drawn up, Ramkup then paid the band back pay retainer wages. In theory, the financial difficulties were over and Samson could plough on. Samson had played two major festivals, headlining Lowestoft's Norfolk Festival and joining the legendary 1980 bill at Reading Festival, on August 24, alongside headliners Whitesnake, U.F.O., Sheffield's Def Leppard, Wishbone Ash and a confident and fabulous, speedily-rising Iron Maiden. It was also one of only a handful of occasions that Thunderstick's expensive cage was used – most of the time it had been too big to fit onstage (he also played inside it in *Biceps Of Steel*). The two gigs, however, were together a rare pair of happy, sun-soaked moments amidst a dark time for the band – although Bruce was bullish enough to see a light at the end of the tunnel, telling *Sounds* that, "as long as you've got something really good to offer and you've got people behind you who believe in you and are willing to give you support, then you can't fail to win through in the end. And Samson will win through, mark my words."[56]

* * *

The management situation may not have helped the band's gigging career to any appreciable amount, but one knock-on effect was that they'd had plenty of time twiddling their thumbs whilst off the road to come up with a new set of tracks – approaching an album's worth. And it was Tony Platt to whom they turned to work on the new material. Platt had just completed work with Iron Maiden, who'd curiously chosen to agree to follow up their Judas Priest tours and chart positions (their first two singles, 'Running Free' and 'Sanctuary' had got to Number 44 and Number 29 respectively) with a cover version of a song that, let's face it, was hardly a feminist anthem, a rather dunderheaded macho rocker entitled 'Women In Uniform'. It was an old Skyhooks number which had previously been released by that Australian band down under, some two years earlier. Platt recalls the events leading up to his working with Maiden on that track.

"The only reason I was doing that was because [Maiden's original choice] Martin Birch was finishing off the Whitesnake album,"[57] says the producer who has also worked with Bob Marley and The Relatives. "They had to make this single, and Martin wasn't available. They were running out of time rapidly and I happened to have time spare so I said, 'I'll go and do it if you want.' They sort of got talked into [recording that track]. I feel somewhat sympathetic in that respect."

'Women In Uniform' is widely regarded in certain quarters as being a rare error of judgement from Iron Maiden; admirably, perhaps, they'd not wanted to mine their debut LP for another single, but equally they'd not wanted to dive into the material earmarked for the follow-up album either. Still, Maiden themselves went with the idea, not least because Platt at that time was being considered for their second album, and it seemed an ideal opportunity to suss each other's modus operandi out.

"I kind of started this whole thinking process that having a singer who had a higher range would be a good idea. At the time I'd just started to work with Samson, and one of the things about them was that the way the songs were was a good sound picture. And obviously coming off the back of working with AC/DC that was fairly prominent in my mind as well – as an arrangement and production technique."

But Steve Harris was not impressed with the results. The mixes, he felt, were weak and commercial compared to the original sound the band had attained in the studio. Actually, to say that the Maiden bassist and single-minded founder was "not impressed" seems a little on the mild side. And I quote… "I just went fucking nuts! I had to walk out … I thought, 'I'm gonna deck him!'… 'You know nothing about us, so you can fuck right off!'"[58]

And, so, 'fuck off' Anthony Platt did; Martin Birch became available, and Maiden started a relationship with the Deep Purple/Black Sabbath producer that lasted many glorious years for all concerned. Platt, these days, is philosophical about 'Women In Uniform', noting that, "on one hand, it's been quite good because it's earned me a bit of money over the years – on the other hand I got a pasting from Iron Maiden."

Back in 1980, then, and Samson and Platt began to chat about how the new material might shape up in the studio sessions for the forthcoming album, which would eventually be called *Shock Tactics*. The producer found that he immediately gained a rapport with the band as musicians, and understood their context within the hard rock and heavy metal scene of the time.

"The total idol that Paul Samson had was Hendrix," notes Platt. "So he really came from that blues/rock side of the feeling. In that respect, Samson were a much more stripped-down band than Maiden, and it has to be said, actually probably more adept musically; then again they were competing in exactly the same arena so there was no point Samson trying to do exactly the same thing that Iron Maiden did."

"*Shock Tactics* had some serious pre-production; we really got stuck into that. The whole idea was to really, really get the songs up to scratch." Pre-production – in other words, chatting about the songs, rehearsing them, playing with different arrangement ideas and experimenting and thus refining how the final versions might be recorded when finally in the studio – duly underway, the feeling was that at least *musically* Samson were moving forward, although it all could have ended in disaster, according to Platt.[59]

"We did all the pre-production in Easyhire Studios, and it was fantastic. It was crazy, right from the start, the whole thing. We were recording stuff, fine-tuning the songs and deciding what we were going to do, that sort of thing, until one day we all started feeling a bit weird and drowsy and we discovered that the room was being heated by gas heaters – one of which was not actually burning the gas which was going into the room. Either that, or the exhaust was blowing into the room – either way we all started to feel heady; when we went outside and the fresh air hit us we realised that there was something decidedly untoward going on. It was wintertime, so you had to have heaters on 'cause it was bloody freezing!" A close call, indeed – not so much *Head On* as *Head Ache*...

This time, the band survived to play another day. Just as well, really, otherwise the rest of this book would consist of blank pages and the whole of British rock music would have been considerably different and one heck of a lot less colourful. And so, 1980 began to draw to its weary and confused close, with a small stop-off for a studio session during which Bruce dubbed his vocals onto the master tracks for the *Survivors* album, the intent being to release that as a free limited edition album as an extra bonus with the forthcoming new release (in the end, the idea was shelved). Remarkable things also happened when the band finally began to *gig* again. However, in contrast to Bruce and the boys' avowed wish to tour Europe to promote *Head On*, instead they found that they had been booked by Ramkup as support act on Uriah Heep's own tour of the UK, playing venues that Samson had headlined in their own right merely months earlier. For many involved, this was entirely unwise, as Rob Grain recalls.

"There were arguments between the band and the management all the way through. In the end it all went too far: *Head On* was out, *Shock Tactics* was just about to [be recorded], and what should have been a headlining British tour to support the album became a support tour to Uriah Heep – who weren't particularly pulling people at the time. The line-up [was weak."

"It was weird," sighs Thunderstick, "because all the progress we'd made headlining on our own ... I didn't know what was happening and I didn't get involved with decisions like that. But we needed to go and do another tour, and really by this time we should have been hitting Europe; that's when we lost ground and it was a *dramatic* loss of ground. Uriah Heep was a great tour; it was playing places that we'd played in our own right, headlining a few months before, hence the reason we felt we were losing ground because we were opening for them. It was a three band package, Spider opening the show, Samson in the middle and Uriah Heep closing it. There were a few more punters there, but not really that many, not really, we were still playing to a real hardcore Samson audience every night. Uriah Heep treated us with a lot of respect and Nick was a great guy to be around with his anecdotes and what have you, because he'd been there, done it and got the T-shirt quite a few times. But we lost out on making progress."

A year – and a decade – that had begun, then, with Samson rubbing shoulders with many of the aspirant acts of the NWOBHM, had ended in confusion, frustration and depression. Whilst Bruce was learning valuable lessons about the vagaries of the music industry, they were lessons learnt at a high cost – namely and perhaps most significantly watching his band's main rivals, Iron Maiden, surge ahead of the pack and become 'The Most Likely To Happen'. Vocally, and as a writer, Bruce Bruce had begun to mature, though, and whilst 1980 had descended into something of a fug, with sessions scheduled during January to record a new album, and the band finally being free to extricate themselves from their management contract in February 1981 in accord with the high court judgement, there was yet much to look forward to. It seemed that quite possibly their collective hair was not yet fully shorn, after all.

chapter six:
Shock Tactics? You Don't Know
The 'Arf Of It Guv

1981 began with Samson shutting themselves away from management problems and outside influences, ensconced as they were at Battery Studios in West London, with a producer that was genuinely enthusiastic for their music. January promised to be a month that reaffirmed the band's status as musicians. Regardless of all the hassle going on elsewhere in their chaotic career, there was one place where the band still had control – and that was in the recording studios. Producer Tony Platt recalls the sessions with a great deal of fondness.

"The sessions were in the strange Battery Studio Two which ceased to exist shortly after!" he chuckles. "It was downstairs in the building that became the main Zomba building, and in order to get to the control room, you had to go through the studios, so once everybody was playing you couldn't get in and out of the control room. By the time we got to the end of those sessions, they were refurbishing all the upper floors so the building was almost completely deserted a lot of the time." Leading, no doubt, to less distractions from the task in hand, namely, making the definitive Samson album. *Head On* had been written, in part, whilst the group were getting to know each other as musicians and people, but by the time it had come to the end of 1980, the enforced inactivity of the previous months had led to a verdant period in terms of songwriting. The musicians had worked together for long enough to know each other's strengths – and weaknesses – and as a result of the time they'd had spare, thanks partly to the court case, they'd also had a significant time to work on the songs and their sound.

"We had a really, really good time making that album," says Platt. "A *fantastic* time – and we had some riotous, riotous nights in the studio. We worked bloody long and hard on that album, we really did."

Famously, Iron Maiden were concurrently working in a nearby studio on their own new album, and the paths of the bands occasionally crossed. At the time, there was also a growing amount of real rivalry between the two camps, although in the case of Samson it was confined largely to their 'cuttings wall', as Platt explains.

"There was huge amounts of competition between the [bands], of course. Maiden were in the other studio so there was all the usual banter going backwards and forwards. All the way through the session there were these big sheets of paper on the wall and we used to cut bits and pieces out of magazines and newspaper captions. And this collage grew over the period of making the record. We'd got all sorts of comments about Maiden stuck on the wall, and somebody told us they'd done the same about Samson on their wall. Certainly from the Samson side it was quite friendly!"

"We nearly got chucked out of that studio," laughs Thunderstick, "because Bruce let a powder fire extinguisher off in that studio as well; it used to be his thing – it went everywhere. You can imagine a powder fire extinguisher inside a recording studio! Fortunately it was not in the control room, it was in the actual studio but – Jesus – it was all in the piano and everything was covered in white."

"There was [also] Bruce's girlfriend Jane,"[60] continues Platt, "who, 'cause nobody had much money, she would turn up every night with a few beers, a load of Chinese food, something like that – and keep the sessions going quite well. It was quite rock 'n' roll and lots of fun." And you can undoubtedly hear the relaxed atmosphere in the recordings. The massive irony of *Shock Tactics* is that it is a blaster of an album, performed brilliantly by a group totally at ease with the material and each other; the events that were to follow also make it one of the great lost opportunities of its era. But at the time, the focus was firmly on enjoying bringing the rock, and creating perhaps one of the more bizarre (and rare) bootlegs that is somewhere in existence.

"I still have a cassette that Paul made of all sorts of stupid outtakes of those sessions; Bruce probably still has one as well 'cause Paul made a copy for everybody," continues Platt. "That started because somebody had left two sweets on the edge of the desk. I was the mug, and one day I asked, 'Whose are these then?' and Bruce, or Paul, said, 'Yeah, they're mine, you can have one if you want.' So I said, 'Thanks' and ate one. Then I realised that everybody was sniggering and I said, 'What the fuck's this then? What's wrong with them?' and they said, 'Well, they're fart sweets.' We all said. 'Nah that's impossible.' And then around ten minutes later we discovered that they were in fact incredibly effective – which meant that everybody then had them. Everybody was then in the studio letting fly with these *amazing* farts. So we stuck a microphone up and hotwired it straight into one of the tape machines – and all the way through the day you'd be able to see somebody, all of a sudden break off halfway through a conversation, run across, set the tape machine up and let fly into this microphone. You can hear all the background stuff of people talking and going, 'Oh no!' and all that sort of stuff. That's the 'fart tape.'"

"There were the phrases that used to go through the session, everything that was bad was, 'Really Dad's'... 'That's really Dad's, that!' All these phrases that went on, it was a very happy album to make, we had a lot of fun."

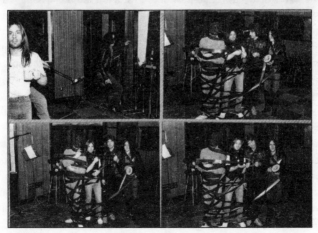

From the opening chords of the album's first track, 'Riding With The Angels', it's absolutely evident that this is a band as tight and together as anyone could hope. To open the LP with a cover version is perhaps a surprise, but the choice of track – which Samson turn into an anthemic, dynamic monster – is a great one. It sets down a huge marker as to the quality of what is to follow; stomping backbeats, great guitaring and vocals that range from gravelly to soaring where the mood demands it.

"['Riding' was suggested by] my manager, Ralph Simon, who was their publisher," explains Platt. "I said it would be good if we got something in there that had a little bit more of a singles-y vibe to it, and this song came up. Being a Russ Ballard song we thought, 'That's got a very good chance.'"

"This is the unfortunate thing. There was the usual thing from the band, 'Why do we have to do someone else's song?' We talked very long about whether we could do something with it. But once we decided to do it, everyone got in there and gave it a bloody good seeing to! And we worked very hard on it. I think we came up with a very, very good version of that song." In fact, Samson's version of 'Riding With The Angels' was such a success that Ballard himself subsequently sent a congratulatory telegram to the band after hearing it.

Following 'Riding' is the galloping, lead-heavy 'Earth Mother', another strong track, beautifully recorded and with melodic feedback and layered guitars introducing a Dickinson vocal streets ahead of anything he'd previously recorded. Salacious and eyebrow-raising, screaming and flailing, it is the sound of a man growing into his voice in every sense. The riff-tastic 'Nice Girl' keeps the pace up, a track inspired, said Bruce, by a sympathy with, "prostitutes, with the fact that women have to go to these lengths to earn a living and it's also about their clients. These blokes who don't get on with their wives or whatever so they settle for a ten minute wife, a ten minute hypocrisy."[61] 'Bloodlust' features one of the great guitar performances of Paul Samson's career, always controlled, incredibly tight, he's therefore able to play with harmonics and control his tone in a way that lesser guitarists could only dream of. Bruce, meanwhile, uses the space atop the sparse licks to layer squeals and squalling vocal lines full of doomy dread, reveling in the darkness – the personality of the *song* comes out with an aplomb that speaks volumes of the time they'd spent in pre-production. More sleaze follows on the insistent 'Go To Hell', with another great solo, before Thunderstick's rain-dance tom-toms introduce the singalong 'Bright Lights' – a classic early 1970s piece of melodic blues-rock – complete with plenty of space for guitar histrionics – that was so close to Paul Samson's musical heart. Bruce's lyrics and delivery were developing to a point where he could step into character at will, 'Once Bitten' showcasing a fictional character firmly in accusative/self-destructive mode. You can almost feel the fingers being pointed – a track with the hefty simplicity of Motorhead, with whom, of course, Samson share musical roots in many ways. 'Grime Crime', according to Bruce, "is about one night when, recently girlfriend-less, I went down to the Music Machine at two in the morning, got rather drunk and spotted this apparition in the corner which, in the half light, looked quite attractive. By the time I got home though she wasn't as attractive what with the streetlights and everything but I, ahem, didn't have any option because she said that unless I did the honours, she was going to scream and call the police."[62] Chivalrous to the last, Mr D, chivalrous indeed.

In one sense, the last track on the album is the most prescient of the lot; given what was later to happen. 'Communion', in lyric an end-of-life, end-of-career, homeward-looking piece of work that surges into an epic, powerful and dramatic swirling musical soundscape that speaks of freedom and breaking out, resting with peace and searching for contentment. It's a remarkable, expansive and evocative work, full of regret, passion, and eventually hope for the future; the only real failing the track has is fading out after a mere six and a half minutes.

To go, then, from the stomping statement of intent of 'Riding With The Angels' through to the dénouement of 'Communion', shows a real understanding of the narrative power an album can have, placing *Shock Tactics* as one of the greatest albums of 1981. Surprsingly perhaps, Thunderstick himself enjoyed the freedom of the previous LP more, as did the guitarist and driving force behind the band.

"Paul didn't like it as an album," reveals the drummer. "He thought that his playing had been suppressed quite a bit, he didn't like the guitar tone that Tony got. It was never really kind of rated as his favourite album. I think, out of the two, *Head On* is my favourite album because of the fluidity of it and the ability to be able to let yourself go and create in the studio, whereas *Shock Tactics* was less of a creative experience, it was more of a workload if you like. In terms of my own playing, the real Thunderstick is on *Head On,* but *Shock Tactics* taught me so much in as much as by the time I eventually arrived in the band, Thunderstick I was actually able to use the knowledge that I'd got from both. I was too Keith Moon in *Head On* and too Simon Kirk in *Shock Tactics*, so I needed to kind of fit somewhere between the two, pull out the mad bits when I need to and [for] the rest of it, keep it regimental. So it's a learning process and you learn as you go along."

It was an album that was absolutely instrumental in the development of the singing style and control of Dickinson, a vital part of the continuing learning process he was going through. "Bruce has gone on record a couple of times saying he learned a lot about singing during that period," says Tony Platt, "and I think his voice developed quite dramatically during that period of time. He stopped shouting and he really became an excellent singer."

Having recorded an LP of such a high standard, it was perhaps inevitable that something was going to have to give. The news came through that Gem, the record company who were to release *Shock Tactics*, was going to the wall, thus taking away any potential cash for touring support. Secondly (and even as Samson were finally freed from their Ramkup management contract and auditioned at the Marquee for potential new management) the only way they were able to extricate themselves from that contract was costly, as Rob Grain explains: "In the end there was the final court case and the only way Samson could get out of the management contract was for the management to retain the rights of the first three albums. So at the end of it Samson came out of the management deal but they didn't own *Survivors, Head On* or *Shock Tactics*."

It was another blow to the band as a whole, but very nearly had a massive effect on Samson. During March 1981, Paul Bruce Dickinson decided to shake off his double-B persona, hooking up with an old friend of his by the name of Stuart Smith, to whom he'd been introduced after a concert at The Marquee the previous year, whilst Samson's future once more looked shaky as a band.

"At the time he was very dissatisfied with Samson, simply because I don't think they had a record deal," Smith told me. "Bruce was a very big Deep Purple fan and of course I was as well, so we started getting together, really just to hang out at the time, and then eventually we ended up writing some material together and we got a bunch of people together and we went into a studio and rehearsed this stuff, just sort of laid it down on cassette. And it was really good, it was great stuff, I mean Bruce's voice of course, has always been incredible. He was very creative as well. I think the first song we wrote was 'Rosetta'."

"We just got together with some people and just played," he continues, "I can't even remember who we had playing with us at the time. But I do remember Bruce really well because it was really him and I who got these people together. But it was great, it could have done something if we'd had chance to develop it."

It is, in fact, one of the potentially great but lost collaborations of the era – tapes exist of Smith and Dickinson jamming, and should they ever come to light, they would be worth an absolute fortune. At the time, of course, it was just two mates playing music together for the sheer fun of it, but had circumstances been different, could the project have *really* got somewhere?

"It could have," smiles Smith. "[Because] you knew whatever Bruce was involved in it was going to do something. I mean he just had so much drive and so much energy. And so did I, and we got on really well, we were great friends and it could have gone further. But in those days we were both just trying to survive, living around London, musicians hanging out trying to make it happen, hanging out down The Marquee and The Ship."

"You know, we were all young, we didn't have real jobs, doing the couch tour a lot of the time. I do remember that as a joke for my birthday he gave me a cheque – he was with the Midland Bank – and he gave me a cheque for a million pounds. I should probably try and cash it now, the money's probably in the account!"

Smith and Dickinson's project was going so well that they decided to try and drum up a little publicity for themselves, so they went to Jennie Halsall, PR extraordinaire, for advice. Bad move for Stuart's growing project, but ultimately very good for Bruce's 'main' band of the time.

"I took Bruce down to meet Jennie because I wanted to tell her that we were going to try and get this project together. Bruce was dissatisfied [with Samson at the time] and he felt that they should have a record deal – which they rightly should – certainly with Bruce fronting the band, who was great even back them. Which is I think why he tried to take the reigns and got Jennie in to try and do publicity for the band. And I think she saw a going concern with Samson, and offered her PR services, and that was it. Basically, I guess Bruce thought that they [Samson] could possibly do something if they could get some good publicity – Jennie was really surprised that they didn't have a deal – I think it was about three weeks later that they suddenly did have a deal."

"It was great for Bruce and Samson, of course, but it basically put an end to what we were doing. But you know, we carried on hanging out during our time in London. Great singer, and a really, really smart intelligent guy. He was always really bright; I think he'd just got out of university at the time we originally met and he was really young. And even back then he was talking about if he makes it he was going to get a swimming pool with heat exchangers in and all this kind of thing. Really bright guy, great sense of humour, we got on really well."

RCA, who were the sister company of the struggling record label, Gem, were the lucky chaps to pick up on Samson's stunning new music, and 'Riding With The Angels' hit the charts in May, peaking at Number 54. *Shock Tactics,* also, was finally released to coincide with a major tour of the UK in June 1981. *Sounds* gave the LP the thumbs up with a four star rating; that magazine's reviewer, Robbi Millar, called it – rather verbosely, but also splendidly pertinently – "a monolithic masterpiece of musical might ... and subtle too!" (unlike the alliteration, possibly). Regardless, *Record Mirror* also loved it, Malcolm Dome going one better and giving the effort the full five marks available.

The tour, part one of which began at Leeds' Forde Green Hotel on June 11, 1981, had been largely booked by Paul and Bruce, and some of the dates were packed tightly but not necessarily with an eye on the geographical implications. It was immediately dubbed 'Don't Give A Fuck About The Petrol Bill Tour', thanks to the often bizarre schedule and often tortuous distances between gigs as the band criss-crossed the country day after day. They'd also gained a new manager at this stage, coincidentally the owner of

Easyhire Studios, one Terry McClellan; his tenure was to turn out, unfortunately, to be rather a brief one.

Keeping busy, Samson were as prolific as ever, writing and demoing more tracks in the run-up to the June dates; 'Turn Out The Lights', 'Firing Line' and 'Red Skies' continued the musical momentum that the band had built up neatly. But things, as ever, were not straightforward in the hallowed halls of Samson. Thunderstick's cage was too big for most of the venues – which turned out to be a symptom of a rather deeper malaise, and one that Neal Kay, for one, had sensed two years previously.

"The Samson shows were overblown," declares the larger than life DJ. "They were completely and utterly overblown and the press reported them in a variety of overblown ways. Because no-one knew what the hell Paul was trying to sell. Was he selling fireworks, or was he selling music? His ability was never questioned, and quite rightly because he was a good guitar player. [But] the roots were wrong and the trouble was that Bruce, in my view, never could really develop the horsepower and performance and use his ability to the full when he was singing the wrong sort of songs. Bruce in actual fact was more powerful than Samson could ever have been; it was the wrong vehicle for him but it did put him in the right place at the right time."

But we get ahead of ourselves; June 1981, and Thunderstick's love for the more theatrical side of performance was beginning to cause a small problem. Bruce and Paul, for all their own love of stage histrionics, and Paul's own fixation for pyrotechnics over the last two years, were largely pulling in the other direction. The album they'd just released was a ballsy, brilliant success and the music, perhaps, was strong enough to stand or fall on its own merits. The band were strong and tight enough to deliver a stunning set, Chris Aylmer's rock-steady bass playing enabling the rest of the band to float round the rhythm with freedom and groove. Speaking at the time, Bruce said that the band wanted to attain the reputation of being an outfit who were, "visually great because of what we do onstage, not because of what the stage does to us. Besides, if I had to sing with lungfuls of smoke and bangs blowing me eardrums in every night, I'd be a wreck inside two weeks." [63] Makes sense from one point of view, of course, but there is also much to be said for over-the-top showmanship, of which the drummer was very enamoured; it wasn't an ideal situation by any means, and it came to a rather final head very quickly.

"Bruce and Paul were quite emphatic at the time that it was to become more of a bluesy, 'We are serious', Blackfoot type of band," recalled Thunderstick. "I was into heroes that I'm still into now, like Alice Cooper. I love the Tubes – anybody that put a lot of money back into the show and gave the audience what they wanted.' Look at Iron Maiden, people go to see the shows when they go to see Iron Maiden, they wanna see the Eddie [character], and they wanna see the [big stageshow and props], whereas Paul was dead against that ... other bands were gaining on us at the time and overtaking us, [and] he thought that it was probably due to the fact that [the character of] Thunderstick was holding it back, basically."

"I decided I'd had enough because we were then squabbling amongst ourselves, they wanted to go in a much bluesier direction. In fact, the last Marquee gig I ever did with them I felt [isolated] because they weren't gonna dress up anymore and Bruce wanted to do the jeans and T-shirts things and said, 'Fuck all this theatrical thing, I'm sick and tired of it, it's a pain in the arse.' Rather than [Thunderstick] being a motif for the band and a selling point for the band, it was actually holding it back. By that time I wanted to take it in even more of a theatrical direction, so we decided to part company and I went starting up [my new band, called] Thunderstick."[64]

Thunderstick's final gig with Samson in this incarnation was on July 8, 1981, at Wigan Pier. After all they'd been through together, it was a shame – but these things happen; Thunderstick's drumming on *Shock Tactics* left one hell of a marker for whoever was to follow.

Samson's great rivals, Iron Maiden, were – on the face of it – forging ahead at a thunderous pace. On the back of their stunning 1980 debut album, the band had undertaken another reshuffle. Guitarist Dennis Stratton had been replaced by one Adrian Smith, a long-time mate of Maiden's other six-string player, Dave Murray, continuing an instantly-recognisable twin guitar attack that meshed together beautifully. After the 'Women In Uniform' single, the band had been out on the road ripping it up left, right and centre, and followed their debut up with the excellent 1981 album, *Killers*, although the press reaction was noticeably more muted to their sophomore release.[65] The lead singer in Maiden, Paul Di'Anno, had all the attributes of a frontman: cocky, confident, cheeky and with a sharp tongue and appetite for life that could be both a blessing and a curse, as Neal Kay recalls.

"Paul was like a kid let loose in a chocolate factory; his eyes were bigger than his stomach," chuckles Kay. "I remember in Newcastle, at the Mayfair where we played on tour [during 1980]. Paul had a penchant for wearing a mod hat, a pork pie hat, and he'd go out on stage in it – which annoyed Steve no end anyway. This is not the way a rock band portrays itself! In the middle of Newcastle-land, in a late set, about half eleven at night, Paul rolls out onstage and then announces to the world that West Ham are gonna knock the shit out of Newcastle. That did it!"

"In one gig we did, I think it was Mansfield, Paul lost his voice and couldn't sing – Steve did the best he could with the vocals ... and promised everyone the show would go back there when the vocalist had recovered. Clive Burr got very sick on that tour; he had a temperature and everything and was throwing up while he played. They carried him behind the kit, gave him a bucket to throw up in, and as soon as the gig was finished, back to bed he went. It was a tour for heroes; it was a time for real men. It was the forging of the legend of rock 'n' roll. I'm proud to have been there to have seen it."

If there was one thing that Harris insisted upon within Team Maiden, it was that – no matter what happened the rest of the time – when the time came for the band to take care of business, they had to deliver. Anything that jeopardised their stage performance was an absolute no-no. As 1981 rolled on, Paul Di'Anno began to lose his voice regularly. Maiden had gone through so much under Steve Harris' guiding hand over the years, and any unpredictable behaviour that threatened to destabilise them as they stood on the cusp of *really* making a go of matters in the music industry was anathema to their ideals and ambitions.

It's a fallacy to blame it solely on the extra-curricular activities, perhaps; in many people's view, more fundamental musical worries being raised were also at odds with the potential of the Maiden vision. Whichever way you want to look at it, the facts are that by the early autumn of 1981, Paul Di'Anno was out of Iron Maiden; something that was kept rather quiet – the press had little inkling quite yet. For his own part, Di'Anno sums it up neatly, referring to the, ahem, rather differently-focussed ambitions he and Steve Harris had, even in the very early years of trawling the pub circuit. His honesty is disarming.

"Every gig was a brilliant experience and a great night for me to show off to everyone and fuck and get blow jobs from as many birds as was possible," explains the rampant Di'Anno. "Steve would be planning world domination and putting the £15 that were made at some shows towards the next show while I was trying to get as many birds names in my little dirty black book as possible."[66]

And as Maiden's stock rose, so did the demands on the singer. "At that age I wasn't also handling things as well as the other guys who were older than me. One minute I was a kid off the street and the next I was expected to handle things like it was sliced bread. Needless to say, I started drinking a lot and I must've done half of Peru up my nose. I screwed up ... I wasn't happy, both with the [Killers] album and myself and I really didn't wanna be there. And if you can't give one thousand percent to a band like Iron Maiden the best thing to do is get the fuck out. I just walked in and told them how I felt and walked away."[67] Say no more. No wonder his autobiography was titled *The Beast*.[68]

* * *

Samson, meanwhile, had signed a stunningly talented new drummer to replace Thunderstick, and were busy bedding him in for their high-profile appearance at the Reading Festival, which would be their last live appearance for a while. His name was Mel Gaynor, with a background in hefty funk.

After some low-key warm-ups, Gaynor and Samson took the stage at Reading on August 29, 1981 – and absolutely ripped the place apart. Coincidentally, the headliners that year were none other than Gillan. Mel Gaynor's immense talent was a massive filip for the band, whose RCA contract was about to expire. The record labels knew it, having seen what Samson were capable of on the *Shock Tactics* album, the Reading set – which was recorded for posterity by the BBC's *Friday Rock Show,* and included another new track, 'Gravy Train' – was an affirmation that this was a band worth investing in. From the new drummer to the steady bassist, the fluid and often fast-fretted guitarist and the remarkable singer, every element was surely finally in place. It has been mooted that it was the sound of a group who were one hit single away from a breakthrough; the Reading performance was subsequently released as an album some nine years later, and the energy and belief emanating from the band is spot on. From the nine minute 'Walking Out On You', to a near-incendiary '... Angels' it's a set that rarely dips from its fizzing rock zenith. It's not without humour, either: when Bruce introduces Mel Gaynor, he draws attention to the fact that, although he is in fact Samson's drummer, Gaynor has nothing on his head or obscuring his face. But the greatest cheers, and they are many, are reserved for Paul Samson. One can only imagine how that must have felt for the guitarist after so many years of near-misses and frustrations.

When a sweaty, hyped, exhausted Bruce Bruce, Chris Aylmer, Mel Gaynor and Paul Samson came offstage, shook hands and parted ways for a much-needed two week break, Samson's stock was once again rising high. Back from the brink once more, the record companies were lining up at last.

chapter seven:
In Which The Central Character In The Tale Finds Himself Being Made An Offer He Cannot Reasonably Refuse, But Being A Decent Chap, He Takes Some Time To Think About It

"With any band you gotta try and get as many components right as you can," says Tony Platt. "Circumstances did prevail against Samson; some were beyond their control and some totally within their control. Paul was a difficult bloke in a lot of respects. I told him on many different occasions that he had a very negative attitude to things, he tended to take the viewpoint that he was being prevailed against rather than take the viewpoint, 'Well, fuck the bastards, I'm gonna get on with it', you know? The problem in any circumstance like that is that you can see that people do have a point. You can see that for some people it gets tiresome, banging your head against the same brick wall week after week and month after month."

Samson had, in a very real way, both predated and outlasted the NWOBHM. The sense is that, come their triumphant appearance at Reading 1981, they'd closed the chapter on rather a strange period in music. Although the band were rightly credited as being a force in hard rock during 1977/8-1981, there was always something that didn't ring true alongside contemporaries like Saxon, Def Leppard, Angel Witch, Iron Maiden and the others. Perhaps it was the classic rock approach – *Shock Tactics* has certainly stood the test of time, without question, and is in a sense timeless, *Head On* also, albeit a little less so, but the Bandwagon crowd, in particular, weren't hugely enamoured of the style. One oft-referenced gig that was sadly memorable for all the wrong reasons saw Samson leave the stage at the Music Machine to total silence from what was a packed crowd, prompting a row between Paul and Neal Kay, who had been previously good buddies.

"Samson had top slot on the bill, with Iron Maiden under them," sighs the DJ. "But Maiden took the stage and basically wiped out anything and anybody with their honesty, their music and their delivery. When Paul

Samson took the stage, people were polite enough but he interspersed his whole old-fashioned style set with explosions and pyrotechnics and all sorts of bizarre things; and at the end of the set not one person clapped. Not one."

After the unfortunate gig, which took place in 1980, Paul confronted Neal and accused him of somehow manipulating the audience so they would show no response. Kay replied in the negative. "[I told him] 'You stand or fall on your own merits, mate, and it's your music they don't like. It's not that they don't like your playing; they admire you as a guitarist, but you ain't going where they wanna go and Iron Maiden are.' That was the problem and he couldn't see it."

And whilst Paul's heroes were in the vein of Jimi Hendrix – a quick listen to the demo version of the track 'Firing Line' brings that fixation home in spades – Maiden took their cues from something altogether primeval, although it is a comparison that perhaps only Neal Kay would think of making.

"Maiden reminded me of Slade," he begins, "I don't mean musically, but Noddy Holder's prime directive is *No Mercy And No Prisoners*. If you've ever stood twenty feet from Slade and watched them do a show, it's one [song] straight into another. There's no fucking around, no long verbals; in those days there wasn't much chat. Maiden were in for the kill, they played their set like I played records, one after the other, bang!"

"And the way Steve and the boys went at it was kinda like that. You were awake, you were being assaulted – visually and by audio. And Slade were like that, completely. They mesmerised me and at Christmas they just shot on stage and killed people. They were so damned good. So Slade were never that pop group you see on *Top Of The Pops* all the time, they were a *fucking rock 'n' roll killing machine*, and so were Iron Maiden."

By inference, then, if Kay's unfortunate difference of opinion with Paul at that notorious concert where Samson came offstage to silence is any indication, Samson was not a rock 'n' roll killing machine. But there was one interested party at that same gig, tear-up or otherwise. "Steve and Maiden were working under them; I was right there in the middle as well and we could all see what Bruce could do," concludes Kay. "I remember Steve coming up to me one night and turning round and saying, 'What do you think of Bruce?' and I think I said something like, 'I'm non-committal, Steve, because I think he's with the wrong band.' And Steve said to me, 'I think he's an *animal!*' Those were his words."

Animal or not, perhaps the problem was the dynamic within the band Samson, none of whom were exactly prepared to fade into the background. "Bruce was a major showman," Platt says. "The one thing that never settled with me was the hooded drummer, which I always thought was a bit stupid. They should've let Bruce be the showman all the way, all the time – but, then, it was Paul's band."

Perhaps it was simply the case that sometimes the team around Samson was unsatisfactory (to some observers) in comparison to other bands of their era. Certainly one of the major aces that Iron Maiden had up their sleeve was their management: Rod Smallwood was an innovative and dynamic character who meshed in with the band's (and ultimately, Steve Harris') vision. Whilst Samson were floundering from court case to injunction, booking gigs themselves or supporting unsuitable bands, Maiden were largeing it round Europe setting fire to audiences onstage and rampaging off it.

"Basically the thing that Maiden had that Samson didn't have," offers Tony Platt, "was a bloody good manager and a much bigger record label. Samson were on Gem Records, a small label, and Maiden by that time were getting the support of EMI. Maiden had Rod Smallwood but Samson [had] Ramkup ... they needed to be properly promoted – and *Shock Tactics* was not properly promoted by any stretch of the imagination." Which, when it comes down to it, is a crucial issue. There's no point making a wonderful album that pushes all the buttons you seek to hit if nobody is able to hear it, is there?

Being a bright chap, Paul Bruce Dickinson would have been more than aware of the failings behind the Samson scenes, and the relentless feeling of kicking against the odds requires a massive amount of energy. Even in the immediate afterglow of absolutely nailing it in front of a massive festival crowd, the underlying problems were not to fade so easily. What happened next is something of an inevitability. In *Run To The Hills ...*, the authorised biography of Iron Maiden, Bruce is quoted as saying that, immediately after the Reading performance, Rod Smallwood came to him in the backstage bar area – right underneath a spot-lit area surrounded by four bars that were "full of gossiping musicians and bloody journalists"[69] and offered him the chance to audition for Iron Maiden. Dickinson replied in the affirmative, and the following day, after running through several Maiden numbers at a rehearsal room in Hackney, the deal was sealed. Bruce Bruce was no more: Bruce Dickinson was the new lead singer in Iron Maiden, and it was as simple as that.

And sometimes life can be; such decisions and opportunities present themselves at, well, the most opportune of times. However, several people close to both the Samson and Maiden camps tell it a little differently, albeit at a quarter of a century's distance.

"They wanted Bruce by the time it came to it," says Tony Platt, who suggests that he had initially planted seeds of wider vocal and sonic possibilities in Maiden's head during his much-maligned 'Women In Uniform' session. "Rod was very much a fan of having a singer who could really pump it out. And, of course, you've got other bands like Whitesnake, already in that arena of having the voice up high – AC/DC were very successful at having that aspect. It made a significant amount of sense for Iron Maiden to have a vocalist who was giving the same kind of edge to things."

Again, being a bright and decent chap, Bruce was torn somewhat between taking what was clearly a positive career step, and doing the right thing by the people who'd got him to that position in the first place. During August and September 1981, Samson were being courted by a number of record labels, including A&M, and were on the verge of being offered a *significant* advance against future album sales that would stabilise things somewhat.[70] It was food for thought. It was the big score. They were one hit single away from stepping up a level, remember. And there was one heck of a lot going on.

Neal Kay remembers his part in proceedings. "I was doing the Green Man in Leytonstone or something. Steve Harris phoned me and said to me that if Bruce turns up that night, would I get him to call Steve. And Bruce did turn up and I did say to him, 'Phone Steve 'cause he wants to talk to you, here's the number.' And that was it, I did my bit." Bruce did his and made the call.

The 'time off' after Reading was rapidly becoming a major headache; Bruce was so much in demand at this time that whispers abounded that he was also being courted by Ritchie Blackmore's Rainbow as a vocalist, something that could have, again, changed this book considerably – and probably given it a better title. Ahem. Samson publicist Jennie Halsall was one of the many people whose advice Dickinson sought at this confusing time. "I can remember one key issue: we were in Henrietta Street the month he joined Iron Maiden, basically. Bruce and Samson had just been offered a deal at A&M [and] Bruce rang me up in a bit of a panic. He said, 'Can I come and talk to you?' and I said, 'Sure.' So he came in and I said, 'Let's go to the boardroom' which was the caff across the road – we used to do all our meetings in there, sat down with a mug of tea. He said, 'I've got this problem, we've just been offered this deal with A&M but it's taken ages, and, well, I've just been offered the lead singership of Iron Maiden.' And I went, 'Oh, Christ, that's tricky…'"

"I remember the conversation really plainly. I said, 'I've come to those sort of crossroads a lot of times in my life and I've done what's right – but not necessarily what's best for me. You'll never get this offer again; it's amazing, it's fantastic, it's where you should be. But the Samson boys are going to hate you, because their deal is going to fall through.' And he knew that, he said that. And I said, 'But there'll be an opportunity for you to pay them back at some point, which obviously won't be the same, but it'll be the best you can do. So you've gotta take it because these offers don't come around very often, and you'd be brilliant at it.'"

"It was frustrating [for Samson] because visionary managers who were business-like in those days were pretty few and far between. That was the problem. Rod Smallwood, and his partner managing Iron Maiden,[71] were meticulous, studied, focussed."

"Not long before that I was looking after [a very famous rock trio], and particularly the band's new drummer, who told me when he joined that he'd taken his own lawyer and accountant with him. One time, a royalty cheque came through to him from Japan. He used to give the cheques to his accountant, send him on a plane, and quite a few times the accountant would go into the record company, do an audit and [the cheque] would be short. But once you cash the cheque, you accept the audit [and therefore have accepted the cheque]."

"It was totally the right thing to do for Bruce, although I knew it would cause casualties. But a business decision is often a tough decision to make, and you have to leave your own personal feelings out of it."

Even guitarist Dennis Stratton, who had recently parted ways with Iron Maiden for non-playing reasons, says he told the 24-year old vocalist that this was an opportunity he could hardly afford to pass up. "I did tell Rod Smallwood there was no way Maiden would ever break America while Paul Di'Anno sang in the band," he recalls. "I was in The Ship in Wardour Street when Bruce Dickinson told me he had been offered the gig. And I said, 'Yeah, take it. And if you take it, Maiden will be big in America,' because he had the range to go up against your Robert Plants and Sammy Hagars and people like that."[72]

Ex-Shots bandmate Bill Liesegang also recalls speaking with Bruce about the options in front of him at the time. "Bruce came over to my house; we were still quite friendly even though we weren't playing in the same band, because I had gone from Shots to Xero, and he had gone onto Samson. And when he came over he said, 'I've just had this offer from Iron Maiden, do you think I should take it?' And I was like, 'Well, you've answered you own question there Bruce, go for it.'"

So after some thought, and lots of consultation with some of the people he'd shared time and trust with, Bruce decided to move on; Samson's constant state of flux in terms of their career, despite the noises being made about new labels and a bright future, was hardly persistent. After so many false dawns, perhaps it was an inevitable that he would decide to part company with the band who had done so much to develop him as a musician and as a performer.

It is a decision that Bernie Torme, Gillan guitarist, has sympathy with. "There was kind of a residual attitude in the Samson camp that Bruce was responsible for the band not really cracking it, because he left," he muses. "But the point is that anyone would have left. If you'd have been asked to join Maiden at that point, basically anyone would have. [Samson] had ended up … they didn't have a situation at all really. And Iron Maiden had probably the best management in the country at that point and they were also on EMI, I mean, who'd turn that down?"

"It was a good decision on Bruce's part," agrees John McCoy, so instrumental in the early career of Samson. "I've been in bands and been offered much better gigs, and because of loyalty have stayed with my original band and then that's all fallen apart, and I've regretted not taking the offer of a better gig. I think Bruce did the right thing, because [Samson] were kind of floundering. And there wasn't any money there to support everybody, and Maiden had their career already planned out for eighteen months to a couple of years ahead. And they had probably the most sensible management of any band at that time."

"[Maiden's management] made sure that the guys were all comfortable, and spent money advertising and getting them on the right tours and, let's face it, they were a good band compared to a lot of their contemporaries. Angel Witch had a couple of good tunes, but they weren't in the same league. There was an energy about Maiden that came through, even in the early days. You know, Steve just had that buzz about him."

* * *

The sparks began to fly; Bruce rehearsed with his new band, and there was a massive sense of homecoming, musically at least. "Samson was heading south, there was no two ways about it, there was nothing happening," continues Neal Kay. "The thing was that Steve had a perception beyond my own in some ways there because I never had the luxury or the opportunity of seeing Bruce try out with Iron Maiden – Steve, of course, after the phone call, obviously took him into rehearsal and Bruce finally realised where he belonged. And he belonged with Iron Maiden. There's no question of that."

"Bruce is different to the rest of the [members of Iron Maiden] as well, as different as Paul Di'Anno … I'm also an ex-public schoolboy and I understand all this, I turned my back on all that shit. Bruce is no different. He's an intellectual, he's got a very powerful, enquiring, inquisitive mindset. He's very, very cut for sport. He is a well-spoken, very, very powerful intellectual being."

"You needed some type of power upfront to combine all the influences and outputs and come up with the definitive lyrics that fitted what was going on. Bruce just gelled perfectly with Iron Maiden. It was a fait accompli. Bruce is the man who was the missing link because once he joined it was frigging obvious what had happened – the balance was finally achieved. In Bruce, they not only had a consummate frontman who could be as funny as hell but he also told great stories that he managed to convey beautifully through the music. He was an Iron Maiden member all along – but I guess he just didn't realise it."

"Arguably, one of the other things about Maiden was that they probably had a better handle as to exactly where they wanted to position their roots," says Tony Platt. "Samson didn't quite have a handle on that. Bruce's vocal heroes were in the area of Deep Purple and that kind of thing. Arthur Brown, very much so, and very much the drama of it all. Bruce was always fairly dramatic and that's what he brought to Maiden. Maiden had to do something more than just 'bloke rock' or 'bloke metal' but the problem was they were [from one point of view,] archetypically Spinal Tap in that they sort of didn't see the joke. There needed to be a bit of humour in what they did to make it go that extra nine yards … The thing about Bruce is that he was able to completely divert that, because his sword and dorkery lyrics were absolutely the perfect thing [to avoid being perceived as over-earnest]."

"And because Bruce is intelligent, he was able to come up with lyrics that had an awful lot of bite and worked musically, lyrically, melodically, in a rhyming sense and everything. Because the guy's eloquent he was able to come up with those aspects quite easily, and make them believable."

Having come to one of the most difficult decisions in his young career to date – leaving Shots was simply not in the same league as the stakes involved here – there was one thing left for the vocalist to do, and that was the tricky and sticky one: to break the news to Paul, Chris and Mel Gaynor.

Rob Grain, closer to Paul Samson than most, relates the moment when a leather-jacketed[73] Dickinson finally came clean. "After a couple of weeks on holiday, Bruce went into a band meeting. Since they'd been away, the band had been talking to record companies and had two confirmed record deals on the table worth [a huge amount of money]. And Bruce came swanning in the meeting and said, 'I've got a bit of news, chaps, I'm leaving, I'm joining Iron Maiden.'" Both offers were subsequently withdrawn.

"[But] on one hand, it was a case of, 'Good luck to you,'" continues Grain. "Even at that point Maiden only had two albums out – but they had toured with Kiss and Judas Priest, and they were playing Hammersmith Odeon-type gigs. You could never knock anybody for wanting a bit of success. Quite a well known Bruce quote is that when he joined Iron Maiden they had the next two years mapped out, whereas in Samson you didn't know what you were doing in two *hours'* time! So, fair play to him. Samson [subsequently] got Nicky Moore in, and got a record deal with Polydor. The two albums that they did with Polydor far outweighed the three they did with Bruce in terms of sales: they did bigger tours, played to bigger crowds, and sold more records."

Paul had discovered Nicky Moore – a magnificent blues singer whose lungs are some kinda weird hybrid between Muddy Waters and Joe Cocker – at a gig at the good ol' stamping ground of the Prince Of Wales down in Gravesend and, of course, must have known what he could do, Samson and The Nicky Moore Band having shared stages many times over the years. As Tony Platt says, "It was an excellent decision; Nicky Moore's voice is fantastic and it really did suit the music they were doing."

Later, Paul was to philosophise that Bruce was in many ways a slightly square peg within the band, in terms of personality at least, "He tried hard but he was never really one of the lads. He tried to blame it on drugs but all we did was smoke a little pot. Really it was that he was from a different social class and educational background. We're working class lads like Iron Maiden whereas Bruce was suburban middle class."[74] So perhaps the situation was slightly skewed from the start, despite the abundance of talent that Paul, Bruce, Thunderstick and Chris Aylmer shared individually and collectively. In a sense, that Samson hung in there for so long is a massive indication as to exactly how good a band they were, despite all the problems and differing backgrounds. But, for Bruce, there was one thing that drew him toward Steve Harris' motley bunch, and one more than any other.

When it really came down to it, it was all about the music.

"When I first heard Maiden I got the same buzz off them I did when I heard *Deep Purple In Rock*," opined the singer. "It was like a steam train coming at you and none of the other bands did that anymore. I really wanted to be the singer in their band ... Paul wasn't surprised when I left and it was a relief to him because he wanted to be more in control."[75]

And if there ever was a band who were in control, it was Bruce's new group: Iron Maiden.

chapter eight:
What's Your Number?

Sensibly, Iron Maiden's first gigs with their new singer were out of the UK. Whilst Bruce had been rehearsing the set to get himself up to scratch during September 1981, the press began to get wind of what was still rather a shock to the system. Di'Anno had always been a rather larger than life character and certainly the eminently quotable focal point of a band of lads that still stood tall as the keepers of the heavy metal flame. Despite having somewhat raced ahead of (most of) the baying pack, losing such a strong personality from their ranks could have been perceived as a very risky strategy indeed, at least from those on the outside who did not yet know exactly the quality of the new addition to Team Maiden.

So the band headed out for five gigs in Italy – beginning on October 26 in Bologna – prior to Bruce's official unveiling at the Rainbow club on November 15, where they were supported by Praying Mantis, still plugging away manfully. Despite some initial nerves, by the time the band hit the UK for that gig, they were united and forceful as if they'd been playing together for years. The rest of November and December were spent in the rehearsal room, writing tracks for Maiden's third album – Bruce's first with the band. But the spectre of Samson – or, more specifically, of those pesky Ramkup chaps, still loomed large over proceedings.

Due to the judgement in the court case, if Burce had written any material on this Maiden album, Ramkup would have had a claim on some monies – thus Maiden's management reached a settlement with Ramkup. Restricted from official creative input into the new album sessions, Bruce later would comment that he had a "moral contribution" to at least three tracks: 'The Prisoner', 'Children Of The Damned' and a little throwaway ditty named 'Run To The Hills'.[76] When it came to lay the album down to tape in the closing months of 1981, with Martin Birch at the helm, Maiden had become a remarkable unit – as yet, the only people to realise exactly how remarkable they could be were a few thousand lucky Italian chaps, the miscreant audience of the Rainbow, and the contents of the Ruskin Arms, Maiden's old stamping ground, where they played a charity gig on December 23. The world was soon to sit up and take notice with some sharpness.

"When I first joined," commented Bruce, "I thought that I could be the best damned singer the band had ever had. I knew that they were ready to do things properly, that the set-up was there. It really was a case of when things were going to happen. When I heard the material for the album that they'd been working on, I knew they were ready."[77]

'The Prisoner' stemmed largely from Bruce's experiences as a youngster. Not only was the TV series – in which Patrick McGoohan plays a secret service operative kidnapped and imprisoned in a very strange village – one of Bruce's favourite programmes, as a youngster moving around from school to school and prank to prank he also deeply identified with McGoohan's character (referred to only as Number Six).[78] "I didn't really have anywhere I belonged, so when The Prisoner turns round and says, 'I am not a number, I am a free man,' I wanted that to be me."[79]

Musically, that song came together from a very simple beat that would-be drummer Bruce[80] had been bashing out, whilst Clive Burr was elsewhere having a cup of tea, then guitarist and bassist Adrian Smith soon joined in the jam, and the track was born. It only remained for Rod Smallwood to attain permission from Patrick McGoohan to use the iconic quote with which Bruce identified so much, and so was born the classic, doom-laden introduction and the song was complete.

'Children Of The Damned', meanwhile, is loosely based round the movie of the same name, which itself was taken from John Wyndham's novel, *The Midwich Cuckoos*, much as is Maiden's wont. The tale is of 'alien' children (hence the 'cuckoo' reference) whose powers of mind control quickly render a typical middle England village under their spell, motivation unknown. The track is suitably taut and paranoid before bursting into the familiar galloping, melodic choruses that Maiden do so well. Bruce commented later that it was heavily influenced – musically, in feel and in structure – by Black Sabbath's 'Children Of The Sea'. Certainly both tracks have a plaintive, eerie gravitas that ramps up the gothic drama with much skill.

'Run To The Hills' is, of course, not only a classic Maiden track, but a song that stands alongside anything ever written in hard rock; it has it all – a slightly political edge, rollocking, romping, William Tell bassline, harmonic guitar leads, solos, and plenty of room for Dickinson to exercise that remarkable vocal ability of his atop the swell.[81]

"It's about American Indians and Western movies," he said, "and the way that American Indians are always seen as cannon fodder, which is not always the case."[82] All in all, the LP is not only light years ahead of *Killers*, but galaxies away from anything anyone else could manage at the time. If ever there was vindication of Bruce's decision to join the band, it was there in black vinyl. And whilst the 'moral contribution' may or may not have been concentrated on any tracks in particular, the fact remains that Bruce's range and technique have freed the songwriters of Maiden to explore sonic territories previously undiscovered. Of the previous work of Maiden and Samson, the closest anyone had previously perhaps come to a track as atmospheric, dark and alternately hefty as *Number Of The Beast*[83] album closer, 'Hallowed Be Thy Name' was Bruce's previous outfit, Samson, whose 'Communion' shares many qualities with that song.

Speaking of the album as a whole, Bruce commented that it was a fresh sound. "It joins together something that was completely melodic," he began, "with something that's completely ... *aaaarghh!*" For Bruce, 1981 had begun with recording sessions for one of the best rock albums that the New Wave Of British Heavy Metal had produced. It ended in recording an LP that was to have rather more significant an impact even than that. 1982 had one hell of a lot to live up to.

chapter nine:
The Rollercoaster Revs Up

1982 was a year of conflict and suspicion, in the wider world at large: the UK's unemployment figures broke through the three million barrier for the first time, a statistic that threatened the very future of the Conservative government. More tragically, events on a small UK colony just off the coast of Argentina escalated into the full-blown Falklands conflict, during which casualties were suffered on both sides as Great Britain fought off an Argentinian invasion force seeking to reclaim the islands as the Malvinas. Margaret Thatcher, the Iron Maiden herself, had already lost her son, Mark, for three days in January when he had got lost in the Sahara Desert on the Paris/Dakar rally (he was subsequently found); the loss of the sons of the UK in the Falklands conflict was a terrible cost of life. Thatcher's government spectacularly recovered in the opinion polls to record a landslide victory in the general election of the following year.

Elsewhere, the United Nations were to pass Resolution 37, which advised the withdrawal of troops of the Soviet Union from Afghanistan, the Soviets having recently become under the new tenure of former KGB head, Yuri Andropov, succeeding Leonard Brezhnev as general secretary of the central committee of the Soviet Communist Party. One of his first acts was to release Polish Solidarity leader, Lech Walesa, from almost a year's imprisonment near the border of the two countries.

It was a time of violence and uncertainty throughout the world as the hippy dream of the 1960s had been shown to be failed through the growing disillusionment of the 1970s; the new decade was to bring a growing sense of self-reliance to the point of selfishness. The Middle East was once more in a state of turmoil, this time seeing skirmishes between Lebanon, Palestine and Israel – where half a million people marched to demand the resignation of the leader of the country, Menachem Begin.

The 1982 World Cup was held in Spain, and saw Northern Ireland humble the host country with a famous 1-0 victory in their own backyard, whilst England's much vaunted challenge was stilled in the second group stage.

Musically-speaking, the very first CD players were released by Sony, although the format was simply too expensive for most consumers, who were still reliant on cassettes and good old vinyl for their sonic kicks. And the sonic kicks of the year included black metallers Bucks Fizz, nosebleed technocore devils Tight Fit, and the rampaging aural assault of ex-Damned bassist Captain Sensible with the vicious buzzsaw thrash of Rogers & Hammerstein's 'Happy Talk', from the banned 1958 slasher movie, the gory *South Pacific*. Punk rock, and rock in general, had seemingly run its course in favour of dressed-up and androgynous pop, a vanguard led by the likes of Duran Duran, Adam And The Ants and, later, Culture Club.

It was to this backdrop that Bruce Dickinson's new band first unleashed themselves on a waiting world. Thanks to an inordinately tight schedule between the recording and the planned tour to promote the band's new album, *Number Of The Beast*, mixing of the LP was not completed in time for the LP to be available during the UK phase of the group's tour, which took place during February, 1982. Happily, however, producer Martin Birch was able to complete the master for 'Run To The Hills' in time for it to be released as a single, on February 12. It soared to Number 7 in the charts, a remarkable achievement by anybody's standards. The first single released by the group with its new singer is rightly heralded as a timeless classic. The band duly embarked on their *Beast On The Road* tour, which would eventually take in 180 dates worldwide, a major step up for Dickinson, who had never previously played outside the UK – not through want of trying, of course. But with a professional, clued-in and innovative management team, visionary and strong-willed Steve Harris pushing matters and the support of EMI, Maiden's stock was higher than ever before; they'd outgrown the loose confines of what used to be called the New Wave Of British Heavy Metal, and were now – in the words of Rod Smallwood – a worldwide proposition. When the LP was released on March 29, it slammed straight to the top of the UK charts. Famously, the group were told of their success during a rather grounding moment, trying to push-start their tour bus which had broken down in the snow on the way to their concert in Zurich. On such moments, perhaps, are band relationships cemented.

Of the album, Bruce summed it up thusly: "When astronomers talk about a planetary line-up," he offered, "a conjunction that happens once in a blue moon – *Number Of The Beast* is the musical equivalent."[84] Things had fallen into place: the gigs were well-received throughout Europe, although across the water there was some trouble ahead. It began in France during April, when Bruce contracted a chest infection, forcing the cancellation of three concerts – something that the band had always hated doing, but needs must, and the unscheduled rest was no doubt well-received in a sense.

The American assault was the inevitable next step, and to that end Maiden had an astonishing 104 gigs set up, mostly as a support act to the likes of Judas Priest, Rainbow and The Scorpions. Given the album's title, and the rising tide of what would become known as the 'moral majority' in the States, a furore began which cast this quintet of rockers in the guise of devil worshippers, satanists, and quite probably also being held responsible for the assassination of Archduke Ferdinand in 1914, the fall of Rome and a slightly underdone sea bass they'd had in a restaurant the previous weekend. The ludicrousness of the laughable accusations centred round the subject matter of the album's title and the similarly-titled single, which had been inspired by a dream, in turn inspired by *Damien: Omen II*, a film that Harris had seen, rather than anything of any further occult significance. Nevertheless, there were burnings of Maiden records, mass-smashings of vinyl and all manner of nonsense – which, as it involved buying the LPs in the first place, quite possibly didn't harm the Maiden cause as much as it was intended. Bruce remembers one particular incident on tour, when a fervent member of the audience protested against this perceived anti-Christian group, and strapped a huge cross to his back to attend the gig.

"We thought, 'That's fantastic,'" said the singer, before chuckling that as the twenty foot cross was so heavy, the protestor had, "fitted a back tail wheel on it." A moment of levity in a situation that could have escalated exponentially as the heat was on. During the May dates, Bruce – perhaps unused to touring quite so heavily – had injured his neck forcing him to don a surgical neck brace for several dates, with a succession of doctors prescribing painkillers – one even going as far as recommending surgery – before the singer finally found relief under the tutored hands of a chiropractor. By now – and if you look for these kind of things, you're going to find them everywhere – the misfit majority were looking for all kinds of Satanic messages hidden within the album, with its memorable artwork by Derek Riggs depicting Maiden mascot Eddie manipulating the devil.[85] Bruce's weary reaction to the tales and half-truths about strange goings on round the band and the album was memorable and definitive, saying onstage at their New York Palladium gig on June 29 that there have been tales of weird goings-on round the album which, "one or two people have attributed to be the work of Satan ... [We] want to say to all the people who play records backwards and burn albums out in the streets, they can ... stick their heads up their arse, 'cause we ain't interested."[86] He was later to comment to *Enfer Magazine* that the problem was that our American cousins were bereft of "the same sense of humour", prompting certain sections to take it all too seriously, and demand stickers be applied to the LP, "warning people of the so-called Satanic aspect of the lyrics." For someone of Dickinson's intelligence and education, this kind of dunderheaded response to art that is essentially slightly provocative, but also slightly tongue-in-cheek, was both puzzling and unexpected. For now, however, there were bigger fish to fry, as the *Beast On The Road* tour thundered its way through the summer, the American audiences much enamoured of Maiden mascot Eddie's antics, as Rod Smallwood explained to the author for an Iron Maiden special issue of *Metal Hammer* in 2005.

"There was the story, don't know if it was a true one, but [Ozzy once inadvertently] bit the head off a bat. So we thought, 'Eddie's always been a very good mate of the bats... we can't have that.' So Eddie will take revenge on behalf of the bats. So we superimposed Ozzy's head [into the picture, indicating Eddie had in turn bitten off Ozzy's head]. And his manager at the time, Don Arden, called, and said it was 'inappropriate' and could we withdraw it. So I said, 'Okay, we'll withdraw it.' So I sent a telex – in those days it was telex – out to all the record companies, asking them could they please withdraw it. But you know, it had pretty well all got out by then, so it created more of a 'thing' about it. Meaning no disrespect to Ozzy, of course." All good clean fun; some twenty years later, however, there would be another clash between Maiden and an Arden. *This time involving eggs!* More later.

By the time August 1982 came around, tour fever had firmly set in, and tales abound of various ways the band would let off steam; one such story, which is possibly apocryphal, places the band's singer entering a bar in Beaumont, Texas, on around August 9. The manager of said hostelry took exception to the shorts and socks combo Bruce was wearing and refused to serve him unless he changed; Bruce went back to his hotel room, and returned with a different kind of shorts – denim, this time, although just as short – and a T-shirt with the rather lovely caption: 'FUCK' emblazoned on it. He subsequently was happily served with his refreshments.

Bruce was later to admit that there was more than a little excess-all-areas activity going on at the time, suggesting that the band – offstage at least – were, 'All fucked up then ... we were young lads, big out in the States for the first time, boilers left, right and centre.'[87] Given that the group were all in their early(ish) twenties at the time, the phrase 'kids in a sweet shop' comes to mind, as noted by Garry Bushell in the 1984 book on the band on which he collaborated with long time Maiden cohort and photographer, Ross Halfin, *Running Free: The Official Story Of Iron Maiden*. This particular tale tells of Maiden returning to the UK from El Paso, Texas, to play a set at the famous Reading Festival, on August 28, 1982. It is a twelve thousand mile flight. To help pass the time, the band's lighting engineer asked Bruce if he might have any sleeping tablets he would like to pass on. Bad plan. "Bruce gave him three horse tranquilisers," says Bushell. "And, mad fool, took three himself. Needless to say, neither of them woke up properly for three days."

The Reading gig was a triumphant occasion. If there were any doubt whatever about Bruce as a member of the band, it had been dissipated by both the huge success of the new material and the growing realisation that the vocalist's range, energy and approach had ramped up matters massively. Following Reading, Maiden returned briefly to the States – as guests of Scorpion this time, who handcuffed Bruce's hands behind his back during one of the gigs – before the band toured Australia and Japan to complete an inordinately busy but ultimately massively successful year in their careers.

Referring to 1982, Jennie Halsall reckons it "was huge, absolutely massive," and, even at this stage, recalls Bruce had one eye on other creative activities. "Bruce always did the cartoon stuff, the images and the writing," she says. "He was also talking about book ideas back then and always wanted to do so much more than just being the singer in a rock band. I don't think Samson, or indeed the Iron Maiden boys, had any other aspirations apart from making it in the music business. He could see the business for the business: as a career and not just the rock 'n' roll stuff. Which sets him apart from the rest, in my view."

"If you saw that tour," says NWOBHM expert, John Tucker, "you'd see there was something really special about them. It wasn't like their third album, with a new singer; it was like a band who'd been doing this for forever and a day. It's a well-paced, well put together set. They had self-confidence, something about them that said, 'We are superstars and we're not gonna look back.' And they didn't."

"Something had to happen one way or the other, because *Killers* didn't do too well in the press. People didn't like the production [on the debut], and though there were good songs on the second album, and *Metal For Muthas*, there's a lot of things people didn't like about what was going on. Whether it was journalistic vitriol or what, I don't know, but the album didn't do particularly well [in comparison]. It was the age old Make Or Break album, and – boy did it make 'em! What can you say? It's a great album."

Neal Kay, as ever, has a tale to tell. "I've got their LP hanging up in front of me," he told me. "*Number Of The Beast*, their third album, presented to Neal Kay for sales in the UK of over 100,000 copies, 1982. A hundred thousand copies! You just think about that – that's fucking awesome for a heavy metal band who never appear on the radio, who never appear on TV, who are universally decried by commercial popular music press as being old-fashioned, out of date, long haired, who gives a shit, it's all dead! Well it's not. That's enough to fill Wembley."

"And the coming of Bruce to Iron Maiden was the final missing piece of the jigsaw puzzle. With Bruce upfront the band couldn't fail as far as I was concerned; it was very gratifying to sit back from a lower position and watch them. I wanted to go with them 'cause I knew what was coming but I had my own destiny and other things to do – they went off touring and I saw them when I could but it was really gratifying to read stories and see pictures of them. They opened up the possibilities for British rock bands of the time and those who might follow in the future, in so many ways. To the far ends of the earth, new territories, new venues and showing the world that no matter what political view you took, or religious stance you had, that nothing actually in truth ever became a barrier to rock 'n' roll. I know Steve thinks like me, and I like he, that in all honesty that's how rock 'n' roll should be."

"I'd moved to the States and Bruce and I lost touch," says Stuart Smith, who very nearly could've put a huge spanner in the works, had his and Bruce's project taken off only eighteen months previously, "I remember hearing 'Run

To The Hills', I think it was when I was getting the tyres changed on my car and it was getting played on the stereo system there and I was 'Christ, that's Bruce!' and I didn't even know he'd joined another band!"

"The music scene in England wasn't really happening [for me]," explains Smith, "and Ritchie Blackmore said, 'Why don't you come over to America and give it a shot there,' so I went and stayed with him in Long Island for a while. But in the first week of being there, I heard Bruce and I recognised the voice, you can't miss it!"

You most certainly cannot; now the world knew all about Maiden. 1982 was the year things started to go ballistic in the career of Paul Bruce Dickinson. As he says himself, the release of 'Run To The Hills' and subsequently *Number Of The Beast* was like, "getting to the top of the rollercoaster – and about five years later, it bottomed out ... we were never just in freefall, it was constant good news."[88]

What a difference a year makes; the band had certainly thrown themselves into it; with this momentum behind them, and ready to settle into a new set of recordings, surely 1983 would bring more of the same.

chapter ten:
Mind Games

It would, however, have to be with a new drummer, Clive Burr having vacated the hotseat following some issues on the extensive *Beast On The Road* tour. The band parted company with Burr in late 1982, replacing him with Michael 'Nicko' McBrain, who had previously supported Maiden with his band Trust. To complete the merry-go-round, Burr would go on to fill the drumstool for ... Trust! Bruce's only comment on the matter was that Clive was in danger of falling into "the same problems that occurred"[89] with previous vocalist Paul Di'Anno.

Regardless of the ins and outs of the departure of the affable Burr,[90] the facts remained that Bruce was standing as the voice of a new generation of metal fans, and yet was still unable to officially contribute to writing new material thanks to the settlement with Samson's old management, Ramkup. On the back of the success of *Number Of The Beast*,[91] and the associated merchandising and tour memorabilia sales, however, the Maiden boys had suddenly found they were comfortably off financially. There was only therefore one thing for it.

"Iron Maiden's management, when Bruce became established within Iron Maiden, was able to go to Ramkup and buy the rights and the publishing and everything," explains Thunderstick, ex-Samson and Maiden drummer.

The practical effect of this was to free Bruce to take up his songwriting credits on the imminent new album, which was largely written in the Channel Islands during January 1983. Maiden manager Rod Smallwood remembers the concept behind the new long player well. "Steve had the idea of Eddie being in a straightjacket," he says. "I thought, 'That's cool but it needs a little bit more than that.' So I got the idea of lobotomising him. And then we had to think of a title, and none of the song titles really seemed apt for it. We were down in Guernsey where we used to go to write the early albums, just trying to think of titles. *Food For Thought* was one for a while! In the inner sleeve, the brains are being served up to the band at the dinner table. And then we were in a pub and it just came out: *Peace Of Mind*. Iron Maiden being for Peace Of Mind, in the normal spelling, was quite a fun idea. Then making it *Piece Of Mind*, it just seemed to work."

Title and tracks sorted, the band decamped to the rather more warm surroundings of Compass Point Studios in Nassau for the actual recordings, again with Martin Birch at the helm. Jennie Halsall remembers her part in the process. "We stayed friends," says the publicist. "Maiden were recording the new album and he invited me out there so I got on a plane with Jane, complete with curry spices which were an important part of the suitcase – [they really wanted] to make curry in the Bahamas! Robert Palmer lived down the road [from the studios] and I met a hero 'cause I went out on a boat with them for the afternoon fishing, which was good fun. We'd stand in the house and watch the storms out in the Caribbean which would flash along."

In that kind of electric atmosphere, Maiden recorded an LP that follows on from their massive hit of the previous year in many ways; aesthetically it is in many ways a companion piece to *Number Of The Beast*, although the themes of *Piece Of Mind* are less occult in feel, and more about conflict, war and resolution. In many ways, indeed, it is a superior album to its predecessor; the band – with whom the new drummer meshes as if he had always been present – are tighter and more together than on ...*Beast*, the year of touring having brought them together as musicians and as people. The dynamic thrust is hefty but with an increasing amount of tuneful moments compared to Bruce's debut Maiden LP; at the distance of over two decades it is a surprisingly poppy effort.

Bruce's first official contribution to the Maiden canon is the ambitious 'Revelations', a six minute extended discussion of religion that features a typically over the top reference, herein the entire first verse is a poem by the social theorist and paradoxist Christian philosopher G.K. Chesterton, plus references also to Hindu and Egyptian philosophy, materialism, mysticism and a character with whom the singer would grapple throughout his career, the atheist philosopher Aleister Crowley; it is an entirely Bruce curveball to throw into the mix, although no doubt the subtleties were entirely lost on those all-too-keen to paint Maiden as evil, as witnessed during the previous year's American clashes with the religious right.

"I take a lot of interest in all the religions of the world and the different forms they take," the singer offered, "because I think that all the religions are the mirrors of the various possibilities and opportunities of life that could benefit mankind."[92]

Following this marker, Dickinson's collaboration with Adrian Smith, the anthemic 'Flight Of Icarus' is self-explanatory, yet its references to touching the sun, and flying on the wings of dreams, are also a powerful reference to the huge rise that Maiden – and the singer himself – had experienced. It was the first track to be released as a single – on April 28, 1983, and reached Number 11 in the UK charts. After this mini-classic comes the call to arms of 'Die With Your Boots On' – a three-way effort between Smith, Dickinson and good ol' 'Arry 'Arris. The sentiment is as impeccable as the control of the arrangement.

Bruce's final contribution as a credited writer is 'Sun And Steel', which he, again, wrote with Adrian Smith. It features a rather unconvincing Harris-pastiche galloping verse structure, and a very Smith/Dickinson venture into a poppy chorus work that, whilst setting nothing alight, sets up a natty guitar-harmony section and keeps the album rolling along.

"It's based on Yukio Mushima, who disembowelled himself," explained Bruce. "He was a Japanese novelist who started living the Samurai code, took up a course in bodybuilding and did the whole warrior bit. He stood in front of the Japanese Ministry Of Defence and decided to start a revolution. It didn't work, so he went inside and disembowelled himself." As you do. "His partner chickened out and did a botched job of cutting his head off, but finally someone decapitated him; all a bit messy ... [it's] a pleasant little ditty."[93] *Piece Of Mind* was released on May 28, reaching Number 3; Maiden could do little wrong, and the singer was enjoying himself. The concerts continued to come thick and fast as the well-received new LP permeated to all corners of the globe. The inevitably-named *World Piece Tour* was to all intents and purposes Maiden's debut headlining world tour, and its 140 gigs spanned the globe accordingly, with occasional controversial moments, such as the band's concert in Buffalo on August 15, 1983, when a local model named Suzette Kolga had won a competition to appear onstage with the band. Subsequently, whilst dancing around the band cracking a whip, she alleged that Bruce had exposed her to the audience by ripping off her top, and sought punitive damages in court for damage to her personal and professional reputation. The matter did not reach the stage of the courtroom.

Under tour pressure, every band is prone to occasional tear-ups, of course, and Bruce captured a particular disagreement between Harris and McBrain on cassette, having stumbled upon an argument after a gig at Allertown, Pennsylvania over a drum solo. McBrain clocked that Bruce was, in fact, whirring away with his Walkman getting the shouting match on tape, and jumped on the cassette in question! However, on the B-side were sketches of new material on which Dickinson had been working for any subsequent new record!

It was a punishing, gruelling schedule, but by the end of 1983 Maiden had retained all the momentum of *Number Of The Beast*, and added to their stock through their consistently hardworking approach; *Piece Of Mind* was later voted by *Kerrang!* magazine readers as 'Number 1 Metal LP of All-Time ... with *Number Of The Beast* at Number 2! Bruce himself was happy enough, although he did concede that it was tiring, and that there must be "other ways to get rich and covered in glory." No doubt, but none so quick, and regardless, the singer, who was still only 25, was never one to shirk a challenge. And approaching fast was 1984 – Orwell's year.

chapter eleven:
Slaves, Death And Glory

After a couple of weeks off at the start of 1984 to recharge the batteries a little, Maiden reconvened during February and March to begin rehearsing and jamming out new material for their fifth album, and Bruce's third as vocalist for the group. In many ways, the material that eventually became the *Powerslave* album draws a line under a trilogy of sorts that began with the breakthrough ...*Beast* album – certainly, when it came to returning to Compass Point during April 1984, the collection of tracks the band had assembled were as assured as anything they'd come up with during their accelerated and hectic schedule of the last two years.

Bruce's collaborations with Adrian Smith were beginning to sound mature and easy; his knack of marrying singalong choruses to Smith's insistent riffing is shown off immaculately in '2 Minutes To Midnight' – a gloriously horrific anti-war diatribe that takes its title from the conceptual Doomsday Clock[94] which, according to world events, is 'set' at closer to, or further away from midnight – the hour of destruction. The first time the hands of the clock had been 'set' to 23.58pm had been in 1953 when the United States Government decided to pursue the hydrogen bomb, a weapon that was many times more powerful than its predecessor, the atomic bomb. In 1984 the clock was set at three minutes to the hour of doom. The track makes no bones about its subject and relishes in its pull-no-punches lyric throughout. It was released as a single on August 11, 1984 and reached Number 11 in the charts, continuing Bruce's good run of chart placings for tracks he'd been involved with as a writer. This was despite a modicum of controversy which was whipped up by certain sections seeking to somehow link parent company Thorn/EMI's military material-building section with other sections of their company – including the record label and therefore the group – and suggesting that Maiden were hypocrites for decrying war whilst being signed to the record division of EMI; very quickly, Bruce dismissed this accusation as ludicrous. "We're observing them in much the same way as a documentary would observe them ... our lyrics have picked upon the points I wanted to pick out."[95]

Bruce's writing is strong throughout an album which – whilst allowing for such relatively weak moments as the instrumental yawn, 'Losfer Words (Big 'Orra)' – is also notable for the genius tour-de-force near-fourteen-minute epic, 'Rime Of The Ancient Mariner', quite simply one of the greatest songs that not only Steve Harris has ever written, but a truly timeless moment in rock history. Ironic, too, that a track whose lyrical narrative sticks very closely to the poem of the same name by Samuel Taylor Coleridge should be released by a band of supposed 'Satan-worshippers'. The poem, and therefore the song itself, has one message writ large: have respect for all of God's creations or be damned to ever walk the earth telling your sorry tale to passing strangers. Not that the religious right would pick up on either the innate intelligence of the material or the fundamentally moral stance of the song; after all, this is a band with *long hair, goldurn it, pass the blunderbuss an' we'll shoot the varmits full of condescending rapturous buckshot in their heathen asses*. Anyway, the track can be said to sum up the album, in truth; every member is playing to their best of abilities, the time changes, outstanding musical arrangement and drama are meticulously worked out – and yet there is room aplenty for the Iron Maiden vibe to come through.

Such heights are rare in music – for a band to have one mighty peak in a career is an achievement – and yet this is an album with two moments where the band touches heaven. The other is Bruce's title track, which not only marks the aesthetic of the subsequent stage show, artwork and Egyptian references, and also discusses obliquely the iconography of celebrity and the rock star pinnacle-placing lifestyle, but is also, brilliantly, a logical extrapolation of some of the concepts discussed on the track 'Revelations' from the previous year's *Piece Of Mind* LP. As was becoming clear with Bruce, one set of lyrics can tell a story on the surface whilst concurrently raising more questions to explore, and that is the mark of a true artist, albeit that it was written in a slightly more prosaic situation than its academic discourse would indicate – Bruce was sat at the breakfast table thinking about 'Revelations', and its indications of Hindu or Egyptian mythology and discussions of mortality, when he suddenly hit upon the crux of the matter.

"There was something missing; the power of death over life, which is a theme you find very often in Egyptian mythology," he noted, "I basically wrote 'Powerslave' while listening to 'Revelations', a cup of tea in one hand and bacon in the other."[96]

Dickinson's other contributions to the album are 'Back In The Village' which is, to all intents and purposes, the sequel to 'The Prisoner', being a slightly dotty but still rather natty collaboration with Adrian and another anti-war workout that builds to a rollocking chorus – and, perhaps most intriguingly, the paean to fencing, 'Flash Of The Blade'.

'... Blade' is a track that revisits one of the singer's main interests, the sport of fencing with which he had become more and more involved over the past year or so since taking it up again after many years. He'd first become interested in fencing in his Oundle days. "A workshop teacher turned up to school one day with an Excalibur-type sword he'd made," explained Bruce. "We were like, 'Cool. Can we make one?' He also mentioned he was a fencing coach and we persuaded the school to buy some kit and I got hooked."[97] The young Dickinson found himself drawn to its cut-and-thrust blend of skill, movement, energy and physical poetry, winning the school tournament and becoming Oundle captain at the age of fifteen, in 1975. He said he was a "ham [who] was immediately attracted to fencing because it seemed like a romantic, melodramatic form of combat."[98] Stuart Smith recalls talking with Bruce about the sport back in the late 1970s. "We were talking one night over a couple of pints about what we thought a good lead singer was, what sort of stage moves he should make. And both of us were big Purple fans and [fans of] the way that Ritchie Blackmore would move on stage. I think I even said something to Bruce like, 'a frontman should hold the stage like how a fencing swordsman would move,' and, of course, Bruce later went into fencing and became an instructor."

Although Maiden's schedule had been exhaustive (and increasingly exhausting), Bruce had found time in-between the bouts of hedonism and rockaround to try, at least, to indulge himself in the sport as early as the *World Piece* tour, although explaining to customs officials exactly what a heavy metal reprobate was doing with a fencing kit was rather tricky at times, as he noted in September 1984.

"You can't imagine the problems I had with customs! I'd learned how to say 'fencing' in ten different languages! And every time I was asked the same question, 'Oh I see, you're a professional fencer!' And my answer was always the same, 'No, I'm a singer!' They look at me pretty suspiciously!" Given that it's tantamount to terrorism to take a bottle of Vidal Sassoon onto an aeroplane these days, one can only dream of such innocent times ...

Although Bruce would enter regional competitions when time allowed over this period, opportunities to pursue this interest were necessarily limited – the *World Slavery* tour was the most ambitious the band had yet undertaken, rehearsals beginning as early as June 20 in Florida, with five days of production rehearsals in early August in Bonn, Germany before the tour proper started on August 9, 1984 in Poland. It was, says Neal Kay, a typically brave move by an act who were still seeking to break down boundaries wherever they found them.

"They were the first band to take a full show behind the Iron Curtain in 1984," he rightly notes. "And they went to all the countries back then that were terribly starved and the youngsters were terribly ill-treated: Poland, Czechoslovakia, Hungary; they took a full three truckloads of gear there and released a four-track video, *Behind The Iron Curtain*. It's wonderful to see; there's all these Polish guards in Krakow standing with their guns by their sides, headbanging, whilst outside on a concrete pillar sits a 1949 Mig-15 – and the kids are just un-fucking-believable. Maiden have truly gone places and touched people that only a mega-successful act has the privilege of doing and I feel incredibly proud to have known them."

That concert, at Torwar Sports Hall, Warsaw, was the first time that a Western band had played a full show – complete with Egyptian Eddie and lights – of that scale. Fourteen thousand people turned up, with five thousand locked outside.

Bruce himself had been more than excited at the prospect, welcoming the change in itinerary from their usual practice of beginning their live activities back at home in the UK. "We never toured over there," he said, "and our fans need to see us because they feel frustrated, forgotten by the rest of the world. They hunger for Heavy Metal, they've never seen any hard rock band and we thought, 'Why not us?' I think it can bring a very positive experience; basically, it's not about selling more records in those countries."[99]

As a history graduate, however, Bruce was more than aware of the still fairly-recent atrocities that had taken place in those countries during the Second World War; the band visited the Auschwitz concentration camp, an experience that put it all into perspective. All the trials and tribulations that a mere rock band struggling to cope with the odd late night and full schedule can only pale in comparison to such unimaginable human-created evil. Bruce later was – rarely for him – unable to articulate the experience. "A black atmosphere just hangs over the place," he began. "I don't think I could ever write a song about [Auschwitz] – words couldn't sum it up. We all felt relieved to walk away."

*　*　*

The tour rolled on for Maiden. In the light of the recently-released film, *Spinal Tap*, the legendary mock-rock-u-mentary tale of a ludicrous metal-ish band on tour, it was gratifying to note that the stage set was still ambitious and somewhat overbearing – a huge Eddie behind the band mirroring the album's artwork, pyramids and the whole Egyptian kaboodle. It was deceptively simple too, with a minimum of complex technology to trip it up, and in fact, more often than not the moving parts were actually powered by stage crew pulling levers! Which makes sense if you are planning to be out on the road for the best part of a year. The *Powerslave* album crashed the UK charts at Number 2 on its September 15 release, and was also well-received in America, where the band were rapidly becoming a major draw. The intention after studio album three – and with a group as together as any rock band could hope – was to release a subsequent double LP, to which end gigs at London's Hammersmith Odeon – during Maiden's four dates there between October 8 and 12 – and Long Beach, Los Angeles on March 17, 1985, almost six months later – were recorded by Martin Birch. This LP became the magnificent *Live After Death*, which subsequently hit the shops in October, 1985, and featured the first vinyl appearance of a new catchphrase, when, in the introduction to 'Flight To Icarus', Bruce exhorted the audience, 'Scream For Me, Long Beach!'

The *World Slavery* tour also took in the unique first ever Rock In Rio series of concerts, which were to become synonymous with Maiden over the years. It was the biggest crowd to which Bruce had played to date, as Bill Liesegang – by this stage playing with Nina Hagen – recalled to the author in an interview for this book.

"At the first Rock in Rio [I was] with Nina Hagen and Iron Maiden were also on the bill so we did run into each other," Liesegang recalls. "Bruce was very friendly and we had a chat. Obviously he was a lot richer than the last time I met him!" The experience was best described, quite possibly, as "unique", with the organisers putting together all the more raucous elements in one place, perhaps to try and contain the madness. Whether Bruce indulged himself in his well-rehearsed fire extinguisher party trick, however, is lost to posterity.

"It was weird," laughs Liesegang. "They put all the metal bands on the bill – AC/DC, Whitesnake, Ozzy, and so on – into one hotel and all the other bands they probably thought were a bit easier, like Rod Stewart and Yes and all that, they put them in the other hotel. Queen were on that bill as well. But we were in the other hotel in the Copacabana. We had a great night out with all the metal bands."

The event itself was impressive, however, both ambitious and well-received in a country that is now renowned for its spirited enthusiasm for all things rockin'. "It was twelve consecutive nights that one, about half a million people (sic) every night so it was quite a big thing. We were there for the full twelve nights, we started it, played on the first night and ended up having the whole week and five days off and having another date at the end, which was quite good." Quite good being possibly the understatement of the century in this context.

And the gigs rolled on, and on, and on, and on: if anyone was under the illusion that either being on the road was fun and games, or that Maiden did not work their proverbials off in this period, then a mere glance at the ridiculously full schedule of dates in the liner notes to the reissue of the *Live After Death* album will very quickly put paid to that. Maiden were on a mission – a mission from 'Arry, originally – and part of that was to conquer the States. The problem was that there was still a massive groundswell of 'moral' outrage directed to heavy metal bands in general during 1984 and 1985, and particularly Maiden. Bruce was amused to find that a particularly fervent follower of TV evangelist Jimmy Swaggart had been sending him religious literature decrying the awful influence that rock 'n' roll was having on the younger generation; even more so when Bruce received one particular pamphlet which featured a rather rockin' picture of Steve Harris himself on the cover. But the tour – for all its good intentions – was the first moment of real schism within the career of Bruce-era Maiden. As the days rolled into each other and the band travelled between hotel and hotel, a full year was passing by with the band members scarcely aware of anything going on in the rapidly-receding farrago of protoplasm and mistakes known as 'real life'. By early 1985, the band was becoming physically – and mentally – exhausted by the pressures of their own success. The Maiden boys were becoming so in demand that dates kept getting added to the end of the tour. It was a Sisyphean task and one that was to very nearly have major consequences.

The utterly burnt out band were rather sinking into a state of depression, having been burnt out by the concentration required in putting on such energetic concerts night after night with barely a day off and waking up from dreams of egg and chips back in Blighty to find themselves on another tourbus in the middle of America. It was as disconcerting an experience as anything that Army training could have offered: the concept of breaking individuals down and rebuilding them as an unit is an intriguing one at the best of times, but when it happens to musicians, they're not necessarily the people who are best equipped to deal with it. Bruce was no different, and eventually was to go to Rod Smallwood – who had a background as a booking agent – and tell his manager that the group had reached their limits. For the first time since joining the band, Bruce was having second thoughts about matters.

"I really thought about ... quitting music altogether," he said, commenting that he was questioning whether any kind of success was worth the trade-off of making him feel 'basket-case material' – he was beginning, he said, to feel like "a part of the lighting rig."[100] It had just worn everybody out, and at the end we were feeling like we were going through the motions every night, which wasn't very satisfactory since none of us are people who like going through the motions or faking it. And I did wonder whether or not, just for the sake of my mental health, to go off and do something else. Very ordinary things were really attractive at that particular moment in time."[101] The tour finished, finally, after eleven gruelling months, on July 5, 1985, at Laguna Hills, California; the culmination of three years of unimaginable success for Maiden, three fantastic studio albums (and one live LP to come, for which the intent was to tour to support it – one can only imagine how that went down with the band). In just under four years since leaving Samson, Bruce had pushed himself to emotional, physical and creative places that nobody could have predicted back in 1981. His band stood at the peak of their chosen field – and he was not yet twenty-seven years old.

chapter twelve:
Caught Somewhere ...

For the first time in half a decade, Bruce Dickinson had some time to think. The past few years had hardly allowed for introspection, being day after day of demands, travelling and tearing it up. Now that immense period was finally over, the long-delayed hangover began to kick in, in spades. A power-slave indeed; Maiden was a monster raging out of control, and having reached the pinnacle of success, there was to be found there only pressure, expectation and people seeking to shoot you down at every turn.

Bruce – who had married his long-term girlfriend 'Jane' Jane in late 1984 – returned to the UK and started to pursue in earnest his multi-faceted – and non-band related – interests for some kind of solace, beginning to train again in his fencing endeavours, taking it more seriously than he had for nearly ten years.

"I wanted to get back into fencing to do something outside rock 'n' roll," he told *Sports Illustrated*. "I didn't want to reach forty and have to say all I'd done was look out the window of a tour bus and get drunk."[102] To that end, he enlisted the help of British Olympic fencing instructor, Ziemak Wojciechowski, who specialised in the foil discipline that was Bruce's speciality. Bruce would spend several months training five times a week with Wojciechowski, refining his technique as much as was possible, and very quickly reached a plateau of skill in a sport that had helped him, rather obliquely but measurably, to reassert at least a modicum of control over at least one part of his life.

The band's four month sabbatical had also left him with time to try and pursue, other aspects of his musical aspirations. There was, of course, the little matter of the follow-up studio album to *Powerslave* beginning to loom on the horizon. Bruce's ambitions were not yet satiated on a pure musical level – the trilogy of ...*Beast, Piece* and *Power* seemed nicely rounded off with the remorselessly brilliant *Live After Death*, and whilst the band were at the height of their popularity, they had surely bought themselves the right to explore other sides of their musical bent.

For Bruce, that meant ripping up the rulebook and chasing down the next challenge. After a period of relative musical inactivity, he found that he was gradually regaining some enthusiasm for working and living in music. However, the tours would have to be shorter, and the music would have to ask questions not only of the band, but – in a typical piece of Bruce logic – also of the audience, and further, stick two fingers up at the cultural pressures and therefore expectations surrounding their success. He set about writing a set of mostly acoustic-based songs, searching for an aesthetic that would inject what was – to him – a much needed freshness into the Maiden machine.

When Maiden reconvened – again in Jersey, and again based there for tax reasons that kept them out of the UK for some nine months every year – Bruce's sketches, riffs and songs that he would propose for the new album were on the whole rather different to what you'd expect from a Maiden record, and these ideas were not pursued by the band. Martin Birch, again producing the new material, felt that they weren't true to the Maiden sound and approach, rather than being poor tracks in themselves, something with which Steve Harris concurred. And Harris always had a very strong sense of what was 'right' for his band, as Rod Smallwood noted.

"Steve is pretty obstinate, I mean, Steve knows what he wants," he says, "and is unbending. If he thinks something's wrong, he just isn't gonna do it. And it's like, you know, the record company come in and say… you know, EMI haven't been in the studio with us since 1980, I mean people aren't allowed anywhere near the band! They make *their* album. It's their album, not anybody else's album."

But there are, of course, limits to how far Iron Maiden can subsume stylistic diversions too. "All the songs I'd written sounded very much like Spanish folk music," Bruce told *Hard Rock* magazine in an interview in May 1986. "I remember playing my serenades to Steve. Everybody was in stitches! So there's only one song from me."[103]

Whilst the group rehearsed the material – sans Dickinson originals – that 'one song' was quietly also dropped for the first time (officially at least) since 1982, the singer was spending any spare time he might have refining his fencing technique, having discovered to his surprise that his relative lack of progress was actually rooted in the fact that, whilst up until that point he had been training and carrying out bouts with a right-handed stance, he – like his father – was ambidextrous, and if anything, stronger leading with a left-handed stance. It was something of – inevitably – a revelation.

"It was strange at first," he acknowledged. "Everything was so much more natural ... my co-ordination and timing had also improved considerably."[104] He still had to iron out problems in his stance, but was more than pleased with this new development in his growing career – by the summer of 1986, Bruce had entered and made it to the last sixteen of competitions both in the UK and the Netherlands – not bad for someone who'd only begun to sort out his technique properly.

The band themselves were torn over where to lay the new album down to tape; the same studio at Nassau was mooted, but Bruce, Adrian Smith and Dave Murray were less than keen, feeling that the laid-back atmosphere and heat were less than conducive to an edgy recording experience. Bruce was also keen to change the routine, although he noted that the bass and drum sound in the Bahamas had been good, hence why Harris and McBrain had happily returned there for that part of the tracking process. The tapes would then be brought back to Europe, with the rest of the lads recording their parts in Amsterdam (a studio had been mooted in Munich – Music Land, famous for being the place where Queen recorded – but it was already booked out). The results, eventually, were mixed; whilst the album had a rather different sonic character to it – and even (gasp) utilised synthesisers – the songs themselves seem to lack a certain nuance. Perhaps that was down in part to the staggered tracking sessions, perhaps it was down to the lack of material from its singer, perhaps the band had simply exhausted themselves more than they realised over the previous three albums' worth of excellence, but the general wisdom seems to say that the LP that was released on October 11, 1986 as *Somewhere In Time* is considerably weaker than anything that had bore the Maiden stamp for many a year. And although the vocal performances are as soaring and full of belief as ever, the singer himself was perhaps still searching for answers. Unbeknownst to the rest of the band, the rebuff to his material had affected Bruce more than was initially evident. His feelings of rejection were strong, and at one stage, the thought crossed his mind to leave it all behind him; the crushing blow and nagging feelings that must have surely reminded him of not fitting in at school all those years ago, however, were tempered by a mixture of acceptance or acknowledgement that the *World Slavery* tour had taken a lot out of him, as well as his growing feeling that being Bruce Dickinson quite possibly meant more than merely being the vocalist in one of the biggest bands on the planet. As he had done throughout his life, he took a step back, took the outwardly-painful blows on the chin, trusted his intellect, and retreated inside, undefeated whilst he schemed as to ways to reassert himself. Bruce trained hard to get into good physical shape before the tour started, running up to five kilometres per day and training five times a week in a club in Offenbach.

Tour life being what it is, there is many an hour to fill between those all-too-brief onstage moments of soundcheck and then the evening's denouement, the gig itself. And whilst in the past, these long hours had been obliterated by means fair and foul; by liquid and by the romp of youth, Bruce's sharp mind would, during the *Somewhere On Tour* months, revisit an idea he'd had way back in 1981: books.

"[Just being the vocalist in a band] was never just enough," says Jennie Halsall, friends with Bruce and Jane – who would sadly shortly split up. "I think he's an incredibly nice guy, he has a brain that can do two or three or four things at once – which is quite unusual for a chap! Of course, as well as the book he was already starting to be into fencing then, he just wanted a balance I think." Something ahead of his time; many people found it very hard to identify the need for a rounded approach to themselves and it was rarely achievable, not least in the macho world of rock 'n' roll.

"I didn't get that balance out of the music business for another ten years, until the early 1990s," continues Halsall. "I suddenly woke up and realised 'This is not the end of the day', although I was freelance, I realised that you must come from the outside and look in, otherwise you get *fucked up*. Because the music business is a *very* bully boy culture, particularly the heavy metal department. If they didn't get a shag, things weren't happening. I used to go on the road quite a lot and [music industry people] weren't very nice to girls – especially girls in offices. But Bruce was different; a great mate." Bruce's self-awareness and sharp intelligence was demanding other outlets, and so, on his latest tour, he began to sketch out the plot to a novel – a flight of fancy, and one which would bring together his often rather child-like sense of humour, whilst satirising the quintessentially English class system – with which, of course, he had had his brushes down the years, not least at Oundle – and at the same time throw in dollops of shagging and scatological humour.

"When you are on the road and working every night," he explained, "two hours onstage running around, you don't have much energy to do much else. You just want to get onto the tourbus and off we go to the next town. In Europe, you do get a bit more time because the distances are less, and I like to travel by train ... you can hop on a train at eleven in the morning and be there by two in the afternoon, and you can get your mind in gear doing something – which is what I did when I wrote this book."

"I would write for two or three hours every day, and when I was on the train or travelling I would rough it out and then I would sit down and write it [when I got] to my destination."[105]

The book was eventually titled *The Adventures Of Lord Iffy Boatrace* – the name of the main character being a play on words from the Cockney rhyming slang for face, in case you didn't know, guv. The basic plot, said Bruce, came together pretty quickly in a succession of hotel rooms and tour buses – and, given he'd been planning to get it together for half a decade or more, it's little wonder that it was so swift a process. Somewhere in the recesses of his skull, some of his grey matter had always been on book duty. Revitalised, he would insist on sharing the day's new words with the crew and bandmates, to the point of near-irritation, as Nicko McBrain explained. "He was unbearable," said the drummer, "because you'd be doing something on the bus and he'd have just finished writing a new chapter and he'd want to read the whole fricking story to you! But he was so excited, you can't blow someone out the sky for that."[106] It was something that was for his own – and others' – amusement, more than anything else at this stage. "I was just curious as to what would happen if I started writing a book," he said. "The only reason I continued is because it proved very popular with people – like the road crew – who would come into my room and I'd sit there and read them the next chapter. They'd all go, 'Well, what happens tomorrow?' I go, 'Well, I haven't written it yet, come back tomorrow.'"[107] And so he did; and soon – even as Maiden were whipping up noisy appreciation on stage after stage – the book was completed.

The Adventures Of Lord Iffy Boatrace is a story that is inspired by the novels of English writer Tom Sharpe, a touch of the jolly what-ho style of the Biggles books, the absurdist, neo-Python humour of the man himself, and a dollop of puerile nonsense straight out of the pages of *Penthouse*. The basic premise of the novel is that the protagonist, Lord Iffy, Laird of Findidnann, and educated at Thigwell Boarding School, is skint. Thirty five years old, a virgin, and a semi-transvestite with a thing for stilettos and stockings, he concocts a madcap scheme to introduce remote-controlled robot grouse into Findinann Hall's grounds, in order that he may be able to offer grouse shooting the whole year round. In cahoots is his butler – 'Butler' – who, unbeknownst to Iffy, has schemes of his own to fulfil, the main money-making idea being a mechanical fucking machine he calls 'Pelvotron'. The hapless Iffy invites a group of old schoolmates to come and experience the shooting; they, of course, all have various sexual and behavioural hang-ups, and confusion and slapstick humour – often on the slightly sick side of bawdy – ensues. Iron Maiden's mascot Eddie appears – as a scowling, leering taxi driver – as the book romps around various plot devices shoehorned in to the shag-and-deathfest. To cut a long, and twisted (in both senses) story short, the book comes to a conclusion with a final car-chase-cum-showdown between Iffy and Butler and Wing-Commander Symes-West, master of disguise, who Iffy had employed to keep an eye on his invited guests, which to be honest I probably should have mentioned a bit closer to the start of this bit, sorry (with it so far? I'm not either and I've read the fucking thing twice). Needless to say that the novel ends with the door held firmly open for a sequel as first Iffy's half-brother, Alphonse, arrives in search of the famed lost treasure of Dub'lune – said to be buried under the castle's pantry (Alphonse swiftly meeting his doom by a mixture of being first buggered, then blown to smithereens) – and, finally, a letter arrives from the 'reverend Jimmy Reptile' inviting Lord Boatrace across the pond to become a missionary. No prizes for guessing whom that represents. As a tale told on the back of a tourbus, it's salacious, extremely silly, and laced with enough filth and squalour to keep anyone occupied for the duration. Bruce admitted freely later that he'd been partly inspired, stylistically, by Tom Sharpe, although he also admitted that, "I don't like him. He's too slow. I only ever read half a Tom Sharpe novel and I was bored out of my mind. They're much slower paced and I thought they needed to be jazzed up. You want a gag on every page. So I just went for the approach of doing a punk version of Tom Sharpe. I thought, there's no point in trying to be gentile about this. Let's just get as pornographic as we can, as graphic as we can, and a gag where you don't know whether to laugh or vomit. A book with a sort of emetic quality. You could actually hurl over the book at breakfast!"[108]

"It's certainly not aimed at the younger end of Iron Maiden fans," he warned, "because it is extremely rude; personally I find it funny. If you like Gary Larson's cartoons, or *Viz*, you'll find it funny. If you look at the cover [which is primary colours, nudity, champagne and cartoonish], everything that is on the cover is extremely filmic. I'd love to have a shot at [making a film of it]. When I saw the trailers of *A Fish Called Wanda*, I thought, 'Oh no! Someone's already done it.' It's a farcical book, everyone's a caricature and outrageous, and if you find that funny, you'll laugh at it."[109] Bruce also enjoyed getting the story out of his brain and onto the page, referring to it later as something of a catharsis. "It's completely lunatic," he laughed, "so I think I've probably got it all out of me. If ever go through a period like that, something good usually comes out of it in the end, as long as you come through it with most of your marbles still intact."[110] Bruce went on to say that he had sketched out ideas for other short stories which he was planning to develop as time went by.

As for the debut book, well, suffice it to say that on its 1990 publication by Sedwick & Jackson, reviewer Mat Snow of *Q* magazine was in rather unforgiving mood, the curmudgeonly old soak.

"[The] shock is not that Bruce is unlikely to be up for a Booker with his first novel, but how very bad it is compared to the worst piece of fiction this reviewer has ever encountered," he intoned. But, to be fair, Bruce himself had admitted that, "It's not going for a Pulitzer Prize, it's not Dickens." *NME*, however, called it "amazingly brilliant", so y'know, depends what you choose to read, one offers.

Still, sales were immense, and on its 1990 release, *The Adventures Of Lord Iffy Boatrace* went on to shift forty thousand copies. Out of print now, it regularly commands a hundred quid in those online auction-type sites, and sales were so speedy-high that the publishers were to commission a sequel in rather quick time. More of which later.

Back in 1986, however, and Bruce's path was to cross once more with an old bandmate, the man who had done so much for his singing career. Paul Samson had been beset once more by line-up problems in the early 1980s, and the band of his surname had effectively split up in 1984. Paul was still determined and full of ideas, however, and by the middle of the decade had settled down somewhat, putting together a new line-up to gig under the moniker of Paul Samson's Empire. The band released their debut LP, *Joint Forces*, in May 1986, and were subsequently invited to join Maiden on tour during October and November of that year, some twenty eight dates beginning on October 10 in Oxford and running throughout the UK to end with a rollocking six night stay at the massive Hammersmith Odeon.

Paul himself knew how to tour; his experience was as a professional. His band, however, were enamoured of the accoutrements of touring life, putting the line-up of Empire under pressure despite the fact that Maiden's audience, rather ironically, had taken to his musical endeavours with a great welcome. Despite the regular four and five figure crowds, the Maiden tour brought the problems within Empire to a head and the line-up changed soon after, just as momentum was arguably once more building up.

There had just been released *Head Tactics*, a compilation of the two Bruce-era Samson albums, something that caused a little soreness within the Samson camp, who of course had no say in the matter as the rights to both the publishing and the release resided now with Sanctuary and Bruce; Thunderstick commented that, "It hurt. It was awful," when I spoke to him. "None of us," he continued – meaning Paul, Chris Aylmer and himself, "were involved with it." Actually, Paul and producer Jo Julian had spent some time re-mastering and mixing the tracks at Music Works studio during 1985. Regardless, Paul, Thunderstick, Chris and Bruce's paths were to cross yet again a few years down the line ...

The *Somewhere On Tour* gigs passed, largely, without much incident, as far as a mega-selling rock band's gigs can; Maiden managed a hefty 150 concerts altogether, including Japan and America – where Bruce would seek out fencing competitions to enter whenever he could find one, including one incident at a Long Beach contest where he did so well that he had to dash back to the venue, with less than an hour to spare before he was due to actually begin the gig.

Whilst in America, and inbetween competitions and gigs, Bruce hooked up with an old mucker by the name of Jimmy Bain. The Scots bassist had been a collaborator with Ronnie James Dio, Phil Lynott and a member of the band Wild Horses, alongside ex-Lizzy guitarist Brian Robertson – who went on to join Motorhead for their excellent (but critically-panned) 1983 LP, *Another Perfect Day*, which was coincidentally produced by one Tony Platt. By 1986, Bain was at something of a loose end, and when Dickinson ran into him at one of the American concerts, the two decided – for the hell of it – to jam some tracks out together. Although Bruce's writing contribution to the current Maiden LP was absent, the ideas were still there, and, as the vocalist says, he, "Went round to [Bain's] house one night and we wrote the bare bones of about five songs, recording the stuff on a little demo machine. It was quite good, quite different – a bit sort of Procul Harum-ish, soul-y."[111] It was a typical spur-of-the-moment collaboration between two friends, a refreshing change to the necessarily constricting boundaries of the Maiden camp. And, although there were plans to expand on these casual sessions, they never came to fruition.

Although there was less exhaustion than at the end of the *World Slavery* tour, nonetheless the camp was rather different in feel than it had ever been before. Immediately after the gigs were completed, in December 1987, and partly – again – because to remain at a lower tax band meant living outside the UK for nine months per year, Bruce decamped to Bonn in Germany. There was another motivation, however: the (then) West German National Centre For Fencing was a world-renowned gathering place for the élite trainers, equipment and athletes. He spent a lot of time training with top foilist Justin Pitman, who was regarded as one of the UK's top practitioners of the sport in the 1980s, and the two spurred each other on to greater feats.

The aftermath of the previous tour had taken a huge toll on all the participants individually and collectively. Ultimately it resulted in an album considered to be something of a weak moment in Maiden's history, particularly when held up against the creative output of the growing groundswell of heavier acts such as Metallica, many of them directly influenced by earlier, gnarlier Maiden (and, in truth, many of the NWOBHM acts, including Diamond Head). The time off after the tour saw Bruce in a better place, although it was not as much of a break as he would have liked.

"What everyone needed [after *Powerslave*] was just a bloody good rest, away from it all," he later commented. "[But] we didn't get that much of a rest, we went straight on to the next tour. I was in a very strange place, if I was going to go off on the treadmill again, I wanted to do something different – something to freak people out. If you're feeling bad about something, it must be somebody's fault, so you look for scapegoats, somebody to blame. And in part, at least some of it is your own fault, for doing it in the first place. But that never occurs to you, does it?"[112] Perhaps only in retrospect do these things begin to become clear.

Although he was newly to be single again, by the end of the *Somewhere In Time* tour, his sharpness and enthusiasm for life had returned, having had a chance to manifest itself in creative ways outside of the relentless schedule. Writing books and becoming something of an expert fencer returned control to his own hands; as it turned out he was, after all, much more than a man famous for merely being the singer in Iron Maiden, as he had told an interviewer from *Hard Force* magazine who had conducted the chat mid-air as the band flew between gigs. Bruce compared the situation in the United States, where money had an immense impact on the way that people conferred status and respect on you, with being in a successful rock band – where people jump to your every whim as you are the 'talent'. Finally, Bruce contrasted this with the grounding effect of being back in good ol' Blighty, where your mates can often bring you right back down to earth again.

"In order to keep sane," he mused, "you need this contact [with everyday reality and] the life most people live; we're not different people. Your mental balance cannot only rest on the name of a band, even if it is Iron Maiden."[113] He went on to explain that he needed to mark a very real compartmentalisation of, or demarcation between, his job with the band and the rest of his private life; in order to do that, he mused, he only needed to think back to those skint-but-independent early days working with Samson, where the pressures were rather different. Being financially well-off, he noted, both, "entices and spontaneously creates a shallow and meaningless entourage," which he studiously recognised and distanced himself from – a theme to which of course he would subsequently return. It is to Dickinson's enormous credit that the realisation of this came even whilst adulation was being placed upon his shoulders; uncomfortable with the pedestal he was being put on, but also revelling in his hammy, dramatic side, the dichotomy was both recognised and to a large extent embraced. There are many pseudo-intellectuals within rock bands – but few people have the actual intelligence and insight to *really* think philosophically about their place within culture, as well as their own place within a wider world as a creative individual. It's fair to say that Paul Bruce Dickinson – having been taken right to the edge during that intense four year period of remorseless demands of touring and, let's say, throwing himself into touring life as a young swordsman – had found something within himself as a result. That's not to say that what he had found provided answers to the madness and magic; in fact, the opposite is probably true. A thousand questions had presented themselves, but the difference is that there was now the bravery and energy to pursue them wherever they may lead. The 1980s were drawing to a close; Maiden and Bruce necessarily had one eye on the new decade. It was going to be, at the very least, interesting.

chapter thirteen:
Sons

Iron Maiden's follow-up to the reasonably-received but fundamentally flawed *Somewhere In Time* LP was to capture the imagination of a refreshed Bruce Dickinson almost from the outset. When Steve Harris rang him enthusing over an idea that was brewing for the album, Bruce immediately jumped on the prospect. This was, certainly, a development that was attractive – it was, finally, to be a true concept album. The band had always threatened to commit themselves fully to a LP-length narrative – but in truth, the LPs thus far had had a thematicism rather than a constructed, consistent tale and aesthetic running through them. The previous artwork may have led the listener to a certain frame of mind in which to approach the constituent musical pieces, but largely it had been based on one particular song; *Number Of The Beast; Powerslave; Somewhere In Time* – or a bit of Smallwood/band cooked-up mischief and play on words such as *Piece Of Mind* and *Live After Death*. This time, however, the approach would be a whole lot more cogent from the very start of the project. Harris had begun to write a song – inspired by the death of spiritualist medium Doris Stokes – which would end up being 'The Clairvoyant'. Intrigued by the concept of second sight, he rang Dickinson to chew over the possibilities inherent in the general theme. As it would be Maiden's seventh studio album, the idea began to germinate as to a full length LP that dealt with second sight, and the character that had traditionally been blessed with this sixth sense was, in historical occultism, the seventh son of the seventh son. It was an inspired moment that put a fire in the heart of Bruce, whose performances on the *Somewhere On Tour* gigs had, whilst being perfectly acceptable by anyone's standards, perhaps occasionally slipped under the incendiary. It was imperceptible, perhaps, but to those involved in the immediate circle, the last album and tour had been undertaken a little too closely to the gruelling *Powerslave* concerts, and the singer had suffered more than most. Newly stabilised, and back from the edge, however, Bruce's creativity was beginning to seek a release in a number of ways.

One of the reasons for this was because he had been spending his hard-earned cash on filling his – let's face it – mansion (not, of course, called Findidnann Hall) with a library into which he would retreat to read and study books that were perhaps a little more involved than *Iffy*. Collecting occult, magical and fantasy/decadent literature from Crowley to Rimbaud, Bruce would sit with his two dogs by his side in his library-cum-study in front of the window, chewing over themes and alchemic ideas and letting them subsequently develop into potential songs and narratives to be used when the time was right. On the back of having written his first novel, a world of possibilities suddenly seemed to be opening up again.

Bruce had been chatting for some months with a friend, the horror author and major Maiden fan by the name of Shaun Hutson, who had brought a script to the table that dealt with Maiden mascot Eddie's back story. Based on the album covers, pre-historic shenanigans and Eddie returning to get his revenge, it was the very early stages of a screen treatment for a movie. Although Shaun and Bruce sat down during early 1988 and tweaked the idea, as with many plans for such matters, nothing came of it, although Hutson – who has appeared on stage with Maiden many times over the years – rejigged the tale as a short story. His books, indeed, resonate with many quotes and references to the Irons, and why not.

Bruce had, however, indulged himself in reading Anne Rice's novels, and was much enamoured by the second instalment of her *Vampire Chronicles* series, a doomy and gothic tale of the undead by the name of *The Vampire Lestat*. The protagonist is also an accomplished musician who uses his position as a member of a successful rock band in the mid-1980s to begin a war between the mortal and the undead which is only resolved in the third volume, *The Queen Of The Damned*. Dickinson and Harris – at this time, getting on famously again, creatively-speaking – discussed the possibility of recording the score to a future movie based on the *Lestat* novel. "We'd love to do some film music sometime," Bruce confirmed, "so somebody should make a film about it and we'd like to volunteer our services!"[114] Prescient, in a sense; the first volume of the trilogy, *Interview With A Vampire*, was later to become a Hollywood blockbuster in 1994, starring Brad Pitt, Kristen Dunst and Tom Cruise.[115]

So the singer was thinking in *very* narrative terms during this period; he had also begun work on a project which was a planned rock opera of the Italian violin virtuoso, Niccolò Paganini, a controversial but stunningly talented 18th century character whose life was beset by gambling, a series of love affairs, mad plans to build casinos, illegitimate children, secret affairs with royalty, many run-ins with the church, and all manner of insane and self-destructive rock star behaviour. Paganini – like Robert Johnson some 150 years later – was said to have sold his soul to the devil in exchange for his extraordinary talent, and there were rumours that he had also been imprisoned for murder. His nickname, 'The Devil's Violinist' no doubt contributed to the fact that he was not buried in consecrated ground until five years after his death. That such a character was interesting subject matter for a rock opera was undoubted, and Bruce would spend much of 1987 and 1988 trying to raise money to move the project forward, having written a synopsis that placed the project somewhere between the films *Tommy* and *Amadeus*, the latter, of course, being the story of another punk-classical artist-genius, Wolfgang Amadeus Mozart.

"The conflicts he had to resolve, the temptations he had to fight," said Bruce of Paganini, "are all relevant today ... on stage he dressed all in black, a bit like Ritchie Blackmore. He was an explosive Italian and would never play one note when fifty million would do!"[116] The project would be considered by many studios, but as yet has not come to fruition.

So, when Harris told Dickinson of his expansive ideas for a new LP, Bruce was already in the mood to make a larger statement with a full-length musical work than ever before. The album was to be called *Seventh Son Of A Seventh Son*, and in musical and conceptual approach it was to take some of the synthesizer-based sonics that the group had established with *Somewhere In Time*, ally it to wider issues – musically, this meant delving back into the group's prog-rock past, with early Genesis and Purple's more psychadelic moments a major influence – and to take the *Seventh Son* theme of clairvoyance and magick to the most rounded degree as was possible.

Recording sessions took place at Music Land in February and March, 1988, and Bruce's direct contributions to the songwriting are a major part of an LP – a record that is streets ahead of its predecessor. He was to comment that elements of his rejected lyrics for the previous effort were to find something of a home herewith, albeit in a different form, but it's clear that from the acoustic introduction to the album and the keyboard riff that sparks off the album proper, this is Maiden in full, epic flow, as the first track, 'Moonchild' kicks into action – a Dickinson/Smith composition with the familiar anthemic chorus, plugging-bass and tension-building middle eight that the pair's collaborations were notable for. The lyrics speak of birth – for good or for evil – of a new day, a new child, and are very close in a literary sense to (him again) Aleister Crowley's notorious Liber Samekh – also known as the Preliminary Invocation – The Beast raising his head in Dickinson's work once more.

Bruce's collaboration with Smith and Harris, 'Can I Play With Madness?' is a true three-way piece of work, announcing itself with a harmonic vocal call-to-arms, it melds Adrian Smith's riffs with Dickinson's lyrical ideas (originally Smith had written the now-familiar, and extremely poppy, chorus as 'On The Wings Of Eagles'); subsequently Harris offered the time changes that are reminiscent of Led Zep, and the resultant track is one of the most-satisfyingly realised songs that Maiden had put together for many years. It was subsequently released as a single on March 26, 1988, debuting at Number 3 and remaining in the Top 10 for three weeks. It even made it onto daytime radio – a rarity for anything Iron Maiden ever released – and its running time of just three and a half minutes slotted nicely into the realms of 'radio single'.

Dickinson explained that at this point in the narrative, "it's where he meets the wise old man, and asks the man about all the bizarre dreams in his head. Should he investigate the netherworld or should he forget about it?"

'... Madness' is followed up by another three-way collaboration, the pacy and edgy – but still extremely catchy – opus, 'The Evil That Men Do'. This time, the lyrics hang around a quotation from Shakespeare's *Julius Caesar*: 'The evil that men do lives after them/The good is oft interred with their bones'. In this context, Bruce's lyrics frame the reference with a tale of lost love, a longing for redemption and living life on the edge. In terms of the narrative, the protagonist, the seventh son, has reached a rite of passage where he begins to accept his fate.

"This is where our Seventh Son loses his virginity," the singer explained. "But not to someone of human origin." Referring also to the furore over censorship in music, and given the chorus' literary inspiration – ie. one of the cultural mainstays of Western literature – Bruce also questioned double standards within those who would seek to pick out the lyrics of musicians, whilst accepting the death and dark themes of other artistic disciplines.

"Shakespeare is a lot more nasty and twisted than any rock 'n' roll lyrics," he continued. "They want to slap a label [on our records] and sell it to Over 18s [only] if there is anything to do with adultery, violence, sex, drugs, alcohol abuse – and that's just about every song in history, including [the country standard about adultery made famous by Tammy Wynette] 'Blanket On The Ground.' It is absurd, and very silly – it's going off on the deep end without engaging brain."[117] A very good point. The writer of the poem, 'Rime Of The Ancient Mariner', God-fearing Samuel Taylor Coleridge himself, was well-known for his opium and laudanum habits; one of the greatest pieces of poetry ever written (or half-written, at least), Coleridge's 'Kubla Khan', was composed whilst he was under the influence of opium he'd taken to alleviate the symptoms of suspected dysentery. Double standards everywhere then.

Bruce's final contribution to the album is also the LP's closing track, 'Only the Good Die Young', a collaboration with Steve Harris, and lyrically also referencing those Shakespearean lines, in spirit, as well as perhaps a pay-off to 'Die With Your Boots On'. It is an excellent ending to an album that regains some of the conceptual and musical ground the group had lost, and the lengthy knockabout ending and reprise of 'Moonchild' complete a very successful project for the group.

As ever, there was an extensive tour to promote the release, although on the back of the problems of previous years, Maiden would insist on more rest days, and, in the case of Harris, travelling in his own tourbus along with his wife and young family. Gone were the days of hedonism and harridans hanging from hairy roadies (most of the time); 1988 was, after all, the year that Bruce turned thirty years of age. And just under two weeks after the singer left his roaring twenties behind, Maiden finally fulfilled a prophecy of their own, headlining a huge concert to take place at Castle Donington under the *Monsters Of Rock* banner. Also on the bill that day were contemporaries including Guns N' Roses, Megadeth, David Lee Roth and Kiss – with one Neal Kay DJing and exhorting nearly a hundred thousand people to yell obscenities back at him. Not that they needed much encouragement ...

The celebrations, however, soon turned tragic; the inclement weather had muddied Donington considerably, and in the crush to watch G N' R's set, two individuals – Alan Dick and Landon Siggers – lost their footing and were trampled to death. What should have been a great triumph for the band had ended in tragedy, although Maiden were unaware as yet of what had happened when they took to the stage for their headlining performance, which Bruce described as being, "a fair old racket."

"If you stood in front of the speakers," he explained, "it was like standing at the back end of Concorde. You do have to be loud to get across to 107,000. The Beatles would have been a lot louder if the technology had existed in those days ... they were using something you would find in a small disco or youth club as a P.A. for fifty thousand people all screaming as loud as they could!"[118] A case of '*Don't* Scream For Me, Shea Stadium.'

Maiden continued to headline the *Monsters Of Rock* tour throughout Europe, the *Seventh Tour Of A Seventh Tour* finally ending with two nights at Wembley Arena – which were filmed for a planned video release – and, finally, back at Hammersmith Odeon for three sold-out nights, ending on December 12, 1988. It was another gruelling jaunt, and although sales of the album had again gone platinum – *Seventh Son Of A Seventh Son* had debuted at Number 1 on its release on April 12 – the critical response had not been great from a music press pack who were head over heels over hell on earth for Metallica's bludgeoning album ... *And Justice For All*, a gnarly, aggressive and thrashy effort that was in spirit and focus hugely different from the cerebral soundscapes that Maiden were offering. In truth, for all the excellence of *Seventh Son*, and its huge sales, heavy rock music had moved in an entirely different direction. Though Maiden had put down a superb marker as to the possibilities inherent in the expanded narrative, a generation was growing up wanting the instant thrust of the noisier and grimier side of life. Whilst Maiden tied off loose ends with a slick, epic and confident touch, Metallica, Megadeth and their ilk were roaring at the skies with an angsty malevolence which Bruce and the boys had left behind some five years earlier. Bruce himself, talking about thrash, labelled it as a limiting style, reminiscent of punk in that, "as soon as it's born, it's dead ... to most people it just sounds like a noise, they can't play their instruments properly and they can't sing in tune." Next you'll be saying there's no tunes and you can't hear the words ... "and there's no tune anyway."[119] Ah.

As 1988 drew to its scruffy close, then, Iron Maiden were happy to prematurely say goodbye to the 1980s having left behind them a body of work that was at turn aggressive, salacious, anti-establishment, streetwise, conceptual, ambitious, stodgy and fizzing. After the triumphs and the hard times, the band decided that 1989 was to be a year off from all official Maiden activity. For a certain singer, it was to prove a year that would allow him to explore further some of the passions that were growing in him, as well as hark back to simpler times.

chapter fourteen:
Daughters

Freed from Maiden duty awhile, Bruce Dickinson – now a qualified fencing instructor – had time, amongst other things, to get to grips with the central heating in his new, smaller house, having moved out of The Mansion after his marriage split. One of his major projects during 1989 was to investigate the establishment of a fencing centre for young people; he felt strongly that the UK was under-represented in that sense.

"I have to find the premises," he told *Kerrang!*, "it won't be in London because there's so much going on there ... I'd like an old warehouse and try and attract a sponsorship deal. I won't throw money at it."[120] Sensible chap. Bruce went on to explain that the West German Government spent twenty five million marks [around £8 million at the time] on fencing, allowing schoolkids to develop their skills whilst being tutored at the centres, and having all their equipment – and, for that matter, their upkeep as boarders in said schools – paid for by state bursaries. As an ex-public schoolboy himself, Bruce could vouch for the educative possibilities (and otherwise) of a set-up like that. His own fencing career was taking an upturn in the last year of the decade, and although his career record was average, during 1989 he was able to rise as high as Number 7 in the British rankings from the previous season's ranking of eighteenth – which in itself wasn't a bad result for a man spending at least nine months of each year on band business.[121]

"I fence," he mused, "and I don't see anything unusual about it. It would be nice if more people got the opportunity to do it, but until Her Majesty's Government sees fit to treat the sport in a proper way in this country and not regard it like *Chariots Of Fire* ... sportsmen today need to be professionals even if they are amateurs. You can't expect to have world-class sportsmen in any sport today unless the person can afford to train full-time – and that means at his peak. When he or she are twenty four or twenty five – they are going to spend most of their early life playing sport."

"You have to be able to create some structure," he continued, "whereby your most talented athletes can have a life after that and not just be chucked on the dole or mini-cabbing or something. It's not fair – and it's disgraceful." Bruce was well aware of the potential inherent in the sport, citing that when cash had previously been injected into development of the sport, the results had been noticeable; and, he mused, not just for the received wisdom of fencers being mostly middle-class boarding school kids, but with results across the demographic board. "[They] were coming, not out of toffee-nosed boarding schools, but street kids were getting into fencing, the sort of kids who were getting into karate or kick-boxing. You get the same buzz out of it – fencing is like boxing without the brain damage. It's a combat sport, it's really exciting and you have to be as fit as hell to do it. It's hard work, and very demanding."[122]

Bruce also felt that with the correct coaching and financial support, the British kids could end up competing at a very high level. A man fired up, if nothing else. In 1988 – on July 25, to be exact – he had taken the first steps toward setting up a company to import fencing equipment from China to the UK, calling it Duellist Enterprises.[123] Bruce's club, Hemel Hempsted, won the National Championships that year – a phenomenal result and an indication that Bruce, when he puts his mind to it, can excel in many different areas.

It was as a musician that Bruce Dickinson was still best known, however, and an opportunity was shortly to come up that would give the 1990s something of a remarkable change of focus. It was also something of a fluke; when the clarion call came out from Rod Smallwood searching for people to contribute a track to the film, *Nightmare On Elm Street 5: The Dream Child*, Steve Harris demurred as he was busy in an editing suite, going through the live visuals and audio that Maiden had recorded on tour the previous year, to pull it together for release on video. Bruce stepped into the breach, looking for things to amuse himself in a musical sense – and looking for a project that he could work on with his old mate, Janick Gers, with whom he'd reacquainted himself in a musical sense by performing the Mott The Hoople classic, 'All The Young Dudes' at a Prince's Trust benefit concert during 1987.

Gers, a near-neighbour of Bruce and a mate from the Samson days, was close to the vocalist, and had in fact replaced Bernie Torme in the Gillan band, although by 1989 he'd been on the verge of chucking it all in after some years of inactivity from the live scene. The pair got on well, and in short order had pulled together a ripsnorter of a track with the lovely title, 'Bring Your Daughter ... To The Slaughter.' The producer for the soundtrack project was the well-respected Chris Tsangarides.

"It happened because my management, Zomba, basically owned Sanctuary at the time and they were also Bruce's publishers as well as putting out the soundtrack to the film," Tsangarides told me. "They needed a song and Bruce had this 'Bring Your Daughter ... To The Slaughter' business, so they thought it'd be a good idea to put the pair of us together, and it turned out to be a right good laugh."

It went down so well with the Zomba chaps that they immediately asked Bruce whether he had any other material that might make a nice solo album for which they could then possibly find a label. Bruce said that, yes, of course he did, and immediately put a phonecall through to Gers informing him that he'd better not sell his gear because they had an LP to write and record, the sessions for which they roped in Andy Carr, bassist for the band 3 Rivers, and Jagged Edge drummer Fabio Del Rio. "I called Janick and went, 'Janick we have to write another album of this shit, quick!' and he said, 'What shall we do?' [And I said,] 'Oh well, we will write a freak sort of tune and a Rolling Stones kind of a tune and an AC/DC kind of a tune and we will just have a laugh because these guys just have loads of money and they will pay for us to make a record so just shut up and have a laugh!'"[124]

"We thought, 'Well, why don't we make an album?'" laughs Tsangarides, who'd worked with the likes of, amongst others, Judas Priest and Thin Lizzy. "It really was a natural thing, just like that, 'cause Maiden were not doing much and he was sitting around scratching his arse, so that's what happened. We thought, 'Let's do a record where it's just fun and laughter', basically. Nothing to compete with Iron Maiden, because it's nothing like an Iron Maiden record. That was the spirit in which we entered into it, and also at the time we didn't have a deal other than the publishers, who happened to own the studios, manage me and Sanctuary etc, so they sort of funded it for us to go in and record it."

"And about halfway through it, EMI said, 'Well, we'll release it.' So, there you go! It was recorded in Battery Studios, in London, in the summer of 1989." Returning to an old haunt meant, in a very real sense, revisiting the relaxed atmosphere of the *Shock Tactics* sessions; the polar opposite to the recent recordings with Maiden, and an unexpected opportunity to get down to writing and recording some classic rock tracks with mates. And to have a bit of a giggle too, of course.

"*Tattooed Millionaire* – as the album came to be called – was purely down to having a good time, making a good record and having a laugh," smiles Tsangarides. "It was eight weeks, something like that. And we just had a bloody good hoot every day. We set up that board game about war and battles on the pool table – Risk – with the armies and whatnot. We were playing that, so that was ongoing at all times. We were also shooting lightbulbs in the studio with air guns. It started off just shooting the odd dead one, and ended up shooting everything! That was quite a laugh."

The back-to-basics approach ranged from the rock 'n' roll tracks that Janick and Bruce had swiftly written together – within less than a fortnight – all the way to the recording process, which, much in common with *Shock Tactics*, was the sound of a band doing what they do best.

"We set 'em up, got a sound, they played it and I recorded it, basically," confirms the deskman who has also worked on releases by Depeche Mode and Tom Jones. "And that was it – it was so old school it was untrue. And still, to this day, that's kinda how I do it. Sorting out what we're gonna do, how the song's gonna go, choruses and arrangements and whatnot, rehearsing it and then doing it. That eight weeks includes pre-production in the studio. The songs were pretty much there already, there wasn't much I had to change. Janick and Bruce had written them, and pretty quickly as well."

The performances, as a result, are to a man, relaxed – and therefore rather excellent, not least from Dickinson. As the producer says, "I think Bruce has done some of his best singing on *Tattooed Millionaire*. It's so confident, it's so upfront and it's so good, really. It's singing, it's not screeching. There are places where he needs to go for it, which he does – but it was proper singing and proper harmonies, the first time he'd really done any harmony work because there's not that much in Maiden." Although we should remember that there was plenty of that kind of thing in Speed, Shots, Stuart Smith Projects, Jimmy Bain demos and – lest we forget – Samson, of course ...

Bruce's other passion seeped into the recording sessions, however; 1989 was – after all – supposed to be his chance to take a year off from music, and so he'd take every opportunity to continue to refine his skills in other areas, to great effect: Bruce finished a creditable thirtieth in that year's UK foil fencing championship.

"When we were doing *Tattooed Millionaire*," says Tsangarides, shaking his head, "he'd be having his fencing lessons every other day. The coach would come in and we'd go and have a cup of tea while he fenced. In the studio! He is a real get-up-and-go character, he will not sit down for a minute. We had a great friendship at the time, as I recall, we were always at each other's houses, my kids used to call him Uncle Brucester, and all kinds of things. It was a lovely thing, a lovely time. I have great memories of it all."

Of course, the track, 'Bring Your Daughter ... To The Slaughter' was almost immediately snaffled up by a more-than-impressed Steve Harris when he heard it. Too good for a solo record! It had to be a Maiden track – and, to be fair, it sounds like one, even in its demo form.

"We did it as a one-off for the soundtrack, and that was that," confirms Tsangarides. "Then the album was something else. When Steve heard what we did for the soundtrack, he wanted to do [similar] for Iron Maiden."

Smashing into action with the forceful 'Son Of A Gun', the album puts down its marker as being a no-bullshit, balls-to-the-wall rocker; it's a track that retreads one of Dickinson's favourite bonnet-bees, that of organised religion – and, in particular, certain hypocrites preaching love whilst concurrently planning destruction, death and double-cross. The solo from Gers wails, mirroring the gruff and vituperative delivery of the singer, who sounds more energised within the first two minutes than he had over the previous two albums. The next track – the title track of the album – is one of Bruce's most personal tracks to date. 'Tattooed Millionaire' is a monster of a pop/rock track directly attacking the LA-based hair metal acts that had so turned late 1980s metal into a competition of the bouffant – those acts that, whilst purporting to rock, would spend more time in front of the mirror, checking out how expensive they looked whilst their ex-beauty queens preened in their brand new Cadillac, dripping in jewellery and falseness. Its ultra-catchiness hides a very strong sentiment against the pedestal lifestyle which certain bands were chasing as the sole goal. As someone who'd always been surrounded by lads from the streets – and spent a lot of time paying his dues – it was a subject close to his heart.

"I'm not a millionaire," he laughed, "and I don't have any tattoos. The song is a specific reference to a lot of heavy metal, heavy rock bands who are coming out of the woodwork now that rock music is suddenly popular again ... They're slapping on the make-up and the mascara, which is something I've never bothered about; there's another outrageous, androgynous-looking band every five minutes. But where were they at the begging of the 1980s when bands like Iron Maiden were going around laying the foundations for all this?"

Bruce continued in his questioning of motives, feeling that perhaps there was a more prosaic – and financial – motivation behind that particular musical fad. "It's an attempt by record companies to cash in on things, but I don't think kids are buying this stuff in vast quantities as they can smell a fake when it appears in their back yard."[125]

'Born In '58' continues the autobiographical tone – a real heartfelt, acoustic-led and restrained mid-paced, almost Springsteen-esque tale of his childhood, and the struggles and terrible messes created since then. Through his personal lyrics, Bruce shakes his head that the lessons of the past have hardly been learned. By contrast, the only real way to read anything more into 'Hell On Wheels' than a straightforward track about shagging is to, uh, shoehorn it in there. At a push, the choruses, talking about nobody waiting at the end of the line, and wondering what exactly is driving the protagonist, could be applied in retrospect to a deeper malaise, but it's tenuous at best. 'Gypsy Road' follows, a straightforward take on the rocker-as-intinerant-lover and the freedom of living by nobody else's rules but your own. The rather juvenile 'Dive! Dive! Dive!' follows – full of more of that *Viz* magazine-type double-entendre Bruce was very fond of – over an insistently funky backbeat, Bruce clearly enjoying himself as he rasps out the lyrics with a cheeky gleefulness.

The aforementioned 'All The Young Dudes' cover follows – Bruce doing a more-than-passable impression of David Bowie in his delivery. 'Lickin The Gun' proves beyond doubt that this is no mere sub-Iron Maiden collection of out-takes, its funky approach and highly-charged earthiness being a world away from *Seventh Son*'s cerebral conceptuality. More of the same follows in the frankly daft 'Zulu Lulu', which is one of the weaker bits of filler on a patchy-but-fun LP with the performances and spirit (plus some more great guitaring) more often than not better than the material itself. 'No Lies' offers an anthemic, singalong feel to matters, and then *Tattooed Millionaire* is complete. Not bad for two weeks' worth of writing! As Bruce was to comment later, the album had done its job, which was to merely be itself without any pressure of expectation on it, although, of course, his profile would always attract certain amounts of interest.

"We had a great laugh and made a terrifically fun sounding record and unfortunately everybody took it seriously," he sighed. "Everybody was like, 'Aha! The singer from Iron Maiden has made a new solo record and it sounds like this.'" To which his response was that it was never something to be taken massively seriously, although he rates the title track, as well as 'Gypsy Road' and 'Born In 58' highly, whilst freely admitting that, "there is a lot of stuff on the record that I am thinking is generic but actually it is just as good as everybody else who is putting stuff out at the time."[126]

* * *

Bruce and Maiden were next involved in the Rock Aid Armenia project, which was a humanitarian single put together by rock musicians in aid of the victims of the previous year's devastating earthquake in that country. On July 8, 1989 a host of internationally famous rock stars gathered at Metropolis, Chiswick Studios in London to record Deep Purple's 'Smoke On The Water' for a charity single; Bruce lent his vocals alongside a stellar cast all doing their bit, including Bryan Adams, Ritchie Blackmore, Keith Emerson, Ian Gillan, Dave Gilmour, John Paul Jones, Tony Iommi, and many others. The recording was filmed and the single duly reached top forty status, with an associated video – and subsequently an album, to which Maiden contributed the ubiquitous 'Run To The Hills'; how very long ago that release must have seemed! Seven years is a long time in rock 'n' roll ...

Maiden did, in fact, break their promise of a year off by gathering for the release party of the *Maiden England* video, which Steve had been working on for the first part of the year. Sanctuary and EMI provided a backdrop of Union Flags and people chomping on fish and chips whilst drinking bitter. It couldn't have been more English if it'd started raining inside the venue. Still, the atmosphere was good and the band were starting to rev up into action.

Thus satiated, Bruce reconvened with the Iron Maiden boys at Steve Harris' music barn in early 1990 to get down to some serious writing for the business of pulling together the first Maiden album of the new decade. The intent this time was to strip down the histrionics and ambition of the superbly-selling, but rather over-earnest *Seventh Son* LP, to bring back the feeling of the very early days, even unto *Killers* would they aim. As it turned out, the new sessions would see the first line-up change in Maiden for a long while. Though there had been persistent rumours for some time that it would be the vocalist who would jump ship – exacerbated by his solo venture – it was actually guitarist mainstay Adrian Smith who would part company with the band. Having been fired up by the exploration of *Somewhere In Time* and subsequently *Seventh Son Of A Seventh Son*, he was not overly enamoured by the back-to-basics intent of the new material. Smith had also been working on solo material, under the *Adrian Smith Album Project (ASAP)* banner, and the taste of creative freedom that engendered far outweighed the lack of relative critical or commercial success of the project. After a decade with Maiden, and a good year off, Smith felt that the schedule for the new LP was too compressed and left the camp, as amicably as was possible.

Bruce, as ever, had the answer, and it was staring the band in the face. One quick rehearsal later, and Janick Gers slotted into Iron Maiden like he'd always been a member. As an old compadre of Samson, Maiden and Gillan, he had the moves, the talent, the attitude and the enthusiasm to make it work, and it worked *extremely* well. He locked in with Dave Murray with some aplomb, and a potentially sticky situation was quickly and seamlessly alleviated somewhat.

Sessions took place between January and April, 1990, with Harris commenting that it was "a more aggressive side of Iron Maiden. I think some of our fans were disappointed in the musical orientation we had taken lately, so I think they'll be happy we're going back to a more aggressive and powerful style."[127]

The new album, to be entitled *No Prayer For The Dying*, was originally going to be recorded at Battery Studios, but because the band were enjoying the rough and ready (but hugely adept) jam/rehearsal sessions at Harris' outhouse, the decision was made to hire out the Rolling Stones' mobile studio, and hammer out the tracks to tape in that very place.

Shorn of his most successful writing partner, Bruce turned to Steve as a creative buddy and the two blasters that begin *No Prayer* ... are so utterly early 1980s Maiden, it almost hurts. Bruce's new enthusiasm for the more simple, stripped-down and filthy straight-ahead rock aesthetic even stretches – as it does throughout the album – to a much more raspy, smoky-throated rock delivery. 'Tail Gunner' – which Bruce said had been 'inspired' by a pornographic film before becoming a straightforward war track – and 'Holy Smoke' – where that pesky character, Jimmy Reptile, is once more taken to task, are a pair of raucous rock tunes that make no bones about the fact that this is going to be an LP set firmly in the no-nonsense realm. As a statement of intent to move away from the ethereal meanderings of their previous LP, it could hardly be clearer. Harris and Dickinson's other collaboration, the atmospheric 'Run Silent Run Deep' is one of the under-rated moments of the project and its galloping bass-lines, piratical choruses and chugging guitars make it one of the tracks that probably could have benefited from a full-technicolour production. As it is, it feels like a demo – albeit a polished one – as much of the album does. The lyrics for this were apparently left over from some sketches that Bruce had in a notebook intended for use on the *Somewhere In Time* album. Bruce's eco-hypocrite-baiting track with Dave Murray, 'Public Enema Number One', is most effective for its twin-guitar harmony than any particular innovation, although its mix of bombast and sense of hopelessness are very much within the slightly paranoid feeling of the LP as a whole.

Prior to leaving Maiden, Adrian Smith had in fact worked with Bruce on what became the AC/DC-esque 'Hooks In You', an update in the long-running 'Charlotte The Harlot' series; the lyrics, double-entendres all over the place, were inspired by Dickinson and his second wife, Paddy, going to check out a possible house purchase, wherein they were surprised to find strange hooks attached to the bedroom ceiling, and the two speculated as to the probable sexual purposes they were designed for. It is a fun bit of rock silliness that could, actually, easily be at home on *Tattooed Millionaire*. Bruce and Adrian always did work well together. The album highlight, however, by an absolute country mile, is Bruce's 'Bring Your Daughter ...' which, by virtue of not having been written specifically for Iron Maiden, stands alongside the greatest songs that the band have ever recorded before or since.

As soon as the Maiden LP was in the bag, Bruce set about pursuing another talent, taking advantage of an offer to appear in an episode of the television series, *Paradise Club*. It was recorded on June 7 and 8, 1990. As a self-confessed ham, and – of course – with the weight of the Oundle Amateur Dramatics Club training bolstering him, he stretched himself to play a musician named Jake Skinner straining to find freedom from a dictatorial boss – in this case a record label. Unhappy that he may, under the terms of a sponsorship deal, only drink one drink, *Rock 'n' Cola*, til the end of his tour, he walks out of the studio where he is meant to be recording. To be fair, Bruce's performance is as natural as could be expected, although his character is a guitarist rather than a vocalist. The track that was used for the performance was 'Wishing Well', a cover of the track by Free, which they would occasionally play on the 'Millionaire' tour. The episode was aired on November 6, entitled *Rock 'n' Roll Roulette*, and also featured Don Henderson and Leslie Grantham – and it is not available on webcam, lest you ask.

Immediately after these recordings, Bruce headed out on his first ever solo jaunt. Replacing the unavailable Del Rio with Dickie Fliszar, the band headed out merrily on a tour that debuted at Newcastle's Mayfair on June 19, 1990 – close to a hometown gig for North East native, Hartlepool's Janick Gers[128] – and was completed in Los Angeles at the Foundation Forum on September 14. As well as album tracks from *Tattooed Millionaire*, the band would encore with such classics as Deep Purple's 'Black Night' – and even, on occasion, Lindisfarne's 'Fog On The Tyne', later made infamous by Paul Gascoigne on his post World Cup-tears 'hit' single. The tour had been preceded by the release of *Tattooed Millionaire*, which was released on May 8 and peaked at a more-than-respectable Number 14, being praised by the major music magazines, including *Kerrang!* That particular magazine opined that it was the kind of album that Deep Purple's Ian Gillan should be making;

something that pleased Bruce immensely. The only blot on the landscape for the *Tattooed Millionaire* project, to be fair, was the concert recorded at Los Angeles' Town & Country Club on August 14, where the intent was to use the footage for a future video release. Unfortunately the audience – at a rock gig, no less – were banned from drinking, for the sake of the ease of technical issues, leading to a rather less-than perfect atmosphere. The budget was very high, and the arena was crammed with huge camera cranes and flying jibs rather than the hand-held cameras Bruce had hoped there might be. The atmosphere was sterilised.[129] Bruce, immediately following the concert, flashed to the van where the tapes of the concert were, and threw them into the the river in disgust. Sanctuary officials later had to rescue them, and happily they weren't damaged to the point of no return. Bruce makes no secret he is not a fan of these clips.

As ever with Bruce, he would not keep still for a second, rushing to join Iron Maiden for the *No Prayer On The Road* tour. 'Holy Smoke' had been released on September 10, debuting at Number Three, an excellent result for a band who many had been writing off for years. The Maiden fans, however, were always the vital component in their success; shorn of radio play, major television coverage, and repeatedly condemned as less-than-credible, Iron Maiden shrugged it all off, got back on the road and worked their balls off with their usual determination, supported in the UK by an upcoming act named Wolfsbane, whose singer Blaze Bayley warmed up the crowds neatly by being charismatic, aggressive and skilful. The travel arrangements at this stage were rather different to the usual tourbus-n-beer days, Bruce preferring to find his way between the British dates by train, indulging a passion that he had had since a child. He confessed, with his usual honest wit, to something that could be considered amongst certain circles as being a little, well, uncool.

"I love railway timetables," he said, "and I love travelling on trains! The British railway timetables are very disappointing these days as they have reduced the number of overnight trains and late night trains, which are the ones I like to use. It's great on the Continent; get yourself a copy of Thomas Cook's *Continental Timetable*, get off at Calais, and the world is your oyster."[130] No wonder he and Paddy had gone on the Orient Express on their honeymoon.

After the tour wound its way through the UK, the album, *No Prayer For The Dying*, released on October 1, went straight in at Number Two; another triumph in what was turning into rather a triumphant year for Maiden and their singer. That amazing return to basics for both Bruce and his main band had paid off in spades. It could only be topped off by one thing.

chapter fifteen:
Top Of The Tree

And that was the feeling when 'Bring Your Daughter ... To The Slaughter' hit Number 1 on January 5 as the first chart-topper of 1991, remaining there for two weeks despite not being playlisted on Radio One or enjoying a great deal of television support. It was a canny time to release a single: Maiden's fans had never been swayed by anything other than the music they loved so much, and whilst the rest of the record industry generally slows down after Christmas as the sales are naturally lower in the pop arena following the huge pre-Xmas splurge of marketing and jostling for that apparently important Christmas Number 1, Maiden's fans would buy a single they loved no matter how or when it was released. Another measure both of the loyalty of the fans, and the consummate managerial skill of Rod Smallwood and Sanctuary Management in terms of excellent timing.[131]

The tour rolled on through America, and ended in Japan on April 5, 1991. It had been another gruelling spate on the road and, as was becoming the custom, the group took the rest of the year off from direct Maiden duty, before they would regroup just after the festive season for sessions for their next album. Bruce spent the time sketching out the plot to the follow-up to *The Adventures Of Lord Iffy Boatrace*, which became a satire on organised religion, a thinly-veiled attack on his old sparring partner Jimmy Reptile, a famous US TV evangelist – it was another novel full of shagging, sick laughs and slapstick, which if anything was possibly even more funny and ridiculous than its predecessor had been. In the introduction, Bruce admits that it was written on night sleeper trains between various British cities, which were, "some of the most productive sleepless nights I have ever spent; sitting alone with my Macintosh portable and a stack of cans of Director's bitter, I doodled and scribbled as the train clattered through the night." Poetic, almost. He goes on to complain about the fate that the trains had suffered under successive governments in favour of the motorway, something Bruce describes as "dismal."[132]

Such strong sentiments and obviously politically adept intelligence must, of course, have helped immeasurably in the writing of a book that ranges from time-travelling sex maniacs to compulsive-eating sex-maniacs, mummified relatives, TV evangelists, coked-up rock managers, cult shenanigans, porn stars, incontinent secret service agents and a plot by a

Japanese businessman to turn America into the world's biggest golf course. It is as bizarre, and bizarrely moreish, as it sounds. A rubbernecking experience, with the deus ex machina being the literal hand of fate. Which is nice for everybody, to be honest. The Germans liked both novels, publishing translations in good ol' Deutschland during 1996 to good response. In a later interview, Bruce was to refer to the experiences with some fondness, but a certain sense of trepidation as to the possibility of taking on another project, musing on the mixed reception that the books had received to a *Moshville* reporter. "Everybody that bought them seems to think they were very funny," he said. "It was only the tossers who write for the music magazines that went all snotty on them. Frankly, some of the literary magazines, some of the regular newspapers and Radio Four gave them great reviews."

As for the writing process itself, it was no deep secret as to the way it all worked, according to literature's latest newcomer. "I know how writers do it," he rightly noted. "I spoke to some and they say you basically get a typewriter and bash away for eleven hours a day and you've got a novel. I wrote the second one more like that. I was told I *had* to write a sequel and it was really difficult. I just couldn't get the pace."

At this stage, Bruce did begin work on a prequel to the *Iffy* series but the process was not as enjoyable this time around. "I got about sixty pages into a third one," he said, "and just thought it was rubbish and ripped it all up. It was Lord Iffy's schooldays. I didn't think it was funny. Maybe I'll have to revisit it sometime." One can only speculate here that there are, more than likely, many characters from Oundle who should probably be sweating slightly on misdemeanours of their past should Bruce ever follow through on that particular project.

Caught up in the Maiden rollercoaster once more, the next project was to begin in January, 1992 with writing and recording sessions at Steve Harris' house – which was now home to a studio of high specifications, in contrast to *No Prayer For The Dying* (which had been recorded in a mobile studio truck). It made sense for the band to decamp there and work on the sequel to the next phase in their career; the back-to-basics albums of the early 1980s had, of course, produced the stunning trilogy of *Number Of The Beast, Piece Of Mind* and *Powerslave* – perhaps *No Prayer* ... would kick off another productive period of technical, creative and explorative musicality for the band.

The differences between 1982 and 1992, however, were marked; whilst in the former year, Iron Maiden had been at the forefront of the New Wave Of British Heavy Metal, a decade later they were something of the old guard; holding onto concepts that were dear to their hearts. Metal had come so far during the 1980s that it had once more fragmented into niches, genres and sub-genres. Maiden's and Harris' wish to keep things as close and true to their ideals, their street-smarts, as possible, was something of an anachronism when set in context amongst the younger, tattooed millionaires that now posed and preened in the rock world. A reaction against these false rock gods was therefore inevitable.

But whilst in 1982 it had been a very British coup, borne on the ideals (and, let's face it, some of the musicians) of punk rock, by the early 1990s those same ideals were causing a raft of street-punks to rise, only this time it was across the pond – and it was called grunge. Seattle in particular was the epicentre of what became a movement that would capture the imagination of a new generation. Nirvana's Kurt Cobain became a kind of reluctant avatar for the disenfranchised. And whilst the punk and NWOBHM movements had been largely led by genuine streetkids, grunge was a repackaging of rebellion for the MTV generation. On the face of it, Iron Maiden were a group clinging solidly to an older generation's set of values; and admirable though those ideals might be, an older generation's values are the only thing that teenagers truly have to rebel against.

The album that became *Fear Of The Dark* also had the spectre of Harris' recent split from his wife hanging over it. It is, altogether, one of the darkest albums in Maiden's oeuvre. His own tracks seem full of paranoia and imagined demons; for Bruce's part, some of the themes he explores in his offerings seem – on occasion – inextricably linked with his own growing restlessness, albeit multilayered and wrapped up in allegory. Janick's joining of the group had given Bruce an extra gear for the latter Maiden album, as only a new member and an old mate can do, and indeed, the two would contribute heavily to the new LP.

Their first collaboration is album opener, 'Be Quick Or Be Dead', clocking in and out in sharp time, Bruce spitting out lyrics that could on one level be about organised religion and the manipulation of the followers thereof, or, indeed, at any kind of authority figure pulling the strings and demanding that people jump into line. Bruce and Janick's second contribution is the moody-but-bluesy, and rather 1970s-toned 'Fear Is The Key', which has elements of Jethro Tull prog writ strong through it. Lyrically, it is an exceedingly pointed attack on double-standards; a song wrapped up in smothering lyrics about being outnumbered, fighting battles vainly, remembering old times when the nights were hot, bodies were hot and the passion, and possibilities were endless. It's also, very clearly, about AIDS, as Bruce remarked to Henri Dumatrey.

"Sex had become a synonym for 'fear'. When we were writing the songs, we heard about Freddie Mercury's death ... in the States nobody really cared about AIDS until Magic Johnson announced publicly that he was HIV positive. As long as the virus was confined to homosexuals or drug addicts, nobody gave a shit. It's only when celebrities started to die that the masses began to feel concerned."[133]

'Wasting Love', a second collaboration with Gers, is another downbeat track, this time dealing with the groupie phenomenon and the emptiness of casual one-night stands; Bruce's days of being directly in that kind of situation were long gone, happily married and a father, it was an anathema to him. Another way to look at the lyrics – and it is very tempting to do so – is to take the lines about the empty days, the lonely years and the desperation on the part of the song's protagonist to finally be honest and find resolution another way entirely. It's a cry in the wilderness, a shout at an empty sky, an emptiness inside. Whichever way you want to reach it, it's damned bleak stuff.

In the absence of Adrian Smith, Bruce and Dave Murray collaborated on two tracks for the *Fear Of The Dark* album, 'Chains Of Misery' – based around a shadowy character preying on the unwary – and 'Judas Be My Guide' which revisits the theme of searching for answers, or being guided by voices that might not be the most advisable. It is an LP that is relentlessly downbeat and though the band are more technically together, than on its predecessor, the darkness that underpins it makes it a very, very difficult album to listen to.[134]

"There's a break between *Fear Of The Dark* and the old Maiden albums," explained Bruce. "I really believe it will make a huge impact; we're going straight into the 1990s this time. But the Iron Maiden style remains, we didn't compromise, we didn't renounce ... we took some of the energy that's currently in the world and transposed it into our music. When [people] listen to it, I hope they say, 'We thought the last Metallica [album] was good, but check *this out*!'"[135]

As had become the norm, the first single was one that Bruce had been involved with, and his and Gers' snappy LP opener, 'Be Quick Or Be Dead' slammed in at Number 2 on its release on April 11, 1982. The album itself debuted at Number 1, on May 11. The subsequent supporting tour saw them playing to massive audiences across the Americas, pausing to play a huge gig in Rio's Maracana on their way back to the UK to headline Donington for the second time on August 22, a gig that went out live on BBC radio, and was subsequently released as the stunningly-titled *Live At Donnington (sic) 1992*. Nervous though the band were, the crowd of 72,500 was ecstatic, Maiden – and Bruce – played a blinder, and things went without a hitch. Adrian Smith even appeared onstage for the encore, slinking his way through the standard 'Running Free' to a roaring reception. Bruce had also found time to contribute to a cover of Alice Cooper's 'I Wanna Be Elected', a charity single for Comic Relief, in which he appeared with comedians Rowan Atkinson and Angus Deayton, which reached Number 9 on April 9, 1992.

The *Fear Of The Dark Tour* then moved on to Australasia, where part one of the two-staged world jaunt was completed, on November 4, 1992. Dark themes, but a band who had absorbed the skilful, playful Gers into their line-up with hardly a stumble. It would, then, be a good and relaxing Christmas break for all those involved with Maiden. Well. Most of them, at least; Bruce took a call from the record company that had released *Tattooed Millionaire*, asking him if he might like to build on the relative success of the first LP with some more solo material. And, Bruce being Bruce and never standing still, he immediately agreed. Chris Tsangarides was lined up to record some demos once more for the project. A sensible choice, as Tsangarides recalls.

"When ...*Millionaire* came out, we had a whole lot of hit singles off it as well, which was a bonus. I suppose that's the way the best things are done – there's no real end to it, you just do it, and somebody likes it, and they buy it in droves thank God, and there you go. Because of our good experiences of that first record, we decided to make another one. So he found a band, basically a pre-set band called Skin, and he went into rehearsals with them on these songs he'd written. Now, I'm not sure who wrote what, or if any of the band came up with whatever but a whole load of material was done, and we went in and did the backing tracks. Then Bruce had to go, he was still with Maiden and they were playing, and inbetween the odd day here and there he came in and we did a couple of days of rough vocals on the thing."

The project, however, was pretty much stillborn, the tracks remaining rough demos. Tsangarides is to this day slightly baffled by what happened next. "I don't know if it was him, or what happened," he continues, "but that was about as far as we got. And to me it was very, very strange because I tend to establish myself with somebody and we carry on to do two or three records, and then it might be time to move on and it's all fine and dandy, you can appreciate that. But it takes a record to learn each other and so on and so forth, you know."

The material was a little different from the classic-sounding *Millionaire* sessions, however, with an edgier, heftier sound to proceedings. "It was a bit heavier, Janick wasn't there. And I think possibly a load of the tunes should have been for Maiden, maybe."

Bruce was having huge doubts about his future over the period of Christmas, 1992, having come to a few conclusions about his status and context within Maiden. "The intention behind that changed after the first couple of records for me," he explained. "Because it became obvious that Maiden worked to a timetable. A 'table that wasn't absolute but it had to be stuck to; 'Now you'll write for six weeks, now you'll make a record for three months, now you're rehearsing for two weeks, now you'll tour for eight months.' It was organised like that and that seemed to suit the style of writing of the band. Maiden was not the kind of band which I would term 'experimental.' In the early days they were doing stuff that was very different, but it didn't stay that different, it didn't continue the process. It pretty much developed into a formula."

* * *

Bruce and Chris Aylmer catching some sleep between tour dates in 1979.
Photo courtesy of Rob Grain/The Paul Samson Archive.

Iron Maiden visit Madame Tussaud's in 1980.
Photo courtesy of Brian Rasic/Rex Features.

Iron Maiden in action in the early 1980s.
Photo courtesy of Brian Rasic/Rex Features.

Samson, 1980.
Photo courtesy of Thunderstick.

Samson on tour, late 1980.
Photo courtesy of Rob Grain/The Paul Samson Archive.

Samson during recording sessions for the *Head On* album, 1980.
Photo courtesy of Rob Grain.

Samson: *Shock Tactics* studio sessions, January 1981.
Photo courtesy of Thunderstick.

Iron Maiden relax backstage at their legendary 1982
Reading Festival appeearence.
Photo Courtesy of Steve Rapport/Retna UK.

Am I Famous Yet? Bruce checks out his career progress.
Photo courtesy of Niels Van Iperen/Retna UK.

Outside Stockholm's Palladium venue, September 25, 1994,
on the 'Balls To Picasso' tour.
Photo courtesy of Henrik Johansson, The Bruce Dickinson Well-being Network.

Maiden model the latest must-have threads.
Photo courtesy of I.B.L /Rex Features.

Enjoying some downtime.
*Photo courtesy of
Tony Kyriacou/Rex Features.*

Bruce with the fruits of success.
*Photo courtesy of
Hayley Madden/Rex Features.*

The 4,700-strong crowd at Valby Hallen screamed
the band's name non-stop for two hours.
Photo courtesy of Polfoto/Empics.

These Colours Don't Run: Stirring up the Ozzfest crowd in
San Bernardino, California, August 20, 2005.
Photo courtesy of Kevin Estrada/Retna Ltd.

Alice Cooper and Bruce at the 2006 *Classic Rock* Awards, London.
Photo courtesy of Brian Rasic/Rex Features.

Bruce along with Ally McCoist, Captain Julian Todd and Walter Smith
en route to Israel with Rangers Football Club.
Photo courtesy of Lynne Cameron/Empics/Rangers FC.

A formula is something that was never going to satisfy Paul Bruce Dickinson. It was becoming clear that for him to move on, he would have to take the decisions for himself – be they good or bad. This quest for personal development – he'd begun taking flying lessons in 1990, and in 1992 had finished twenty-second in the UK foil fencing championship – permeates everything that makes him an artist of constant surprise and excellence. It is, as much as anything else, ingrained in his personality; the two strong characters in Maiden were beginning to find that their creative paths were taking very different directions.

"It's just the way [Steve] is, you know. He knows pretty much what he wants and I think he tends to exclude a lot of options. He's never taken a drug in his life, he doesn't smoke, he never smoked dope, he's never taken acid or anything that would alter his possibilities. He very rarely gets drunk even, because he likes to stay in control and I think that's the fundamental difference between me and him. Sometimes you have to be in control of things and there are times when you need to be out of control."

But for someone as well-read and psychologically ambitious as Bruce Dickinson, who had a library many academics could only dream of, and a penchant for alchemy and the altered imaginative states of creativity and magic, that was an anathema to him.

"That's sometimes when the best ideas happen – when you just take a big leap into the unknown and you don't know what's gonna happen. That can be very creative and it can be absolute shit but some of the best and the most exciting pieces of music have been created out there on the edge of destruction. But people have different interpretations of that and, fundamentally, to me, 'being on the edge' means being on the edge of actually destroying the creativity. Not being on the edge by playing fast, technically, but to try stuff that's so out there at a gig that the whole show might fall flat on it's face or it might be completely brilliant."

"I saw my position in the band as being the one to try and take Steve's ideas, reinvent them and fuck around with it as much as I could, or as much as he allowed ... when we got to *Seventh Son Of A Seventh Son*, I was quite optimistic about that album. I think it was the last really good record the band made and it was a record where everybody was really trying hard to come up with directions, but it was so slow developing that record and it took such a long time to record it and it was so *terribly* expensive. But it was a pretty good record and there were several ways the band could have gone at that point – but as it turned out, the next one *No Prayer For The Dying* was a huge backward step, I thought."

"The idea was to do something low-key and not particularly complex, to do something that was the opposite to *Seventh Son* – something that was very street, very happening and something that was gonna sound good. The fact is that it sounded terrible and everybody kind of acknowledges it now."

The much-vaunted mobile system that had been instrumental in Adrian Smith's growing creative distance from Maiden; in retrospect, it had also affected Bruce. Even though he'd enjoyed the process, as all the band had. "We all collaborated with it and we all had a great time making it because we were out in the middle of as field making a record in a barn on a twenty year old mobile truck. But basically the [ex-]Rolling Stones mobile [that we used] was a piece of crap! It's exactly the same as when Deep Purple recorded *Machine Head* on it. And the only reason they recorded *Machine Head* on it was that their real studio had burnt down! It wasn't because it was such great sounding equipment, and it certainly sounded much better twenty years ago. They didn't even have a pair of monitors in it that were suitable for mixing on so they got in a pair of small monitors – and I believe they mixed the album on the Rolling Stones mobile as well which, I think, is completely crazy. Martin Birch suggested that we'd do the album in a proper studio at the very beginning but everybody was like, 'No, no, no, this'll be really cool.' And Martin did the best he could."

As is the job of any producer worth his salt; Martin Birch, being one of the greatest producers *of all time*, would have understood that one of the key issues is not necessarily producing a box of tricks to make everything sound magnificent, and pushing the band into a sterile white THX-type studio to attain pristinely-tracked music, but to keep the client happy and relaxed in order that they perform to the best of their abilities. And though Birch had semi-retired but for the Maiden albums, the quality of the mobile truck was not ideal.

"Steve, at that point, started getting very interested in the idea of himself being a producer," explained Bruce, "and he was already editing Iron Maiden's concert videos ... Then we did *Fear Of The Dark,* and I took Nicko aside and said, 'You heard this band called Dream Theater?' I had some demos of theirs and I played [our] album to him and I played some of their demos and I said, 'Listen to these, these are 24-track demos, no samples, no nothing, no machines, listen to this band.' and then I said, 'Now listen to *No Prayer For The Dying*, this is our album, and these are their *demos*. It blows Iron Maiden's sound into next week and it shouldn't.'"

"*Fear Of The Dark*, then, was recorded in Steve's studio because he wanted it to be. I think it was the first album where we were attempting to recapture something in the past. In many ways, I think that we were looking backwards to other albums that we've done in the past while other bands are looking forward to something new. And that was the last studio album I made. Shortly afterwards I just woke up to the end part of the twentieth century and went, 'Shit, I'd better try and do something different.'"[136]

And so he revisited the Tsangarides tapes, and asked his manager Rod Smallwood for an opinion. Smallwood's reply was along the lines of advising Bruce that if he were to want to do something different from Iron Maiden, musically these tapes were perhaps not what he was looking for, because they sounded too much like Maiden. Then Bruce dropped his bombshell: he was going to pursue whatever it was that was driving him to look for new adventures …

… and he would be leaving Iron Maiden to do it.

chapter sixteen:
Balls, Balls And More Balls

The second half of the *Fear* dates – known as *A Real Live Tour* – were played with the intention of recording and releasing two live albums, one of 'classic Maiden' and one of newer material. Before the shows started, Bruce – with his decision to leave made – took himself off to Los Angeles to try and extract some new material. The producer was a little befuddled by Dickinson's change of heart.

"I got a call into [the management office]," remembers Tsangarides, "who basically told me that my services were no longer needed because the record company had decided they needed to explore more with the vocals ... I remember feeling very befuddled and thinking, 'Well, we really haven't done any vocals, what's going on, what the hell?' Really at the time I thought, 'What's happened here, what have I done?' You know, you look and think, 'What's the matter with me?' But quite frankly it was nothing to do with me, to be honest. I think that's when he sort of decided that he didn't want to be in Iron Maiden. I think that's kind of what really was behind it, when you look back with hindsight ... I mean, I was paid for it, but it was just very strange."

The fact remained that for Bruce to leave Iron Maiden was a huge deal; leaving Maiden to do something that sounded similar to that band, conversely, was pointless. So in early 1993, Bruce flew to LA to seek out Keith Olsen, another absolutely legendary producer who had worked with the likes of Fleetwood Mac, Grateful Dead and Sammy Hagar.

"He had just left the band," remembers Olsen, "and I think that exacerbated the problems because he didn't want to do anything that reminded anybody of the band." The early 1990s were also a time of experimentation, with one particular record setting the scene for many rock and hard rock artists.

"So with it being 1991, with Peter Gabriel coming out with 'Shock The Monkey' that didn't even have a single cymbal on it anywhere, not even a hi-hat, [that was a very influential approach].[137] Everybody wanted to be Peter Gabriel back then, everybody. And I think that he had that influence also. Instead of wanting to be Maiden he wanted to 'shock the monkey'. So everything was changing. Stuff was changing in front of our eyes. Sounds were starting to change, you know, Nirvana was there, the grunge sound was just starting to attack everywhere, Pearl Jam had just been released. It was a very confusing time for an artist. Especially an artist from a very, very popular, world-renowned rock band. For the lead singer to kind of go off on his own, to leave that very happening band and go try to do something different [was unprecedented]. It was all troubling him, he saw the end of Maiden, because of the change in music"

What Bruce brought to Olsen was a clutch of ideas, but as the Skin/Tsangarides material had been dismissed as not hitting the mark, there was no band as such with whom to work. So the singer and his new deskman set about discussing how to approach the new project. As the producer remembers, Bruce was adamant that he moved away from the Iron Maiden approach as far as was possible – and to experiment with new studio possibilities.

"Groups like Dream Theater and people like that at the time were using technology a little bit better than Maiden were. Maiden had kind of hit a rut I think, they were just kind of doing the same thing over and over," agrees Olsen. "And that's the thing with Bruce, we were saying, 'We'll take a shot, we'll see if it works but let's at least give it a go' and that's kind of what he was trying to do. As a shot to see if it worked and to see if he could be a little more theatrical and broaden his musical scope a little bit. That's where it made sense. It was interesting in the way that we put it together and tried to be as unique and creative as we could because, God only knows, we had Bruce's name. Because if someone was going to pull it off, maybe it could have been Bruce Dickinson. So that's kind of the wrap of what we did."

Stripped of a band, Bruce's intent was to push the boundaries further than ever before; to work with sequenced drums and backing tracks rather than hit on a band vibe, and to construct painstaking keyboard lines and percussion completely in a digital realm. In a contemporary context, this is as commonplace as auto-tuning the drunken bassist's backing vocals – but in 1992/3 it was absolutely at the cutting edge of studio and sonic technology.

"He wanted to do something really radically different," confirms Olsen, "and we did. He wanted to have it programmed instead of played, he didn't want to have any metal in it at all. So I went 'Oh, that's unique.' He basically wanted me to construct and programme kind of beats around what [he had written]. We worked with Jimmy Creighton, as a programmer. Because he was taking about being more 'Euro' in the programming. Kind of euro-programmed. 'Prock' I call it, you know, pop-rock? So you know, euro-programmed, non-German-but-sells-in-Germany Prock."

"He wanted to be a hundred and eighty degrees away from Maiden. So because of that we tried this stuff that he wanted to do. And all that I can say is that we tried. It was unique. It had some merit to it. But it's not what he does best. And the songs were not a strong as they should have been. For me it was unnerving, the lack of direction and trying to be something that he's not. Bruce is a great hard rock artist and he's got to be a hard rock artist. That's why he's been successful all these years."

"Technologically," Olsen feels, "we were trying to do something ahead of its time, trying to do something kind of the way they make records today, back then. You sit down with a programmer and you try to put together something with an approximate feel, and the right length, and this, that and the other. And you make a copy of those files and you go off to a guitar player who's great, who puts on a bunch of stuff; you take your hard drive underneath your arm and you fly to Austin, where they have really great drummers that won't kill you with their price. Then you put drums and percussion on. Then you fly back to L.A. and you do vocals, background vocals and mix. Tim Pierce did play guitar on it. And then we had a percussionist come in and do some work on it."

"And that's kind of the way it's done today, you're going from project studio to project studio till finally a [real] studio to mix it. And that's kind of what we did. We did all that stuff in that little studio of Jimmy Creighton's, then we went over to Goodnight L.A. to do vocals and mix. And it was different, it was unique, it was okay."[138] Keith Olsen knows what it takes to make a hit; this is the man who, after all, is responsible for The Scorpions' 'Winds Of Change'. You may want to whistle along at this point.[139] Although the radical approach had satisfied the side of Bruce that was desperate to experiment and move from the Maiden blueprint, the sessions themselves had yielded only very modest amounts of useable material for his second solo album.

But in early 1993, it did not ring true for Bruce; even as he was recording with Olsen in Los Angeles, Rod Smallwood was telling the rest of the Maiden camp of Bruce's decision to leave. Bruce had said that he was at the mercy of the rest of the group; should they want him to leave immediately, then that's what he would do, but he did not want to let the band down either, and in the end he was to play the scheduled concerts during 1993. It was, in retrospect, something that was no good for anybody involved. The gigs were nearly all sold out, and it was intended that Bruce's last tour was something of a final farewell to the fans who had been so instrumental in the success of Maiden in the Dickinson heyday. But tensions were inevitable; the general feeling among many observers was that Bruce was, at best, inconsistent during his final gigs with Maiden, and by the time the tour finale came about, it was a relief to all concerned.

Inevitably, under the pressure of touring life, and when tiredness begins to take its toll, people can snap and come out with some things that appear stronger or harsher in the cold light of day than they were necessarily meant at the time. Add this to it being 2a.m., post-gig in Bremen, having had a drink and being asked for the umpteenth time about Bruce's imminent departure, it's understandable that eventually seemingly harsh words were going to be said. So it was with drummer – and very good friend of Bruce – Nicko McBrain, who in a notorious April, 1993 interview with *Kerrang!*, said that Bruce was "going his way, we're going ours – fuck 'im, let's get a new singer. That's it – cut and dried." When the journalist asked if Bruce had "shit on Iron Maiden" by leaving, the response from an obviously tired drummer was immediate and vituperative. "Course he has! He's said, 'Fuck you, I'm off.' If that ain't shitting on you, then what the fuck is?" McBrain went on to criticise Bruce's recent Los Angeles jaunts, and speculated that perhaps pressure had come from other influences goading him to leave Maiden's "bunch of has-beens behind" in favour of a solo career. But the drummer was also defiant about the future, raging that rather than the current tour being *Bruce's Farewell*, it was still the *Fear Of The Dark* tour, no matter who was screaming up front. He likened Maiden to, "the phoenix rising; we will rise again, as a stronger and more positive bird."[140] Strong stuff, heartfelt at the time no doubt, but also exacerbated by a mixture of alcohol, the demands of touring and a pervading tiredness. Bruce was relatively philosophical and later told an interviewer from the French magazine, *Hard Rock* that, "the journalist spent three days ... trying to dig some dirt. And he couldn't. In the end he got Nicko a few drinks and, after about five hours, he finally got three sentences out that made that bloke's day. I didn't mind, I've known Nicko for too long."[141]

Bruce was philosophical about matters in that same *Kerrang!* Feature, commenting that completing the tour was, "easier than the other way of leaving Maiden ... [sitting] there, gnashing my teeth and dumping it on the band after the tour's over. This way, it's out in the open, and all I see in the audience is people smiling." He went on to comment that generally the fans had been understanding, and although *Fear Of The Dark* could have been better, it was still his favourite LP since *Powerslave* some seven years earlier. Downplaying any reports of friction within the camp, Bruce comes across as basically indulging in the archetypal, 'It's not you, it's me ... I need to change and find myself' type of break-up conversation. The remarkably adult feel of matters – bearing in mind that the band still needed to tour together – was continued by Steve Harris, who took the old 'this band is bigger than any one member, and if anybody's not into it 110% then it's not gonna work out' line, whilst also expressing surprise that Bruce felt he could not pursue parallel careers both in and out of Maiden. An uneasy peace, but it all was during a dark period of the bass player's life in general, and Harris was to comment that it'd come, "at a time when I was at a bit of a low ebb anyway. But you have to pick yourself up and steam back in ... Bruce quitting knocked me for six, and I thought maybe the rest of 'em would be looking to me to be a leader. For a week or so I didn't feel like that, but now I feel stronger as time goes on."[142] Stronger indeed; there is very little under the heavens or for that matter below the earth that is powerful enough a force to knock Steve Harris' vision off course, and once the *Fear Of The Dark* tour finally came to a close, Maiden were to begin the search for another new lead singer with renewed vigour and self-belief,

That last 'gig' was a particularly crass affair, a televised piece of silliness on August 28, 1993 alongside magician Simon Drake, during which a member of the audience was 'killed', Dave Murray had his arms 'sawn off'; finally, Bruce himself was put inside, fittingly, an Iron Maiden torture device and summarily 'killed'. Completely over-the-top, possibly ill-judged, but certainly final. The show was recorded at London's Pinewood Studios and broadcast on pay-per-view television, subsequently to be released under the moniker *Raising Hell*.

Afterwards, the various members of Maiden – arms restored – and one newly-ex-vocalist, sidled off to their respective homes – and that, as they say, was that. The Worksop chap was no longer Iron Maiden's singer; he was, once more, Paul Bruce Dickinson, itinerant musician, fencer, pilot and bon viveur, and he was looking for the next challenge. He was, he said, bored of the cycle of long tours revisiting the same set-list and similar performance; the inside of a tourbus held no fascination for him. Musically-speaking, he admitted that the recent albums he was listening to were Alice In Chains' *Dirt* – but also, surprisingly, *The Soul Cages* by Sting, an LP he praised for being, "beautiful and consciously naïve ... it describes a multidimensional universe quite well and with a lot of honesty."[143] He went as far as to label larger rock concerts as boring and overly-controlled, and admitted that he was occasionally prone to attending rave parties – which, to him, were reminiscent in spirit and freedom to the concerts he had grown up with in the 1970s. "That's where you can find drugs, girls and the freedom to react the way you really want ... in rock, the artist on stage has all the rights, he's the boss for the night, the audience has no prerogative and just waits passively for the show to end. In rave parties, each individual can participate. It's no longer just a circus show for the crowd, people are part of it."[144] And although he was not planning to release a rave-anthem, smiley-T-shirted techno LP, he was intrigued as to the possibilities of marrying that spirit with a rock sensibility. A collision of concepts and cultures that is Bruce Dickinson all over – but not one that would ever be viable within Iron Maiden, of course.

John McCoy, who'd been a factor in the music scene since the 1970s, postulates that in part, it was quite possibly down to the differing backgrounds of the musicians. "My impression was that Bruce was just trying desperately to fit in," he says, "as he was in the Samson camp. The Samson camp was kind of an ongoing comedy show, and the Maiden camp was like rock and football and football and rock. I think he was just trying to fit in really, to be one of the guys, but unfortunately that's never gonna happen because of background and education and he's just from a different world. But it's strange in bands because people come from all kinds of different lives and backgrounds, but it doesn't really matter, if what they contribute to the band works then you put up with their sort of [differences] in personal life, or you try to." It can work, and work well – as it had in the case of the Gillan touring band of the very early 1980s – but, conversely, sometimes the constant flux of having to create a viable working relationship can get exhausting, and rather stifling after a decade together.

"He just outgrew it," offers Tony Platt, who also gives a rather interesting insight into the perceived insularity often inherent in the Maiden camp. "I saw him a couple of times after he had joined Maiden, I happened to be in Germany and somebody phoned me up – they were doing a warm-up gig in Hamburg or Cologne. And I was working in a studio just outside Cologne; I pitched up, Bruce had organised passes and it was really great to see him and meet his wife for the first time, it was really nice but there was definitely a frosty atmosphere from the rest of them. Nicko was the drummer and I had a huge history with Nicko because of working with him in Trust. We were great mates, Nicko and I, he used to come down to our house in Sussex and we'd spend the weekend. That was even stranger in that circumstance. The Maiden camp was very much a closed rank thing. So you could potentially think he'd outgrown all that ... And, of course, he'd got other things to do; other fish to fry as they say."

Indeed he did, not least on the material he had been trying to pull together outside the often restrictive confines of the Maiden Machine. For Bruce's part, the experience of the stuttering solo recording sessions to date had been a valuable – but expensive – one. Dipping his toe into the water of something so *extraordinarily* radical – creatively speaking, and in terms of his career to date – had been of great interest, but ultimately of little use to his immediate plans.

"I took Myke Gray over," recalls Bruce, "who did the original guitars on the first album but I didn't use him on all of it. I used some session guys over there in the States and I used the keyboard player and the bass player from Saga to do a lot of programming. The recording was basically put together electronically, written on computers, keyboards and shit and I then got human beings in to replace that. It was an interesting experience and I learned an awful lot about what I *didn't want* to do out of that record."

However, what he had achieved, if nothing else, by virtue of indulging in those LA-based Olsen sessions, was meet a character whose talent, approach, humour and production ideas not only matched his own, but surprised and often bemused him. That character is Roy Ramirez, who had been around and about the So-Cal rock scene since the late 1980s, playing with the likes of Warrior and Royal Flush before renaming himself Roy Z and forming his own band, Tribe Of Gypsies, in 1991.

"I grew up in the valley in a place called Pacoima, explained Ramirez. "It was a very very bad part of town. It's famous 'cause of [cult film stars who, uh, like the odd smoke] Cheech And Chong, a lot of shootings. A lot of gang activity. Lots of friends of mine are either in jail or dead. People that I grew up with. But it's a beautiful part of my life 'cause we were happy! I did not know that I was poor. I come from a very traditional family, very family orientated. We still see each other all the time. Very close knit. I am proud of who I am and what I do and where I am from."[145]

Roy Z was also an accomplished producer and engineer, with a real feel for how sounds go together. When he and Bruce met in Los Angeles – courtesy of Shay Baby, who had been Keith Olsen's engineer on the ill-fated second shot at the new album sessions – the two musicians got on famously, both personally and on a creative level.

"He played me his band, the Tribe Of Gypsies," continued Bruce. "And I just listened to his band and said, 'Fuck – what am I doing fucking around with computers and all this LA crap?' And he was really into writing some songs with me, so I said, 'OK, let's do that.'" Roy's fearless approach was in part down to his upbringing, although he felt the meeting was, "surreal and wonderful. It was pure destiny. The scary part was that he was so enthusiastic about my music. It vindicated what I was doing, for me. Trying to do Heavy Metal in the past never got me to meet these kinds of guys – or I would meet them and they would not think about working with me. Then here I am doing this, what you could call traditional-type music; and then you get noticed! I thought it was so strange."[146]

The original intent was to collaborate with Z on three or four new tracks, band-based, to complement the six songs Dickinson had accumulated through the Olsen sessions. But despite the fact that Bruce had dipped into his own coffers to fund the recordings, he came to the conclusion that it would be a fudge, and something of a betrayal of his ideals, were he not to scrap *everything* on the second album so far, in favour of starting again in cahoots with Roy Z and his merry band of musicians. It would be a case of Third Time Lucky; The Tribe were a stunningly proficient bunch, and Bruce had found a solo band – and a collaborator – with whom he could work extremely well.

Bruce and Roy began to write together, and in short order had come up with a collection of songs that at last matched the vocalist's vision for what his second album should be. Roy would play him material, he'd scream along – to the point of almost crashing on the freeway more than once – and the pair came up with a raft of material which they began to lay to tape, with Shay Baby at the controls, at Metropolis Studios in London. Shay Baby had been enthusiastic about the possibilities of utilising African and Spanish rhythms alongside the Gypsies' skilful, but streetwise, approach, and was well aware of the talent of Roy Z as a guitarist and creative force. When the call came to produce the Metropolis sessions, Shay Baby and the band were somewhat disturbed by an occasionally odd ambience in the facility, which was The Who's hangout and was said to be visited by the ghost of Keith Moon.

"Weird things were happening," laughed the producer. "Mic stands were moving; we would tune the drums, and we'd come in the next day and all the drums were out of tune."[147] They even found a weird, gooey substance on the kit one day; even from beyond the grave, Moon was playing the prankster – settings would be changed on the studio desk and there were several occasions in which takes had to be redone when mysterious drop-outs appeared on the tape.

The sessions were notable for a real willingness to try different sounds and equipment out, as Baby recalls. "We used 1950s Fender guitars, vintage Gretsch guitars ... and even hunted down a Hendrix amp ... we used some of Brian May's amps. So we got to put Roy's stuff through the amps Brian used with Queen."[148]

So Bruce had finally managed to negotiate through a very difficult creative period in his life; whilst there was a certain amount of sniping in the media between himself and his old bandmates, he'd got on with it and – eventually – recorded his second solo album, which was to be called *Balls To Picasso*.[149]

The album opens with a sense of foreboding on the atmospheric, sinister, 'Cyclops' – one of the first tracks that Dickinson and Ramirez had written together. Its blend of doomy-funk, metallic bass and robotic samples is offset by a sinister, *sotto-voce* vocal from Bruce that speaks of secrets, lies and falseness; as the texture thickens into a passionate chorus it's pretty uncompromising stuff and although it's one of the heftiest tracks on the LP as a whole, it's as far from the Maiden days as 'Run To The Hills' was from 'Vice Versa' – and miles away from the knockabout daft-romps that permeated *Tattooed Millionaire*. This is serious stuff, as evidenced on the Latin-tinged percussion and scales of 'Hell No', another set of lyrics about belonging, and starting afresh on his own terms. It doesn't take a huge leap of faith to extrapolate what that's all about. Roy Z gets an opportunity to show what he can do as a guitarist on the expansive anti-war track, 'Gods Of War' with an evocative and squealing solo; there are more digs at politicians and double standards, two pet themes of Bruce's, on the growling menace of '1000 Points Of Light', before it kicks into one of the greatest tracks of Bruce's solo career, which on the LP cover is credited to B. Dickinson/Roy Z/A. Dickinson.

If you were wondering who the mysterious A. Dickinson might be, it is an artist making their lyrical debut. Step forward Austin Dickinson, Bruce and Paddy's second son, who inspired the track with one of those phrases that only children – with their mix of unfettered imagination and open-eyed naivety – could come up with. "'Laughing In The Hiding Bush' is about my youngest son, Austin, playing with his cousins. He said, 'Look, Daddy, I'm laughing in the hiding bush.' I thought it sounded cool, so I wrote it down and Roy came up with a cool riff. It made me think of all of these fucked-up things kids think of. It makes me think of what we teach our kids."[150] Bryan May's amplifiers must have come in handy on the soulful, introspective 'Change Of Heart', which recalls Rush in their more pensive moments and discusses lost days and strength of love. 'Shoot All The Clowns', by contrast, is an insistent Aerosmith pastiche that had its genesis in a particularly, peculiarly record company-type moment when an album, *Aerosmith Rocks* by that band was slipped underneath Bruce's hotel room door by a Mercury Records gofer, with a note to the effect of "the album's cool, but can we please have a track that sounds like this?" (whilst Bruce was in discussions with that label to seal a deal in the US). Three days later, Bruce and Roy had dashed one off, nonsense though it is, and despite the obviously superior musicianship, it cuts across the rest of the feel of the album somewhat – although it is notable for Bruce Dickinson rapping on record for the first time, which is a mark of how open to new ideas he was by this time. "It was a bizarre experience," commented a bemused Bruce in the album's sleevenotes, "and my worst in the time-frame of the *Balls To Picasso* period."[151] Regardless of record company meddling, the cautionary tale of 'Fire' brings the album back to form, followed up with another track featuring Dickinson rapping, the chuggy, funktastic 'Sacred Cowboys' – a tightly-controlled exploration that, musically, sums the album up entirely, and again features some rather insightful lyrics – Bruce sings that there aren't any indians to kill anymore, they're not on the hill – harking back not only to his own work but also perhaps talking of having faced down the enemy one by one, and now looking for a new challenge. There are similar nods and cues throughout his solo work.

The album ends with the only song Bruce is credited as having written alone, and that is 'Tears Of The Dragon' – the only track also to have survived through all three ...*Balls* attempts, and the only one to have retained Dickie Filszar's original drum part. It is an evocative piece with more lyrics about escaping from an oppressive past into an uncertain future. It's Bruce as an artist at his most vulnerable, and in sentiment, arrangement and delivery, it's as poignant and mature a statement of regret – and hope – that he had ever allowed himself to be associated with. It is a brave, soft-rock, epic-feeling song which rams home, via a beautifully-delivered and occasionally understated vocal, exactly what the motivations of leaving Maiden and pursuing solo ideals were, and rounds off an album that is, at times, pertinent and pointed, but one which is – '...Clowns' aside – an honest offering.

The music press agreed on its release on June 6, 1994, including the venerable *Kerrang!* to the tune of three stars, and though they also felt it a little patchy, they praised its occasionally 'magical' moments. Generally, however, the response was muted from a press who were either obsessed with grunge, or simply didn't understand the point of the project. On his own website, Bruce later said they were talked into making a softer album and should have produced it differently.[152] Slightly more sinisterly, and unluckily it must be said, after three short months, Bruce's contract with Mercury Records, was terminated, along with several other artists, as that organisation had to cut its roster due to financial difficulties. And touring was out too; the Tribe Of Gypsies were unavailable, busying themselves with their day jobs – being a damned fine band and rockin' the free world. Although the initial intent had been to rip it up together, circumstances dictated that the Gypsies' career was rightly at the forefront of their minds. After all, they'd only been 'borrowed' for the project in the first place.

As for Bruce, he was now becoming an accomplished pilot, clocking up the airmiles during 1994, as well as finding some time to collaborate with the band Godspeed on a cover of 'Sabbath Bloody Sabbath' for the tribute to the Sabs, *Nativity In Black*, which also featured a raft of artists that includeed Biohazard, Megadeth, Therapy?, Corrosion Of Conformity, Ugly Kid Joe and 1000 Homo DJs.

Despite the relatively modest impact of *Balls To Picasso*, it was still a refreshed Bruce Dickinson who, after finally having got the second LP recorded, had conquered some of the questions he was asking himself. Having put creative, physical and temporal distance between himself and Maiden, a rejuvenated Dickinson set about looking for a new bunch of musical reprobates with whom to enter the next phase of his career.

chapter seventeen:
In Which Our Gallant Hero Realises That He Hasn't Been In A Band Starting With The Letter 'S' For Quite Some Time, And Thusly Sets About Rectifying Such An Oversight, With Excellent Results

The new project was to be a little different. Having had such a difficult and long gestation, the second solo album had brought one thing home to Bruce in spades: a solo album is all very well, but being part of a *band* has many upsides. The experience working with the Gypsies had reminded the vocalist of the inter-band dynamics that could work wonders with creativity. Having been out of Maiden for nearly a year, officially at least, Bruce was also on a quest to find his place in music and clarify his cultural context.

On his own website, he mused about avoiding ending up on the "metal or rock cabret circuit" (highly unlikely!)[153] To that end, Bruce recalled that some seven years previously, whilst out for a pint of Ruddles Bitter near his home, he'd been very impressed by a young guitarist who happened to be rocking it up with his band, Gun, down the boozer that night. As Bruce says, the pub is often the "best place to find most things." Particularly if you're looking for beer. Regardless, and despite the difference in age, that young guitarist – Alex Dickson – was called up again by Bruce, the two bonded over common musical interests and began to write and jam together. The next thing was to try and put together a touring band, as the Tribe were busy wowing record executives with their own material. Specifically, a bassist and drummer were needed. Following a recommendation from old mate Myke Gray, Bruce set about tracking down ex-Atom Seed bassist, Chris Dale.

"[Atom Seed] did quite well touring the UK and Europe," Chris Dale told me. "We had a deal with London Records, but it all went bottoms up, as many bands do. After that I did a few more projects and was looking around for a new band to commit to. I auditioned for Thunder (whoops, don't think I meant to say that), then I read in *Kerrang!* that Bruce was looking for a band. I was working with a very talented young Italian drummer at the time called Alessandro (Alex) Elena, so I asked if he wanted to do it too. He was, like me, a Maiden fan, so we sent in the demo of our latest band together. I also knew a couple of the guys from Skin, who were also on Sanctuary Management, and Janick Gers, so I asked them to recommend me to Bruce. We got called up to go to a meeting with Rod Smallwood first, then a first audition."

Elena recalls it well, and looks back on it with a lot of affection, having previously worked with Dale in the band Machine. "Oh man, that's a silly story. I was in London obviously. I had pretty much just arrived from Italy and it was funny because I didn't quite speak English. And so Chris and I went and it was a pretty funny audition, I must say. It was amazing to meet Bruce because when I was a kid I was like a major Iron Maiden fan, I used to go and see them play and stuff, I like all of their records. But then when I turned fifteen or sixteen it all died. I was like 'Oh, *fuck Iron Maiden*, now I wanna listen to something else!' You know. Meeting him was a trip, he was super-cool, man. He like helped us unload the gear from the car and, you know, he was super-friendly. We started playing, you know, we played a couple of songs from *Balls To Picasso*."

In fact, guitarist Alex Dickson, Alex Elena and Chris Dale clicked immediately on a personal and musical level to the point where the three continued to bring the funk long after the 'official' audition was over. "Bruce went out," laughs Elena, "and me Alex and Chris kind of kept playing for probably a couple of hours, from Chilli Peppers songs to Kiss covers, anything. Alex and I clicked immediately, and again he's still one of my best friends, and he's a sick guitar player, he's fucking *crazy*. And he kind of always wanted to get into funk, and funk was always my thing, so we kind of clicked on that. And I remember Bruce asked Alex, 'Should we get these guys?' and Alex was like '*Fuck YEAH, man!*'"

"So we got the gig," confirms Dale. "It was all quite exciting. The first new material we heard was *Balls To Picasso*. That was already recorded and Bruce needed a live band to go on tour with it. I was pleasantly surprised that he was making a brave move and doing something quite different from Maiden. I love Maiden, but a change does everyone a bit of good doesn't it? I just wanted to join a good rock band, go on tour and play bass a lot. The fact that this band had Bruce Dickinson singing for it was a bit of a bonus!"

"So after the audition we ended up going to Maidenhead," continues Alex Elena. "There was an airfield where Bruce used to keep his plane. An airfield for me was a *trip*, imagine, man, I was eighteen years old, literally just arrived from Italy, which compared to the UK is like a small village, you know. I don't quite understand what's going on around me because I don't speak English that well, and I'm kind of like thrown into this. And at the time I was *completely* broke. I was living in Kennington in some housing project, and next thing you know I have a limousine that comes to pick me up to take me to *Top Of The Pops*, I was like 'Okay, what's going on here?' you know. And that's kind of how I got into it. It was trippy man. And it was kind of bizarre because I got so much media attention back home, I was on like the front cover of the national newspaper, 'What's going on here?!' And obviously my parents were super-happy because my dad is also a drummer and my mum is an artist, so they always kind of supported me doing my thing."

Bruce also had another impact on the twenty-year-old Italian drummer's life, as he happily acknowledges. "It was kind of like a life changing experience. I was really lucky, because at the time Jamiroquai wanted me in their band. But Bruce is a really cool, grounded, wise person, he's a good friend. And for me at the time – man – I could have gone either way. I could have gone down the route of rock 'n' roll, drugs, fucking mayhem, bullshit, you know, fake people. But he kind of trained me in a way, you know. He kind of took a liking to me."

"Like, at first I lived in his house, he's got a couple of houses in Chiswick and said, 'Alex, you know, come and live with me, I'll rent you one of my rooms and you can live there. So for a while we used to hang out a lot. I used to go to his place at night time and drink endless amounts of vodka. He's got a freezer full of vodka man, from all over the world! And I remember leaving his place *completely* drunk, not knowing, like I couldn't even walk home and home was like four blocks away man, it was ridiculous!"

"He's been, at least for me, he's been a bit of a mentor. You know at the time he taught me a lot of really, really good things I must say; he was one of the people who first taught me to speak English. He was always very patient with me and I would ask him like, when I was learning I wasn't the guy who would just always say, 'Yes' to things I didn't understand. I would be like, 'Hey man, what does that mean? How do you use that word?' And because he speaks incredibly good English, very proper, and he is a great writer as well, I got the best out of it, you know, I had a pretty good fucking teacher right there."

Band duly sorted, Bruce and the boys spent the rest of 1994 playing what was, effectively, the *Balls To Picasso* tour throughout Europe and America, ripping up a series of small clubs with a tight-arse band, and playing far smaller venues than you'd associate Bruce Dickinson with in his Iron Maiden days.

"The States was really crazy," laughs Chris Dale. "We were supporting Jackyl across the Mid-Western states. Remember Jackyl? They had a song called, 'She Loves My Cock', which was a subtle little ditty they performed most nights. They also fired shotguns and played with a real chainsaw, sawing up chairs and stuff. They had a bucking bronco type thing which they'd get girls from the audience to have a go on, all this onstage during the gig. They were full-on, good-time Southern boys, nice guys actually but kind of scary to be around for a lad like me from a small town in Wales! Outside in the audience and the streets, things were more mad with strippers dancing to Kiss, cab drivers trying to sell coke at gunpoint and chalk outlines on the ground to show you where their last customers had been. Looking back I'm amazed we survived – the food was good though. When we did the US leg of the *Balls To Picasso* tour Bruce flew us in a little seven seater twin prop plane all over the States. He might be a wild metal frontman but when he's in the pilot's seat he's a proper pro."

"We flew to Dallas, I believe it was," laughs Elena, "and we rented a plane there. He had a co-pilot, just because of us in the back, but we basically flew for months straight, man. We had the crew travelling on the bus and we basically flew from place to place. And we went through storms and, you name it. But the guy is a monster of a pilot man, you never feel scared, it was amazing."

"Europe was a bit calmer, at least more familiar," Chris Dale explains, "Alex Elena was, of course, Italian, and we'd all been on European tours before with other bands so it wasn't so alien to us. We had a lot of fun here, I seem to remember, we were headlining clubs and it was very cool to meet all the fans and have a few strange beers."

Alex Elena also threw himself into it, and remembers the European dates as being both exciting and, occasionally, a little surprising – and the experience of watching a true master at work was something that made a huge impression on the drummer at the start of his career.

"Playing live was a trip, man," he gushes. "It was really a trip at first, because the guy has got *total* control over the crowd. We spent six weeks touring Germany, we played every fucking venue in Germany – man, it was ridiculous. And Germany is not a great place to play, because the food is crap, the chicks don't look that good and German people don't quite have a sense of humour, so it's kind of a weird combination. A lot of history, you know, but besides that it's very, very exciting. The funny thing about Germans, man, is that people come to your show and they don't clap their hands. They are really still. But Bruce has got this thing where he can literally get people going, even when people don't want to go anywhere, he's just got this energy." Which he used to great effect as the tour wound through the Continent, both on and offstage, as Chris Dale remembers.

"It was great fun, we used to jam around a bit, occasionally throw in a different song in the encores, and generally have musical fun onstage. For me, although I'd toured Europe before, it was my first time in the US, South America and later Japan – they were all great experiences. We'd all have our little jobs on tour. My job was to check if the beer was up to standard in the dressing room. If the promoter had given us Fosters or something, it was my job to get some proper beer in. Bruce trusted me there. At some of the German venues it was amazing to go into their cellars, see what they'd got and pick out *a case of this ... and two of that please!*"

Before too long, however, the tour was on its way back to good old Blighty. "The UK tour was great fun," remembers Dale. "It was quite a small club tour – by Bruce's standards. They were mostly venues I'd played before in previous bands but this time it was all sold out and the crowds went crazy. After just coming back from touring the States and Europe it was nice to see familiar faces in the crowd." That UK tour included a raucous date at The Marquee Club, which was recorded for posterity.

"I remember there were a couple of mistakes I'd made during the Marquee gig," recalls Chris Dale. "It was a crazy gig with stage diving and everything going on, I'd had a couple of beers and mistakes do get made. We discussed whether to fix them or not later. But when we listened back to it all, I didn't think they mattered much, so I said I'd rather leave them in there and keep the vibe live and real. Isn't that what live albums are about?"[154]

Those recordings ended up being released as *Alive At The Marquee*, which was the 'bonus' album released as a double CD with *Alive In Studio A* (which itself was intended, originally, to be broadcast live to U.S. radio); essentially it is an extended radio session which shows off how the group had come together during the 1994 tours. It was one of many plans that were flying around at the time, says Chris Dale.

"There were loads of ideas going around all the time from management, record companies and Bruce. It was quite exciting – not all the ideas happened, of course, but it was good that there were loads of them. Radio broadcasts, live albums, tours of Eastern Europe, camcorders for everyone to make video diaries, B-sides written by the daft bassist, living in LA for a bit, Frisbees with the band name on ... all these ideas were bandied about. The more stupid ones worked better, we found, hence I wrote some B-sides and we got the Frisbees made up! It was a day or two after we'd finished up our tour at The Marquee. So we just played the live set as we had on the tour, the only difference being we set up in a studio rather than onstage. The studio was Metropolis studios in Chiswick where we'd previously recorded some B-sides for 'Shoot All The Clowns'. I think most of the original *Balls To Picasso* was done there too. We recorded this live stuff in room A, hence the title. The vibe was good, it was just like a gig except not in a concert venue."

Notably, the performances on *Alive In Studio A* take the blueprint of the Tribe Of Gypsies, but morph the songs onto and into the skills of the new musicians performing the material; something that Dale feels is inevitable.

"When bands tour for a while, the songs start to change and evolve a bit," he says. "In this case more so, because we weren't the band that had played on the original versions of these songs from *Balls To Picasso* and *Tattooed Millionaire*, so we took them and played them in our own style. We jammed around and improvised a bit with songs too. Alex Dickson particularly improvised new solos every night on tour, most of them were incredible.

Bruce fully encouraged this. He's a big Deep Purple fan and liked the way they jammed for hours back in the 1970s – while we weren't quite going down that avenue, it was a similar vibe."

The idea behind *Alive In Studio A/Alive At The Marquee* was to counteract the growing trade in unofficial releases of live gigs, often recorded badly and therefore giving something of a false view of the band. "I think part of the idea was to beat the bootleggers at their own job," agrees Chris Dale. "There had already been a bootleg out of the Milan show on that tour. Inevitably, bootlegs do come out and die hard fans will buy them all, I can't blame them, I've got loads of Kiss bootlegs. I think Bruce has done a good thing by releasing a live album or live video on almost every solo tour he's done. The fans can then get hold of a live recording of the tour they saw and at least they know they won't get ripped off. A lot of bootlegs are expensive, have awful sound quality and poor packaging. This double CD was priced as one CD, it was recorded well and had loads of cool photos inside from the tour. A lot of those photos were from my personal collection when I was snapping away with an Instamatic. I used to take loads of photos on tour, and most of the fully clothed ones ended up on that CD cover."

Both the *Alive* albums are fizzing with energy, but, crucially, also have a superior sonic outlook; the fans were not short changed, although on the February 27, 1995 release of the double CD, *Kerrang!* rather uncharitably asked whether people really wanted to spend their '1,299 pennies' on it. *RAW* magazine, however, saw it for what it was and enthused about its moody, clinical precision and generally splendidly-performed spirit, awarding it four stars.

The months together on the road had brought the band even closer together, as people and as musicians, and when a rather odd call came from *Kerrang!*, the group jumped at it – of course, they'd love to play the gig that was on offer. The only small problem was that it was in war-torn Bosnia.

"They were asked by UN protection forces in Sarajevo to get a gig together with a local rock society," explained Bruce. "Motorhead pulled out at the last minute, Metallica said they didn't want to do it, 'What the fuck, we'll do it!' It was an *amazing* five days. We basically drove ourselves through a war zone, sleeping on the gear in the back of a truck for seven hours with no military protection or anything. Just a civilian driving up front in a soft-top truck."

Chris Dale remembers it very well. An unforgettable experience, and one that brought the rest of the fun and frolics back into sharp focus. "Sanctuary, the management, got a call from a British UN officer asking if Bruce would play in Sarajevo. Bruce is always up for an adventure so he said yes. At the time, December 1994, the war was still on but had dropped from the headlines, so we assumed it had probably all quietened down over there. As had happened before, we were wrong. We flew into Split in Croatia and were met by the United Nations at the airport. They said, 'Thanks very much for coming but things have got a bit worse here recently and we can't guarantee your safety so we advise you to get back on the next plane home.' Which was a bit disappointing. Bruce, meanwhile, had met some guys from a charity who regularly drove trucks into Sarajevo despite it being under siege at the time. They said we could go along with them if we wanted a lift."

In for a penny, in for a pound, the band decided to press on with their planned gig. After all the preamble, they'd not come this far to turn back at the first hurdle; it would however become clear that this was no ordinary drive to a gig.

"So later that night, we got into the back of a couple of brightly painted trucks and drive overnight towards Sarajevo," continues the bass player. "Straight away it became obvious that this wasn't just a little trip through normal countryside. There were shell holes around, some roads were destroyed, there were military road blocks. But the really odd thing was there was no-one else on the roads, and very few signs of life anywhere. It was mostly just dark. No houses with lights on, most of the electricity was down. One of the few signs of life was hearing sporadic gunfire throughout the night. We were told it was mostly fired up in the air by drunks, but that didn't reassure us too much. We only stopped once or twice on the journey, and never saw anyone except for soldiers at the road blocks. When we did stop we were warned to stay in the middle of the road, even to have a piss. You didn't know who might be in the hedges or if the side of the road was mined. It had suddenly become quite serious."

The group pressed on through the war-zone, toward their destination, which by now had taken on rather a more serious tone than the on-paper 'adventure' which had enticed the band in the first place.

"We arrived on the outskirts of Sarajevo just as dawn was breaking. At a Bosnian army checkpoint, we switched from the charity truck into a UN armoured personnel carrier. We were warned to keep our heads down as snipers were common around here. Going into Sarajevo, we saw most of the buildings had bullet holes, some were riddled with them, some had a whole wall missing. There was a bullet hole in the wall next to my bunk in the UN barracks when we got there. I found that a bit disconcerting. There was a discarded tank here and there, some houses had smoke billowing out of them – people were cooking inside on open fires."

"And this was the amazing thing, life went on for the people of Sarajevo. They'd lost the roof off their house, had no electricity or gas, no shops or money to buy things anyway, they were cut off from the world, their brother and sisters were all dead, their sons were conscripted and at the front line and yet they carried on with life. When we met people from Sarajevo, they were mostly quite cheery, very generous with the very few things they had and [they] just had tremendous spirit. That affected me most."

"You know back here in Britain and the West, we're always complaining about everything – the weather, day-to-day life, the price of things, getting home from work late, not having the latest DVD ... over there they had nothing, it was all taken from them. And yet they smiled."

"The gig we played became a very minor part of the trip in a sense. It was a good gig and the audience were very, very appreciative, but the major parts of the trip that stuck in my mind were a visit we made to an orphanage (for which I cannot describe the emotions in words) and conversations with locals where they told me things that were so horrific, and yet day-to-day life and death for them. Then we left Sarajevo via Serbian army checkpoints, a Sea King helicopter and Hercules transporter plane into Britain in the middle of pre-Christmas consumerism and over-indulgence. We were all still a bit shocked and stunned by what we'd seen. I think it made a deep impression on us all. As far as I know, no other foreign bands played in Sarajevo during the siege."

Were there any proof needed that Paul Bruce Dickinson was rather more than a heavy metal singer in a bombastic band, it was surely here; such experiences are neither planned nor bought, and moments of that humbling nature would certainly never be possible within the strict, and restrictive, confines of a major metal group touring sterile enormo-domes – this gig is as far from the concept of the tattooed millionaire as could possibly be imagined. As the band returned to the UK for a quick Christmas break, they'd bonded deeper than many bands do over a ten year career. The group duly toddled off to South America, where the single 'Tattooed Millionaire' had been a huge hit for Bruce, and where the audiences had always been enthusiastic for the singer's work within and without Maiden.

"The audiences in South America are the craziest in the world, second to none," confirms Chris Dale. "They scream the loudest at gigs and all through the gig, they don't stop. They camped outside hotels all night, tried to climb over high fencing to get in to the gigs. There were riot police called out in Chile at the gig. It was all quite crazy – but then, when we met the fans, they were the nicest people in the world, really open and welcoming."

Dave Pybus, now bass player in Cradle Of Filth, recalls the UK dates that he played with his band, Dreambreed, who were supporting during April 1994 having only just released their debut record; by now Bruce was guesting on the Radio One rock show as a DJ, where he first spun Dreambreed's disc. Subsequently, as Pybus reports, matters took something of an unexpected turn.

"Bruce played it a few times on the show," he told me, "which was a great buzz for us. Then, totally out of the blue, I had just gotten up with a terrible hangover and was having breakfast when the phones goes and it's Bruce on the line! He asks me how things are and *would the band like to go on tour with them around the UK for a few gigs*. I was like, 'Erm ... sure, sounds cool to me.' I was in a bit of a daze. So he said, 'Great!' and told me his manager would give me a call later to arrange things. Rod Smallwood was from Huddersfield, which was like five miles from my town, Heckmondwike, so that went down well with him. It totally didn't sink in for a few hours. I mean, there I was eating cornflakes at my mum's at eleven in the morning, and Bruce had just called me to ask if we'd go on tour ... surreal. The word got round pretty quick 'cos our label was good at networking. We were all over the moon to even have one show, never mind a whole tour with Bruce!!! We were very excited."

"For the size of my band, the venues were bigger than we'd ever played or hoped to play on our first release," continues Pybus. "I mean, on average we were playing to five or six hundred a night. Most of the audiences were into what we were doing, very receptive and respectful that Bruce had asked us. It was great. We were three band and three crew sleeping in a Transit van with our gear. It was great, looking back. Some great memories, like a lads' camping trip but with lots of people to play to every night! [Bruce was] quiet, but fun. He'd pass by and tell a joke or two, ask how things were and if we needed anything we just had to ask his crew. All cool. But we never really saw much of him, as he'd fly to each show and the rest of the band would go their own way, train or whatever, so we'd see more of them."

Pybus got a chance to chat to Chris Dale and the others a little more than he did with Bruce, who was often engaged elsewhere. He recalls the tour with great fondness, no doubt because on more than one occasion his band hit such a chord at one particular gig that their free alcohol quotient was doubled. "Obviously going round the UK in a van has its moments," continues the bass player. "We were sleeping on the beach in Weston Super-Mare, and a police-woman knocks on the van door at 6am simply to warn us the tide was coming in! We used to drink Special Brew[155] back then just to get to sleep – so some memories are lost, as you can imagine. One of the best buzzes for the band was in London. The venue promoter thought we were so good he paid us double! And in Nottingham a local record label wanted to take us out but we asked for a crate of lager instead so we could get to sleep later. I sometimes reminisce with the guys about it even today." He remembers that there were often calls for tracks from Bruce's old band, which he was still firmly distancing himself from. "Obviously everyone was like, 'Shouldn't you be singing Maiden songs?' But I guess it's down to the person at the end of the day, if they want to follow something else, that's their business, right?"

And, so, by mid-1995, it was clear that this wasn't merely a Bruce Dickinson solo project any longer; no, this was a band, of which Bruce was merely one member alongside three compadres, and the band were to begin recording some new material of their own.

They even had a name: Skunkworks.

chapter eighteen:
Pivot Point

Although the band were as tight as you could possibly get, the fact remained that – certain B-sides aside – they were still by and large performing the *Balls...* material which, of course, had been written by Bruce and Roy Z. That was soon to be rectified, and in order to facilitate a contemporary sound as well as stretch the boundaries, Bruce brought in a rather surprising producer to the project.

That man's name is Jack Endino, whose stock during the mid-1990s was of the highest order, having been at the helm for albums by most of the major movers and players in the worldwide phenomenon of the grunge era, including Soundgarden (a favourite of Bruce), Mudhoney, and a huge number of the bands coming out of the incredibly influential Sub Pop label in Seattle, including the band who had blasted their way to the front of the new movement and were capturing the imagination of teenagers all over the world; a small outfit named Nirvana.

"I produced the first album of a Kilkenny band called Kerbdog," Endino explained to the author, "who were managed by Sanctuary. Bruce heard the album and liked it. The following year he just called me up, at my home in Seattle, out of the blue. He explained his whole solo situation, and how he wanted to make a modern-sounding hard rock record that didn't necessarily sound like what he'd done before. He seemed to know a lot about what I'd been up to in Seattle."

From the outset, Bruce was keen to get away from the concept that this was just the latest folly by the ex-singer in Iron Maiden; the obvious comparison being David Bowie and his Tin Machine project. Bruce, at this stage, was driven strongly by the part of him that was trying to cast off his baggage and be recognised merely for his work. The band would be named after something that Bruce was increasingly obsessed with: flying history.

"*Skunk Works* is the name of the design bureau of Lockheed Aviation company that make very secret and advanced aircraft," he explained. "Planes that can't be seen on radar, and the Blackbird, which is the world's fastest and highest flying aeroplane. They designed the U-2, America's first jet-fighter back at the end of the Second World War, the F-104 Starfighter, all kinds of really very revolutionary jetplanes. Skunk Works is their nickname, which became the semi-official title. We changed it from being two words to just one word."[156]

"Bruce was adamant that it was a *band*," Endino told me. "He told me he would have preferred to just call the band Skunkworks and not had his name on the album cover. He didn't treat it like a solo album. He went out of his way *not* to seem like he was calling all the shots, and to treat the other guys respectfully, but at the end of the day, you still knew he had the final say on things. So the power relationship was a little strange, and maybe a little bit artificial. The other guys knew they were working with a heavyweight who was almost twice their age, but Bruce really tried not to act like one too much. Maybe he should have. But they were good players and Bruce respected that. And I respected the fact that Bruce acted a *lot* less like a "rock star" than some Seattle people I've known!"

"We did about six weeks worth of pre-production in Fulham," recalls Alessandro Elena. "We used to rehearse upstairs from this old pub called the Kings Head. It was run by a bunch of Irish people from Belfast. Honest to God, it was like one giant room with two fireplaces and two gigantic windows. And Robert Plant and Jimmy Page were there rehearsing before we got in there! It was just like a gigantic room with a PA, you had to bring your own gear, but the vibe was amazing."

"We did a lot of pre-production there with Jack Endino and again, for me, it was amazing working with him man, the stuff I learned is priceless. And he is like one of the *mellowest* cats. He would come out for dinner, I'd cook for him and we'd sit down and listen to music. At the time, Alex Dickson was also living with me. We were both renting one of Bruce Dickinson's multi-pads in Chiswick. So it was me and Alex, drinking ourselves stupid at the time, it was so much fun. And you know Jack would come over and discuss songs and arrangements and stuff."

Chris Dale recalls how the tracks would come together. "Alex Dickson recorded a load of instrumental demos which he gave to the rest of us. Me and the two Alexes would jam them about a bit, while Bruce came up with vocal ideas. We went through maybe thirty songs like this and picked the best. He's good fun to work with. He works hard and plays hard. He has a good work ethic but once the work's done, it's time for a pint!" Quite right too. Music-wise, the producer had also been well-primed for the tracks. "It was pretty much what he had led me to expect," recalled Endino. "In fact, I think I agreed to do [the project] before I even heard anything. At their request, I was actually present much of the time while they were writing the songs."

"The only songs I had a hand in writing were 'Innerspace'," remembers Dale, "which was a riff me and Alex Dickson came up with together, and two of the B-sides: 'Americans' and the 'Italian Drummer' sketch. They were just silly songs I'd written for fun. I'd written a bunch of tunes like that. They weren't intended for Skunkworks, but Bruce heard them, laughed a lot and said we should try recording them. As I'd written the music and lyrics, I was kind of directing Bruce how to sing them – that was fun – here's me telling one of the best metal vocalists in the world how I think he should sing a song!" The tracks Dale wrote would end up resurfacing a little later ...

The recording sessions took part at Great Linford Manor, a studio in an impressive amount of grounds, and a very comfortable environment in which to work.

"It's in Milton Keynes," explains Elena. "It's like a castle from the 1600s. And that was an amazing learning experience, because we were all together. I mean, Bruce was hardly there, but us as a band and Jack were there every day. We would sleep there. And we would literally listen to music all day and dissect it and learn from it. It was incredible. We learned more during that process than anything I can think of. When you bond with a band like that and they all want to grow as musicians – man, that was amazing. And we were getting paid to learn, that's like the most amazing gift. So anything I did in the past during those days was like, 'This is my only chance to do this and learn as much as I can so I can have a career on my own' as a drummer and now as a producer. So it was brilliant."

"Cool old manor house," offers Endino. "Very big, though, with a tiny control room. Nice gear, and there was excellent cooking for us while we were there. Pete Winkleman, who ran the studio, was a funny guy. There was a canal nearby with a walking path that was obviously an old railroad bed or something. I walked it all the way from Milton Keynes to Newport-Pagnell a few times, quite a distance. Being able to exercise like that in the mornings was very good for my head. It was a pleasant environment, a lot like Rockfield [Studio, in south Wales]. Bruce seemed pretty sharp, open-minded and also a nice guy; in fact he's six months younger than me, so it turned out we had a lot in common as far as the 1970s records we grew up with. He has broad music taste. Recording in the UK is always a good time, there's some great studios. And I liked the idea of trying to make a 1990s hard rock record with Bruce. If I could work with Soundgarden and Nirvana, why not Bruce? Why the hell not? He was done with Maiden, he could do whatever he wanted, so I was intrigued. Working with great singers is a pleasure."

As for the Skunkworks band, Jack Endino loved the vibes coming back from the youthful musicians. "Musically, it was excellent," he continues. "There was a chemistry. But they were young so it was hard to get them to stay focused sometimes! Bruce and I are, of course, total workaholics. But those guys would break into Kiss tunes at every opportunity! The music and the whole creative process was pretty collaborative. Alex, Alessandro and Chris would come up with riffs, or demo them on a four-track. Bruce would pick the ones he liked, and we would all get together in a rehearsal room and just start throwing ideas around. The melodies and lyrics are all Bruce; the music was largely from the band, though with Bruce pushing in particular directions. I sat in the corner taking notes, noting the tempos they were playing at, making comments like, 'Why don't you try playing that part four times instead of eight?' or, 'What if we went back to that other riff after the solo section, and then into the verse?' I tried to be a catalyst and keep things moving along."

The sessions were also a good opportunity for Bruce to continue his full-paced lifestyle, and according to Elena, the singer was never still. He recalls a certain early morning with a lot of affection.

"I've got this image in my mind that I think I'll never forget. We were doing the record out in Milton Keynes in that old castle thing and in front of it we had this gigantic park, man, I mean it was so fucking beautiful. And I woke up early in the morning, [the rest of us] used to smoke a lot of everything at the time, as the band, and drink a lot. So I woke up at six in the morning, I think I was still drunk and stoned from the night before, [and] went for a piss. And as I was pissing, I looked out of the window [and] there was Bruce Dickinson dressed in his white fencing, you know, suit, whatever it's called, practicing in the park, man. Literally, it was kind of like, 'Am I hallucinating here?' The way he was moving and the discipline and just the technique I guess, that he's got was amazing, flawless, great man. And, you know, he tried teaching me a couple of times. But with him, he's so fucking crazy and he will stab you and it's really hard to stab people with those fencing things, but it hurts. I tried a couple of times and I was like, 'Dude, you know what? I need to practice by myself first before you can stab me fourteen times,' fucking *ridiculous*, man! Sometimes we would tour Europe and he would organise fencing events and so he wouldn't turn up for soundcheck because he was killing somebody somewhere else with his fucking sword, you know! But it was cool and I liked that about him, man, that he had all these crazy hobbies."

There was also the matter of refining the songs in the studio, and Endino made sure that the band would stretch themselves out as much as was possible. "There was one funny moment," he remembers. "After weeks of watching them painstakingly putting together all these heavy mid-tempo songs, I suddenly realized that what this band was lacking was, simply, plain old bashing rock and roll. There was not a trace of punk rock in this band. Or irony. Coming from such a bunch of wise guys and comedians, the songs were all so damn *serious* and earnest. In Seattle, I well knew, hard rock and metal and punk had kind of blurred together – that was how grunge came about. So one day I just got fed up, and I challenged them to write a fast song right on the spot with just *three* chords, NO MORE, and a guitar solo with almost no notes in it! It was like an exercise. *Could they do it?* That's how the B-Side 'God's Not Coming Back' came about – to my eternal delight, especially with Bruce's lyrics. They welcomed [my input into the arrangement of the tunes]. You see, it was a brand new band, and they were just starting to write together as a band, throwing ideas around. Arranging is one of my strong points; I tried to make sure the songs and riffs didn't get too clichéd or repetitive, and also, since I had thirty years of rock history in my head, it was easy for me to see if anything was unwittingly plagiarizing something earlier."

"So the Skunkworks songs all sound fairly original. It's pretty hard to be original in guitar-based hard rock these days, since so many have gone before us, but I think we did a good job of creating something with its own strong identity. I also kept pushing Bruce to try new things, both with his voice and his lyrics. 'There will be no dungeons and dragons on this record!' was our motto. Bruce has a very keen sense of humour about his past, and about heavy metal in general. We had many a good laugh. The concept of 'wheels and rainbows' became another running in-joke. Perhaps you had to be there!"

The material is strong throughout a record that stands and falls on its members; Bruce having brought the players together had created an unit of some force, but he was still suffering from the fact that he was such a recognisable character. Unfortunately, the record company refused to allow the album to be released without his name on the front, thus negating the point of the project somewhat.

"The idea was to have [a band] all the while, but we never really got the timing right to get things together," he mused. "So the first opportunity I got to do something sensible with a bunch of people, you know, we got *Skunkworks*. And it's *shitloads* better than anything else we've done. Loads better. It's really fresh, it's really new. It's nothing like the old stuff. From the next album, it's just going to be Skunkworks. There's just no point in persisting with this 'Bruce Dickinson' nonsense. So what you're seeing now is the last vestiges of it. Promoters somehow cling onto this thing. You know, Bruce Dickinson – ex-Iron Maiden – and people will turn up. People aren't turning up for the *real* Iron Maiden, never mind *ex*-Iron Maiden!"[157]

Which was a good point; since Maiden had signed up Blaze Bayley, formerly of Wolfsbane, to front the band, and with the groundswell toward the grunge generation, interest in that band – aside from their ever-rabid and extremely loyal fanbase – had declined, relatively. Unsurprisingly, perhaps, given that Maiden were in their twentieth year of consecutive activity. Bruce, meanwhile, had achieved his aim, at least according to his producer.

"We succeeded in what we set out to do," said Endino. "But it didn't really do much for his career, or for mine. People who know me but never heard it, imagine it must be a typical metal record, and wonder why I would do it. And some of Bruce's hardcore fans were upset that it didn't sound more like Maiden, though there were a smattering of people who totally *got it* and seemed kind of amazed. Other than that, I think I would have mixed the vocals a little louder!"

Endino recalls it being a little more difficult than other records had been to make, with perhaps a slight lack of true focus amidst the group as a whole.

And although the songs on the album rock along merrily, the process itself had become exhausting. Away from Bruce, those extended jam sessions between the Skunkworks band had produced a real hunger for the three younger players to form a funkier band, playing the dafter songs of Dale's, eventually under the moniker Sack Trick; although they were focused on the job in hand, it began to become clear that perhaps their destiny and Bruce's lay down different paths.

"I think Bruce might have gone even heavier, in a kind of Sabbath-y direction, if he could," muses the producer. "But the band wouldn't go there. With hindsight, it's easy to say now that Skunkworks was essentially Sack Trick impersonating a metal band! Their hearts did lay elsewhere, and about halfway through the project, I realized this; that was when I knew in my heart it would not be a long-term band for Bruce. It did not come about organically: the guys were picked, or hired, or invited by Bruce to 'become a band.' It was like a grand experiment; everyone participated willingly in it, and the results were good, although years later when talking to Bruce I compared it with trying to animate a sort of Frankenstein's monster, built from dissimilar parts. We agreed, however, that the monster did actually come alive and even sit up and look around a bit. But it was a pretty hard record to make. I had to apply relentless will power and total focus for almost four months. Even thinking about it now I feel tired. Records should not have to be forced into existence like that. But some of those songs are pretty good, regardless of how hard it was to make the record. 'Space Race', 'Strange Death', 'Meltdown', they're *killer*. I still *like* the record."[158]

Alessandro Elena, the baby of the band, agrees that although it was a great deal of fun – and he had learnt an enormous amount from the process – the future did not look great for Skunkworks as a band.

"The Skunkworks album is a pretty cool record. We, as a band at the time, were listening to Soundgarden, we were really into the Chilli Peppers and *majorly* into Jane's Addiction. And if you listen to the record now, you will find bits and pieces from those bands everywhere. Or if you check any of the live stuff, it was a crossover, literally, between the Chilli Peppers and Jane's Addiction." He feels, however, that Bruce could have taken things a little further even than the huge steps the singer had taken to destroy his past, and speculates as to whether there may have been pressure from other angles – still – to create 'hit singles'. Whatever the reality of it, things could not carry on for long in their present form.

The band, however, embarked again on tour during 1996, including a stint as special guests to Helloween, putting in the hard yards on the road backing up the release of *Skunkworks* in the time-honoured manner, the increasingly masterful pilot Bruce again flying his group from gig to gig. The album was released on February 26, 1996, and although it barely scraped the Top 40, the music magazines were much-enamoured of this new swerve in the increasingly winding path of Bruce Dickinson's career. *Metal Hammer* felt is was a "tour de force of modern metal", and *Kerrang!*'s legendary British Metal expert Malcolm Dome gave it four stars, opining that Bruce had successfully harnessed the skills learnt over the previous decade-and-a-half near the top of his profession, whilst also releasing an album with the vigour to appeal also to the grunge generation. Sadly, despite ripping it up on tour, the band's days were limited, and it was, seriously this time, down to that age-old concept/excuse of 'musical differences'.

"I think he wanted to challenge himself musically. Before he left Maiden he'd never rapped on a track, never done acoustic songs, I think he just wanted to try something new and see what happened with it," says Chris Dale. "He'd tried doing something different and I think really enjoyed it. But to be honest, the fans weren't enjoying it that much. It was kind of a love/hate thing. Some people loved it – some absolutely *hated* it. I remember one fan in Spain told me, "Bruce is a traitor to heavy metal," which made me laugh at the time – but these people take their metal very seriously and, well, they should. I think the *Skunkworks* era was like a holiday from metal for Bruce; at the end of the day, Bruce is a metal singer, he loves metal and that's what he's best suited to doing."

"I don't think any of us regret doing the *Skunkworks* album, but it was a one-off. I think of it in Kiss terms – I think of most things in Kiss terms – as being like *The Elder.* I'm glad Kiss made *The Elder* – but I'm glad they went back to *Creatures of the Night* afterwards. And if I could choose just one Kiss album to have played on, it would *The Elder*. So of all Bruce's albums, I'm proud to have played on his most different and the one that causes most controversy amongst fans. If you don't try something, you'll never know. Maybe we could have done it a bit more commercial, maybe we could have had a more metal single or video ... nah, we did what we wanted to do with no outside pressures to conform to standard and that's the best anyone can do. People say it was a commercial failure in that it sold less than Bruce's other albums, but Bruce's least selling album is still a lot more than many bands sell!"

Alex Elena feels that the experience was something that money could not buy, despite the group splitting after their 1996 tour. "That's how I started my career professionally, pretty much," he offers. "He opened the doors to me becoming a professional musician. Because if you don't do it professionally, you will never learn how to do it correctly, you know? You can be the best drummer in the world, but if you don't go on tour for three years straight and if you don't record in proper studios with proper producers, you'll never learn. You'll never know the gap between people that make it and people that don't make it. Like, 'Why didn't I make it?' Because it's obvious that *you weren't good enough*: that's always my answer. Obviously there is always bad luck that always plays its part with some musicians. But everyone you see out there doing stuff is [doing so] because they deserve it or because they're good at doing it. Whether you like it or not, they are good at doing something."

Bruce made his debut on the musical gameshow *Never Mind The Buzzcocks* on November 12, managing to deal with the innuendo of Richard Fairbrass of the band Right Said Fred as well as the aggressive sarcasm of host Mark Lamarr; and in an interview around the same time he was to explain how the band decided to call it a day. In mid 1996, there had been talk of a second Skunkworks album, but, "the direction that, particularly the guitarist was going in, was like east and I was going west. I wanted to do a much heavier album. I was quite prepared to call it *Skunkworks* and carry on with the idea – but the stuff that was coming through from them was really so far removed from hard rock music, so I was like, 'This is not gonna work.' Skunkworks was kind of a *Tin Machine* – [type] project, basically, and you commit yourself to that as long as you can and as soon as it became obvious that it wasn't working, you just have to abandon it and start again. I think we had a situation where I think the guys weren't as committed to the idea of Skunkworks as a band as I was, you know. Otherwise, when I suggested that we cancel the whole thing they would have gone that, 'Oh no, What a shame', you know, but everybody went, 'Oh, okay.' Just like that!"[159]

It was time to find out what Bruce Dickinson could do again: as 1997 dawned, despite the relative disappointment of Skunkworks' reception (and the pride in the achievement), two individuals were to return to the creative sphere of the Worksop chap. One, a relatively new collaborator – and one, a very old friend. Things were about to be flipped on their head once more.

chapter nineteen:
Rebirth ...

Whilst *Skunkworks* had been somewhat of a catharsis, a project that released the urge to pursue his craft in an entirely different direction, the response had been – at best – lukewarm. In truth, for Bruce to be able to shake off his fame and recede into the confines of an unknown band to begin an assault from ground level once more was unfeasible and unlikely; working with such a high-profile producer as Endino, in any case, was bound to attract attention. And although the LP remains an under-rated and excellent set of tracks, it had neither made a mark amongst the grunge generation or entirely satisfied those fans who had stuck with Bruce from the Maiden days. Sales were respectable, although anything would feel a failure when put up against the multi-million selling albums of the past. With the Skunkworks band, effectively, going off to do their own thing, Bruce was left once more pondering his place in the world of music. Was anyone really still interested in what he had to offer? Or was he to be unjustly written off as yesterday's man? The questions were maddening and circular; had anything really changed for him since he'd left the Maiden camp? Sure, he'd pursued his imagination and developed many projects outside music, but at root, music was still a passion. And in the aftermath of *Skunkworks*, where was there left to go?

"I was devastated by the *Skunkworks* thing," he said. "I was on the verge of saying, 'This business is so fucked, I just don't care anymore,' you know. *Skunkworks* was a record which I tore myself apart to make and nobody seemed to give a shit. I don't think anybody in the management really understood what was going on either, because otherwise we wouldn't have been touring with Helloween. They were totally the wrong band for Skunkworks to tour with."[160]

However, he also saw the inherent value in his expeditions into different sonic valleys, not least because it was like, "a bucket of cold water for a lot of people, 'cause it was like, 'What is he doing?'" In particular, Bruce remarked that he rather enjoyed the fact that [the album] was hated by the hardcore Maiden fans and those with the narrow-minded attitude that he should do only one particular style of music. "I took great pleasure in that," he continued. "They were feeling something other than this kind of numbness that you get when you get the same old shit day after day after day." Avoiding that restrictive routine was one of the things that motivated Bruce to leave Maiden in the first place and pursue his own path. Otherwise, he felt, the danger was that he would, "Sleepwalk through tour, album, tour and just keep on going and suddenly realise that I would be forty nine years old. Hey, pension in ten years time. Another tour, another album, another tour, another album, get the Grecian 2000 down, another tour ... I used to wake up getting night sweats about it going 'AARGHHH!! You might as well be dead.'"[161]

Admirable indeed; but a combination of record label problems once more meant that the LP was almost bound to be a lost cult classic as soon as it hit the streets. Bad luck? Bad timing? Or a combination of more factors? Regardless, as the vocalist approached his late thirties, a crossroads was presenting itself. Kicking these concepts around in his head, and wondering where to head next, Bruce's world was to change once more when he took a call from Roy Z, who was enthusing about some new riffs he had been playing with. What Roy played him suddenly made a huge amount of sense. It was, unashamedly, balls-out metal. And though Bruce had some initial reservations that it was re-treading old ground, the facts were that during 1997, metal was considered to be a spent force much in the same way, perhaps, in certain quarters the singer was being written off. In actual fact, the thought of doing a metal album again appealed both to Bruce's musical instincts as well as his well-developed sense of mischief. If metal was by now the last thing that people expected from him – after all of his well-publicised pronouncements that he was done with a certain genre, and after all of his avowed aims to explode preconceptions – if he was expected *not* to come up with a hard-driving, heavy metal set of songs, then perhaps that was *exactly what he should do.*

And, so, that's exactly what he planned to do. Going into sessions along with Roy Z, things started to click into place.

"So there I was, boom, in Los Angeles, on my own, it's kind of sunny and I thought, 'Let's see what happens.' So I went in and we came out with 'Accident Of Birth' and I was like, 'That sounds great.' And then it was like a big light went on in my head: 'I can do this, I know exactly what to do on this record, *exactly*. I don't know any of the songs yet but I know I can write them.' It was almost a huge relief that I was going to do something that I knew exactly what to do ... I just wanted to make an album that fucking rocked and I guess that makes me sort of some kind of weirdo because nobody's making an album like that."[162]

There was also a huge sense of fatalism about the project; a determination to see things through to their natural conclusion and *que sera, sera*. "Then I thought, 'If this fails this will be the last album I ever make,' and I thought, 'I don't give a shit. If this is gonna be the last album I ever do, I'm gonna do the best straight heavy metal album I ever made in my life.'"

And so Roy Z and Bruce sat down together and began to write a set of songs that took metal as their starting point and, melding the genre with the possibilities of the studio, ripped the paint off the walls. That was also achieved by virtue of the addition of another musician to the mix, a shock to many, but a well-received bit of news: Adrian Smith would be adding his guitar skill to the project. Smith had been relatively quiet since his own step back from Maiden almost a decade earlier, working on his own solo material and putting together a new act of his own – Psycho Motel – who by 1997 were on the verge of releasing their second album. The material was rooted in classic influences like Hendrix, melded with a more modern approach engendered by the group's other members, who brought a contemporary touch of Alice In Chains and Soundgarden to the mix. Psycho Motel was a lot of fun, and musically satisfying, but the temptation to work on a true metal LP was strong for Smith, and he agreed to put down some guitars to the Z/Dickinson material, and renew his long-standing and successful writing collaboration with Bruce. Needless to say, Smith was reasonably easily persuaded to stay on for the tour too.

"When we were in Maiden, we always talked about maybe doing a joint album outside of the band," said Smith. "So, I heard he was going to get in touch with me and he did. He got an idea for this next album and called me up, he'd already written some songs with Roy, I had a couple of ideas that I thought might suit and we wrote two or three songs and that was it."[163]

The album that became *Accident Of Birth* was bound to have Maiden-esque elements, not least due to the metallic approach and Smith's guitar contributions. However, it would be churlish to pigeon-hole the LP as such; Bruce's vocals are hugely controlled, as fluid as any Smith guitar line, and as gravelly as any heavy Z riff, but only when the material warrants it. His development as a singer during the solo years is perhaps often left unsaid, but having explored many different styles since leaving the Maiden camp, and with the passing of time, there's a richness of character in a timbral sense on *Accident Of Birth* that allows for even more expression. If *Shock Tactics* had been the album where, in the words of Tony Platt, Bruce stopped shouting and started singing, *Accident Of Birth* is where he added consummate, classical technique and maturity to his still-incredible vocal range. There is not a moment on the album where Bruce is not in control, despite some very demanding melody lines and interval jumps that would test lesser vocalists beyond their capabilities. It is, in many ways, the best set of vocal performances of his career.

Lyrically, also, *Accident Of Birth* is much more conceptual than the sometimes brutally-honest personal nature of its predecessors; there is passion here, but more often than not it's couched in allegory and imagery. Bruce always was a good storyteller, after all. Bruce, indeed, returned to the source material of an old friend, Mr Aleister Crowley, for the epic 'Man Of

Sorrows', which – in concept at least – was a track he'd been playing with for nearly five years; the lyrics outline neatly the quest for answers and alternatives that also was, in part, based on Crowley's childhood sketched out for a movie treatment entitled *The Chemical Wedding*, which Dickinson had also been toying with for a while. 'The Magician' also referred to Crowley, but *Accident Of Birth* is far from a concept album; the themes and tales, although sharing a certain aesthetic, are wide-ranging and each track stands on its own merits. The title track, indeed, is both self-aware in terms of its references to freedom and homecoming, as well as, "about a family from Hell. Except they're in Hell and one of them has accidentally been born, and they want him back and he doesn't want to go. For all the same reasons that you wouldn't want to go back to your family if they're a pain in the arse."[164]

Of the approach in general, Bruce's take was that he, "had a lot of fun writing the lyrics, because I just went back to the idea that this album was going to be about escapism, you know, in terms of story-writing and story telling." He said that although every song was bound to have an element of a personal theme behind it, it was more about the interesting stories he wanted to tell. "I had to construct quite an elaborate story-line and then maybe only tell half of it in the lyrics. I had to do that just for my own benefit to show that I could, you know, daydream properly. There's not a single thing on this record which is not rooted in imagination in some way, with the with the exception of maybe 'Man of Sorrows'. All the other songs were written in the space of five weeks."[165]

Notably, also, the cover art was provided by long-term Iron Maiden cover artist, Derek Riggs – who, similarly, had not worked with that group since the early 1990s. The cover was a Mister Punch-esque character jumping out malevolently from the belly of his parent, and again the themes of rebirth and mischief are writ strong therein. The character is even named Edison – no prizes for guessing the reference there.

On its release, on May 12, 1997, *Kerrang!* awarded it three stars, reviewer Liam Shiels remarking that it was something of a return to type for Dickinson, who was saying, "hello again to preposterously overwrought vocals, [and] great big hooligan riffs." The reviewer went on to note that it was an album that Maiden fans would snap up after being, "sent reeling by the dour, plodding *X Factor* blunder," an inevitable comparison given that this was the first Bruce LP that directly and unashamedly reveled in its metal, whilst *The X-Factor*, Iron Maiden's second stab at an album with latest singer, Blaze Bayley, sounded rough, tired and quite fundamentally hackneyed in the face of Bruce's slick sonic assault. Particularly praised were tracks including 'Darkside Of Aquarius' – which the reviewer felt echoed 'Revelations', and the Smith/Dickinson collaborations, 'Road To Hell' and 'Welcome To The Pit'. Dave Ling, meanwhile, writing in *Metal Hammer*, praised its "thrilling vibe" and awarded it four out of five. Referring to

Bruce's intent to play Maiden songs on tour, the legendary journalist ended with the words, "Bet Harry's worried!" As well he might have been, because the prevailing feeling was beginning to be that Blaze Bayley and Maiden were suffering from a certain lack of energy, and sales – whilst remaining healthy – were down across the board for metal acts.

After a quick week of acoustic and instore appearances to push the LP, Bruce's full band embarked on a tour that scooted round Europe before hitting America once more, beginning at the Mastetrax Festival in Madrid on August 5, and culminating with the group's concert at Springfield, no less, on October 4. Whether Otto and Bart were at the gig is unverified, of course. Of that American tour, Smith commented that it was real ground-level stuff, and that as the band, "moved across the states it seems that the audiences have been getting bigger. In the 1980s, with Maiden, you had video, MTV and all that kind of media stuff and loads and loads of rock stations. Now we're doing it the hard way, going across doing the clubs its getting around by word of mouth and it's kind of paying off."[166] And although the crowds were more like five hundred than fifty thousand, he felt refreshed and challenged by the experience, enjoying standing there, in the moment, soloing and watching Bruce work the crowd once more. By the time the group joined Lynyrd Skynyrd as special guests for their tour, they'd managed to build their profile to the extent that audiences were now touching around a thousand. Bruce himself was pleased with the reaction, citing the sense of excitement and anticipation there seemed to be for the album and the return to the metal roots. "I actually feel fairly confident that its going to continue," he predicted in October, "cause the band is so fantastic, and what we're doing and what we're going to do on the next record is going to be as good, if not better, than this record."[167]

The band continued to gig all the way through to November 22, 1997, after several dates in South America hooking up in Brazil, Chile and Argentina with the Monsters Of Rock Festival. There was no doubt about it; Bruce was back, and the addition of Smith to an already great band of Roy Z, Eddie Castillas and Dave Ingaharam made them a unit of some force.

So Bruce's reservations were unfounded; far from being the last album he would make, *Accident...* had returned fire to his belly, and received critical acclaim that had been previously (perhaps unfairly) absent from his solo work. "All the reviews came in," he mused, "and all of a sudden I was back up there on the Richter-scale and everything was cool and I sat back and thought, 'Wow, what do I do now.' I could do the same again but it would be fake."[168]

Given that Bruce had also found the time to duet with opera singer Monserrat Caballe on a recording of 'Bohemian Rhapsody', complete with a forty-eight piece choir, direct the video for 'Inertia' (his second as a director after the previous year's 'Back From The Edge'), as well as keep his hand in with radio work and television appearances, 1997 had been some year for the singer, but the following twelve months were to be *astonishing*.

It all started in February, when Bruce teamed up with DJs Tommy Vance and Krusher Joule to serve up rock on air throughout the month on Manchester's All Rock Radio; an increasingly confident Dickinson becoming more and more comfortable on air. It was well-known that Bruce was a talker, but often putting a microphone in front of someone in a radio context dries up their verbosity. Anyway, it was clear that a follow-up album to *Accident Of Birth* was not only advisable, but inevitable, and to that end Bruce, Adrian and Roy began to get their heads and riffs together for some more metal madness. This time, remarkably the results were to be even heftier than *Accident Of Birth*.

Bruce and Roy had been sketching out ideas for a while before the singer found himself, as is his wont, wandering to a second-hand bookshop to browse for some idea-pie to feed his hungry brain with lyrical and thematic ideas. And what he stumbled across meshed in perfectly with the idea of alchemy that he'd already been formulating from the original clutch of songs that had begun to shape up for the new album, which he'd already decided to entitle *The Chemical Wedding*.

"This thing caught my eye which was an encyclopedia in art history of alchemy, a big thick book with loads of great pictures in it, ranging from early pictures of alchemical engravings, right up to H.R. Giger and stuff like that. And what's linking them all together is that they all have an alchemical thread to them. And Blake features very heavily in this book, both his paintings and his poetry." Bruce had hit upon the central theme around which the whole concept could be hung; the English artist, philosopher and visionary was an outsider in his time, but author of some of the most remarkable social commentaries and esoteric literature of the period; Blake's world was an often preternatural one where the boundaries of internal and external consciousness were blurred, where demons and angels could co-exist with the physical plane, and heaven, hell, madness and love often meant the same thing. The theme of alchemy, of transformation of base materials into wonderful and magical substances and experiences, was as close to William Blake as it was to Aleister Crowley's seeking of darkness, of the poet Arthur Rimbaud's cross-sensory destructiveness, and had huge parallels with any esoteric medium that demanded sensory interaction; music, of course, being the ultra-powerful transporting force it is, made Blake a perfect inspiration for a set of tracks as uncompromising as they are intriguing. And, in one of those moments of circularity that occur in life, Blake had of course written the poem 'Jerusalem' – for many, England's unofficial national anthem, as well as a hymn that proud Englishman Bruce had sung many times in his Oundle days, and one he now revisited, in his fortieth year, for the basis of the track of the same name on the LP. One of Bruce's heroes –

and, by now, one of his mates, Arthur Brown – also appears on the LP, reciting sections of Blake's poetry, something that pleased Bruce immensely.

If it is, in one sense, a high-concept album, in another way it is one of the most immediate, straightforward and downright *brutal* records Dickinson was ever to put his name to. One reason for that – in addition to the very heavy riffing and often dark-magick themes – is a particular guitar set-up that the group perfected during the recording sessions in California. They called it the Molossian Guitar, after the huge, two hundred pound dog.

"We took the D string off a bass guitar," Bruce told *Terroriser*, "and put that as the E string on a normal guitar and started with that, tuning the other strings in proportion. This guitar was just a fucking monster!" Not least for Roy Z and Adrian Smith, who were charged with playing the beast. (For non-guitarists, the experience is something akin to playing a football match with one boot made out of lead ... bloody difficult but when you shoot for goal, ain't no goalie gonna get in the way.) The sound, ultimately was an enormous, bassy one, taking the concept of detuning guitars to the *n*th degree. In the same interview, Bruce expanded on his affinity with Blake, feeling that the parallels were many, particularly with Blake's single-mindedness and willingness to tear deep into his own soul to pull out the art that lay therein.

And the LP reflects that; the press went absolutely bonkers over it on its release. Ian Glasper of *Terroriser* rated it full marks, commenting that when it came to doling out the album to the journalists in that office, "almost all of us regular contributors, be us Hardcore hooligans or Metal maniacs, were scrambling to review it." He was much enamoured by the "vicious grit of the guitars" and the "heaving menace of the chorus" of the track, 'Trumpets Of Jericho'; the title track itself was "more typical Dickinson territory, with a soaring vocal hook carrying the chorus' mighty riff sailing up into the tempestuous skies, destined for the halls of Metal greatness with all the languid doomed majesty of the bottom-bound Titanic." He concluded by referring to Bruce as "the cheeky jester who pulled the rug from under the throne of the cursed Hype King."

Liam Sheils, of *Kerrang!*, found 'King In Crimson' and 'Killing Floor' akin to bulls charging around "in search of china shops, all bottom-end groove and duelling guitar dust-ups" before comparing those tracks to a "down-tuned Thin Lizzy." The reviewer referenced Dio-era Black Sabbath, and Led Zeppelin, in the album's more epic moments including 'Trumpets Of Jericho' and 'The Alchemist' before commenting that, although to make an LP like this was resolutely unfashionable, it supplied "enough piledrivers to send you reeling." It was given four Ks, a very good result indeed. Meanwhile, Dave Ling at good old *Metal Hammer* gave it eight out of ten, finding it a meaty and powerful offering from his old acquaintance, and one that saw Dickinson out to claim, "the unwanted middle-ground between the heaviosity (sic) of Fear Factory and Pantera and the more accessible end of progressive rock." Ling namechecked 'The Book Of Thel' with its precision, an indication that Bruce was on his way to claiming exactly that.

By all accounts, then, the album was a triumph; a masterful concept delivered exceptionally well via some exemplary performances of great songwriting and Roy Z's excellent production skills. *The Chemical Wedding* was also notable for being released on a new label – Air Raid, which was Bruce's freshest project. After many years of dealing with the excruciating politics of record labels, and being pressured by time and money to hit ridiculous deadlines and – if Keith Olsen is to be believed – create radio-friendly tracks, the vocalist had taken matters into his own hands and set up, with a little help from Sanctuary Management, his own independent label.

It was, mainly, a vehicle for Bruce's own work, being wary as he was of the financial and time pressures of signing unknown bands and trying to help them through to the next phase of their development, although he did express a wish to sign up those cheeky chaps, Sack Trick. The previous six years or so had certainly taught Bruce a great deal about the overheads inherent in marketing records and, of course, the lessons of the Samson days were still with the singer – when management and labels seemed to be falling by the wayside one by one, and everything that could have gone wrong went *horribly* wrong. So much so, in fact, that he planned to re-release the four Samson albums on Air Raid during the next year, partly to reappraise his past, and partially, perhaps, to try and generate some income for his former bandmates from any sales that might be forthcoming. The band were, in fact, still active, more or less.

"Over the years, Paul, Chris and Barry [Thunderstick] would occasionally get together," explains Rob Grain, tour manager of Samson and member of that band's inner circle. "They would book a rehearsal room for two or three days and just go in and play. It never transpired to a full-on reformation at first, but because 1998 was like twenty years of the NWOBHM, they thought they'd do a few more rehearsals in case anyone wanted to put on any shows to celebrate it."

"Suddenly out of the blue, Paul got a phonecall from Bruce, who said that basically he'd heard through the grapevine that the three of them had been rehearsing, and were they thinking of doing anything – or was it just for fun? But if they were gonna do anything he hoped that they would involve him. So everyone thought, 'Great, we can probably do something here. Have a bit of success and maybe at last earn some money, get the back catalogue sorted out.'"

Bruce, interviewed in October 1998, also said that there had been talk of some one-off concerts with his old band, and admitted that, "the phone-lines have been active [between he and Samson], and Thunderstick is back with the mask and Chris is back as well so the ingredients are all there but nothing is certain."

"Paul and I had been out to America," Thunderstick told me, "and done a couple of gigs out in the States which kinda prompted it. We said, 'Fuck this, let's go back to England and write some material.' And we wrote what I consider to be some great, mature, adult Samson material, it really was."

"And this is what we sent to Bruce. He said, 'Yeah, great, let's do this.' His solo career was doing really great, he had no need to come back to us but he just wanted to do it as an old pals thing and just another challenge for him."

"The comeback from it was, 'Yeah I'm interested [in a reunion]' and we had [a concert in] Japan in the offing, and it was all kind of the fact that, 'Bruce Dickinson on board, that'll be great!' But we ended up doing Japan as a three-piece, playing stuff from all those three Samson albums. Bruce was really interested and saying, 'I'm thinking we should get together and do this anniversary thing,' even though his solo stuff was successful at the time. Bruce felt that at best it would be a temporary reunion, however, saying that he had plans for a follow-up record to *The Chemical Wedding*, which would be recorded in 1999 but released in 2000.

More imminent, however, than all the talk of reunions with old bands, was the tour schedule for the latest LP, and the band set out on that familiar trek round the world to promote their stunningly-received latest release. Blackshine were the support act on the European leg of their tour, which weaved its way through Scandinavia during October 1998. But the tour did not get off to the most auspicious of starts, as Joakim Stabel, the Swedish band's guitarist recalls.

"The first venue we were supposed to play at was *way* too small," he laughed when I asked him about those days. "It was like a strip club or something, there was some major trouble there, and the stage was like big enough for the drum kit or something and we were definitely not going to play, if there was to be a concert at all. But somebody must've made a lot of phone calls to the right people because they fixed that we played in a bigger venue, more suitable for it. Which was really great, sold out as all the gigs were, great."

"Bruce and Adrian, we felt very shy meeting them because they were like these major people to us, as we are huge Maiden fans, we felt we weren't like worthy or something so they must've thought we were really strange! Actually they were the ones that started saying hello to us and everything, because we didn't want to get in the way and so on!"

The gigs were at venues holding anything between five hundred and a thousand people, which didn't faze Bruce and the band in the slightest. "I can tell you one thing, he gave 100% no matter, I don't think he cares if it's like a hundred people or ten people or ten fucking thousand people – he gives 100% anyway. It's really amazing to see that kind of professional at work."

"The audiences, yeah they liked us, but when Bruce and the guys came, it just went crazy every night. It was *amazing*. They played 'Powerslave' and I think 'Flight Of Icarus' as well and, let me see, '2 Minutes to Midnight.'" Although Roy Z was unable to tour due to other commitments, his place was taken by Richard 'The Guru' Carrette, the band's guitar technician. He'd had to learn the set in a very short space of time after Bruce had contracted a virus ten days before the tour started and was therefore too unwell to rehearse fully during this period, but The Guru nevertheless rose to the challenge, held up his end manfully, and played a blinder to boot. Elsewhere, Bruce and Roy ran through The Scorpions' track, 'The Zoo', for an *Extreme Wrestling* CD, and similarly 'Trumpets Of Jericho' appeared on the soundtrack to the movie, *Bride Of Chucky*, the album released on October 6.

1998 wound up, then, with Bruce and the boys ripping it up with the heaviest LP he'd created outside Iron Maiden. Inroads had also been made into reuniting with one of his previous bands, and the singer's stock was at its highest point creatively for many years. It wouldn't hurt at all were he to hook up with some old mates and play those classics one more time, now ...

... would it?

chapter twenty:
Reunion

1999 began, then, with Bruce's schedule starting to fill up; first he and Adrian's contribution to an Alice Cooper tribute LP was released in January (they played on a cover of 'Black Widow', alongside Bob Kulick, Tony Franklin, Tommy Aldridge and David Glen Eisley); there was to be a tour of Brazil in April with his solo band, with those gigs recorded for a planned live album; recording sessions would then take place; and a new Bruce Dickinson solo album would be added to the Air Raid release roster, which would also include repackagings of *Survivors, Head On, Shock Tactics* and *Live At Reading '81*, the live BBC set that had been originally put out by Repertoire in 1990; following a swift drinkette for the pesky Millennium, activities would then begin in earnest in 2000 with more of the same. The future looked bright.

Nothing ever goes to plan, though, does it? Whilst the calls continued from the Samson camp, things were taking rather an unexpected turn. Rob Grain remembers it well. "Bruce was in the States with his own band, and [mentioned that in] April 1999 there was a festival in New Jersey, a Heavy Metal festival. Paul took a call from Bruce, who said, 'Look, I'm compering this show, how about I get Samson on the show, we'll bill it that you'll do it as a three-piece, but actually on the night we'll do it as a four-piece.' And he asked if they had crew and all that, and it got to the point where Paul was phoning me to get a crew together to do it. They were rehearsing, they'd sorted the set out and Bruce was asking them to send him the set so he could learn the songs. It got to early 1999 and it all went quiet."

The reason why the trail had gone quiet? Since January, Bruce, Rod Smallwood and Steve Harris had been sitting down together discussing a reunion of another sort. Six years of solo work had taught Bruce a lot, but conversely, so had the Maiden camp. And, according to the authorised biography of Iron Maiden, all the resentment and suspicion that may have been gathering during Harris and Dickinson's years apart, simply fell away in what amounted to a summit meeting in Rod Smallwood's Brighton bolthole in early 1999. "We were both a bit nervous," said Bruce. "But as soon as we walked in the room we gave each other a big hug and it evaporated."[169] The pair chatted well into the night, revisiting old times, talking about possibilities for the future, sharing a pint or three, and eventually resolving any problems that might have existed between them.

And so came the announcement that shocked the world of music. After years of denials from both sides, years of fending off journalists fishing for any hint of a reconciliation, the impossible suddenly became the reality.

In March, 1999, it was announced that Bruce Dickinson was to rejoin Iron Maiden full-time. Tony Newton is well placed to give his view on the situation, having played footy with Steve Harris for many years before Harry found out his tough-tackling teammate was also a musician; subsequently Newton's lot – Dirty Deeds – toured with Bruce – on the *Accident Of Birth* tour, and also Blaze-era Iron Maiden.

"The great thing with Maiden," says the Londoner, "is that everything's behind closed doors; if they've got problems or whatever, you never seem to know about it. They somehow really keep it in house."

Newton also feels that the time was absolutely right for the heavyweights to come together once more, having laid some ghosts to rest. "Bruce probably got [his keenness to experiment] out of his system," he continues. "He'd probably be the first to admit it didn't all work out how he probably would've hoped but the bottom line is he's got it out of his system, and I'm sure they all missed playing in the big places." Fair comment; Maiden's huge crowds in the 1980s simply dwarfed playing in front of five hundred in a strip club in Scandinavia, an utterly different beast no matter how you looked at it. And though the reunion seems to make perfect sense in retrospect, at the time it was a jolt to most.

"To be honest with you," confirms Newton, "I never saw it coming, I *never* expected Bruce and Steve to get back together, it shocked even me. I remember Steve telling me when we went to play tennis one day, that Bruce is coming back, but part of it is that Adrian's coming back as well, and I said, 'Is Janick gonna go then?' And he said, 'No way, no!' And in actual fact Jan, when he heard, he phoned Steve up and said, 'Look, I'll step down, Steve.' And Steve wasn't having none of it, he said, 'No, you ain't going nowhere, I want us all in there.' But that's what they're like, they're very loyal, what with the management and a lot of the crew have been around, from almost day one, you know, It's like family, the whole thing – and that's why it's remained so strong. It really done 'em a favour, being apart, it really did."

"Bruce's solo material is stuff he would never have been able to do in Maiden, you know. Steve's off the wall sometimes on arrangements and this and that, but he's also very focused ... on certain other things that he'd never have happening in the band. Like, he'd never de-tune and play a song that wasn't in concert pitch, you know what I mean, he'd *never* do that, I know him. Like, just coz everyone else is going drop-tuning he wouldn't go down that road. Bruce obviously has experimented with all that stuff and whether he's got it out of his system or not, I dunno, I'm sure he'll do [another solo album]."

"It was the best move they could make," says producer Chris Tsangarides. "I was surprised that they'd got what they had got. It didn't surprise me that they went back because that's what the fans wanted. Maiden sales went down and all the rest of it, so they needed to get the band back – and I thought it was great that they got Adrian as well, and kept Janick and them all in the band."

NWOBHM guru, the author John Tucker, agrees with Tsangarides' overview of what happened. "I guess they needed each other," he says. "Yes, Bruce was writing good songs and making a living but never gonna be bigger than that. And like a lot of these bands, people wanted to see them back together. I could never understand why people would flock to see Thin Lizzy but not Phil Lynott's Grandslam. The same songs, by the same guy – but played with a different band. He had his die hard fans but a lot of people just wanted to see Bruce Dickinson fronting Iron Maiden. And their popularity had gone down; Blaze is not [the same] frontman and they'd gone to playing Odeon-sized venues, two and a half thousand. It's quite respectable but you're back doing one day in each, like you were in 1983. And now look at it: Earls Court, NEC, Download. I can appreciate why, in their forties, they wouldn't want to go back to thirty four-date treks of the UK. In the early 1980s, the Gillan and Iron Maiden tours stretched on forever; there must come a point when you think, 'Let's do a couple of really big gigs and go for it.'"

"I don't blame Steve for it, he knows what he wants," says Thunderstick. "He's made millions from it and he's got a world-class band there who have the back-up behind them. They really have – great. You wouldn't have thought a band like that would have held that longevity and been able to achieve what they've achieved."

However, Samson's long-discussed reunion was one of the first things to fall by the wayside in the Maiden melée, as Rob Grain puts it, "Suddenly you picked up the papers and it was 'Bruce rejoins Iron Maiden'." Never say never again.

Bruce, however, was still thinking of his Air Raid Records project, rolling out plans to release a compilation of his solo material, and rarities left in the vaults (the planned album being called *Catacombs* and due for release in 2000), as well as re-release the *Metal For Muthas* compilations. He had not forgotten his Samson compadres, either, and pressed ahead with plans to re-release those four albums. "There's still quite a bit of money ending up to get paid off," Henrik Johannson was told, "because we invested quite heavily in the records to buy them off of the record-company which was going bankrupt."[170]

Rob Grain, speaking in 2007, was philosophical about things, telling me that, "the Air Raid releases didn't sound very good. They weren't mastered very well and there were mistakes on the covers, they spelt the name wrong on one of them, [down the spine of *Survivors* the band's name was mis-spelt as] 'Samsom' (sic) Paul later got in touch and said to Sanctuary, 'If you're going to do them, let's at least do them properly.' So he then had a bit of input when [Sanctuary] reissued them properly in 2001, Paul supplied the pictures and stuff, and licensed some additional tracks, but that was basically because at the time there was a Samson reformation going on and it all helped."

Rob Grain, the tour manager and close friend of Paul Samson feels that there has been a misunderstanding, or missed communication over the years, that has led to some perhaps unnecessary bad feeling between old friends. "Having spoken to Bruce recently," he now says. "I think that he probably thought that he was helping his old mates out by releasing the Air Raid things, and is probably unaware that nobody was getting paid from them [as they are still unrecouped]."

Thunderstick still feels let down, sadly, and opines that press interviews over the years have concentrated more on the extra fuel that the band would indulge in, rather than the music that Samson produced. "I get people on MySpace telling me they have these albums and they're from the most bizarre places!"

Nicky Moore subsequently rejoined Samson for a series of dates, bringing the reunion to some kind of conclusion, at least, but tragically Paul Samson was to lose a battle with cancer, and he passed away on August 9, 2002.

April 1999 saw the very final dates of *The Chemical Wedding* tour, which was now to be the final set of solo dates for the foreseeable future. The gigs were held in Brazil – home to some of Maiden and Bruce's most fervent fans – and in the immediate aftermath of the shock announcement of his and Adrian's return to the Maiden fold, the concerts were hugely-well received by around seven thousand each night. The live album, *Scream For Me Brazil*, is simply Bruce at his bombastic, metallic, solo best, running through the heavier moments of the latter two albums – no 'Fog On The Tyne' nonsense to be found here – or even 'Tattooed Millionaire' for that matter. It is a wonderful, gnarly, full-on fire-bastard metal performance, and an absolutely excellent live album by anyone's standards. *All Music Guide* agreed, thinking it a release full of, "consistent, inspired performances", on its November 2 release. By that time, of course, Bruce was full-on into pre-production for the first Iron Maiden album with which he'd been involved for almost eight years. Maiden had been bedding themselves in with – by their standards – a short tour between July and October 1999, playing a set of classics to coincide with the release of their new compilation, *Ed Hunter*, which also featured a computer game based on the antics of their mascot. Bruce flew the band from gig to gig, although there was a rather scary moment when one of their engines apparently packed up on them over Greenland (it was later found to be a loose wire causing a false alarm). It wouldn't have done reluctant flyer Steve Harris a lot of good nerves-wise, although his singer's calm mastery of the aircraft was beginning to change 'arry's mind as to the pleasures of air travel. In general, the tour served both to reintroduce Bruce and Adrian to the fold, as well as whip up anticipation for the forthcoming original material as the new Millennium beckoned.

chapter twenty one:
After The Tempest

Returning to the fold meant largely returning to the set-up of old: rehearse, write and release an album, and subsequently tour the hell out of it, have a break, and do the whole thing over again. The contrast, however, to the early 1990s, was that Bruce's multitude of other interests and activities were as important to him as was the musical aspect; it was now a matter of time management rather than prioritising one over the other, which – along with his perceived view of a slip in recording and even quality control standards – had been instrumental in his leaving Maiden in the first place.

Brave New World, then, was one of the most eagerly-anticipated albums of all-time, as far as metal was concerned. The questions were hanging in the air all over the place: would Steve and Bruce get on musically and personally? How could the group accomodate three lead guitarists? And, most of all, what would the album be like, sonically? The last question was answered in no uncertain terms: it would sound, simply, like classic Iron Maiden, at their storytelling, imaginative, and occasionally very dark, best. *Brave New World* is more *Seventh Son...* than *Beast*, of course, with the six-piece band allowing themselves to stretch out on some tracks that refine and expand the Maiden blueprint to a very contemporary level, with the returning singer putting in a sterling and confident performance on top. Less heavy than Bruce's latter two solo efforts, the LP nonetheless faces down the weight of the band's own past and looks to the future with assurance.

Bruce's writing on the album is classic Maiden; his album opener, 'The Wicker Man' (not to be confused with a song of the same title he'd written a number of years earlier) stomps in with an insistent guitar riff and Steve's busy bass before exploding into the melodic choruses that uplift and soar with an essence of a new rise. Appropriately so – this collaboration with Smith and Harris locks in as if the three had never been apart. It was released as a single on May 8, 2000 and reached Number 9. The second track on the LP is a collaboration between Bruce, Steve and Janick (who was at the time sharing a house with Bruce and his clan); the expansive 'Ghost Of The Navigator' which peals on for almost seven minutes as Bruce indulges himself in a tale that takes in a sea journey as a metaphor for life, fears, aspirations and the fundamental wonder as to what might happen when the journey is completed. Fairly involved stuff, of course, but hey – there's a great ol' solo in the middle to help speed things along.

The title track, written by Bruce, Steve and Dave Murray, is a prog-tinged effort that recalls the themes of Aldous Huxley's book of the same name, which speculated on a dystopian future, whilst taking an image of a dying swan as its central tenet to hang round a rather relentlessly dark and broody number that essentially is the flip side of the previous track. Bruce's final writing credit on the album is the second single to be taken from the LP, 'Out Of The Dying Planet', released on October 23 and reaching Number 20 in the charts. Again, it clocks in at over six minutes, the theme this time being based on the film, *Forbidden Planet*, the 1956 B-movie ... which was based loosely on Shakespeare's Play, *The Tempest* ... from which Huxley had extrapolated the title of the book ... which became the Maiden album ...! Maybe. Or perhaps it is just about, as Bruce remarked, "a bunch of aliens who have destroyed their planet and now ... they're coming to get us." It is a fun, gallopy Maiden track that pulls and pushes itself through typically complex changes of tempo and rhythm, retaining a live feel that, more than anything else on the album, sounds like a band *enjoying themselves*. If there were any further clues needed as to the fact that the air had been cleared, Harris' album closer 'The Thin Line Between Love And Hate', with its lyrics of respect for the right of each man to take their own road in life, is so strong you'll trip over it if you're not careful.

Dean Karr directed the evocative video for 'The Wicker Man', telling the author that he had admired the original 1973 film, featuring Christopher Lee and Britt Ekland (we all admired her contributions to it, in truth). He said that inspiration, allied to Maiden's first single back together, gave him the opportunity to put something amazing together. "I put my own twist on the film," he said, "working closely with Bruce more than anyone else. We hung out all week prior to the shoot, looking at wardrobe and having tea. In the end, we [made] the film current, featuring my green 1970 Dodge Challenger, which Eddie claims in the end of the video, and a bevy of beautiful women, who flank the actual Wicker Man – which was the biggest thing I've ever constructed in my career!"

The only problem, explained the acclaimed director, was the weather, which was so heavy it cost half the day. "It rained so hard in Los Angeles," he laughs, "that when the band jumped out of their motor home, they sunk in mud up to their knees." That same bad weather meant that Karr – a perfectionist – still feels he and Maiden missed some important shots, "but I just can't fight Mother Nature!"

"I had wanted to do the aisle-way of Pyro balloons gag for years," he continues. "And I thought of no better band to do it with than Iron Maiden. I had each of those giant weather balloons – inspired by the TV show, *The Prisoner,* electronically connected to live detonators, to blow once the man ran past it – it's a miracle they all went off in perfect sequence!" He commented that everyone got along "famously" and that he was personally extremely pleased to see Adrian back in the band "where he belongs", as well as the return of Bruce.

The *Brave New Tour* began in earnest on June 6, 2000 – on the back of the album hitting the UK charts, reaching Number 7 after its release on May 29, 2000. As ever with Maiden, it was humungous in ambition, and although this time around there were more rest days built in, the touring behemoth nevertheless kept raging until January 19, 2001, at Rio – a concert which was recorded by cameras and a huge sound rig. It was part of the *Rock In Rio* festival and the crowd of 250,000 was treated to a set full of old and new classics. It was subsequently released as a live album and DVD. "It sounds really, really strong," said Bruce. "It was the last show of the *Brave New World* tour, it was in front of a quarter of a million people, it was broadcast live on TV to over 100 million people ... it was a great place to do a live DVD and CD! So, that is why we decided to do the recording in Rio, and since it was only one show, we knew we had to do it right so there was a lot of pressure on stage, knowing we've only got one shot at this."[171]

Dean Karr recalls the huge logistical pressures that were involved in facilitating the project successfully, recalling that he and his crew had travelled with Maiden's crew through Mexico City, Argentina, Chile and Brazil for what he terms 'The Big One'. "We edited footage from the other countries into the Rio gig," he explains. "Those other locations were covered with four or five cameras each night, whilst Rio was covered with eighteen."

"In Chile we fastened the cameras onto the tips of the guitars and locked onto Bruce's shoulders to create that cool, lockdown effect. It bummed out the crowd but it was necessary to create something fresh for this DVD." Fresher than the band's clothes, at least; for continuity they were required to wear the same wardrobe.

"My favourite memory," concludes the talented photographer and movie maker, "was rolling in above the crowd in a helicopter, feeling the excitement below. There were multiple choppers and I had Steve Harris, Bruce Dickinson and Jimmy Page in mine – pretty cool stuff. I had goosebumps bigger than Lemmy's warts!" There was another very memorable moment, Karr recalls, although it was more than a little unsavoury. "I saw a partially decomposed 'skull' roll up to my foot whilst I was on the stairs below Dave Murray, filming," he laughs. "I reached down and picked up the skull – which had been thrown onstage by a fan. I was sure it was fake – until I stuck my finger into the spine hole in the back and held it up to Bruce, suggesting he took it from me and sang like *Hamlet*." Alas, poor Janick, I knew him, Horatio ...

"While the once-occupied head of someone's was next to my face, I noticed a horrible reek coming from within the inner cavity and quickly threw the head onstage, cleaning my stinky finger off as good as I possibly could! I have worked in graveyards for many years and I never had an experience that gross! Later in the DVD, when the band is winding down, you can see Janick and Dave hold the skull – and quickly get rid of it! It had some crazy voodoo painting on it, and leather strings tied to the cheekbones."

"Obviously some maniac fan had dug it up to make an offering to his favourite band – and, hey, it made the DVD – I would have given the dead man credit if I'd known his name!" Some people would do anything to get on TV.[172]

For Bruce, 2001 was also a year where his involvement ended in a rather daft film that was all about 18th century zombies, postponed from a 1999 project that was supposed to have been brought to fruition by a Swedish company, and due to star Dean Cain. After original filming sessions – in the beautiful city of Prague – were postponed that year, the project, as often happens, had fallen down the list of priorities and was subsequently canned. He had, however, found a spare day to fly down to Holland to lend his vocals to Dutch curio Ayreon's project *Universal Migrator 2: Flight Of The Migrator*, Bruce singing on the title track. The artist was ecstatic to finally get Bruce on to the album. "I was a fan already of Samson, Dickinson's pre-Maiden band," he gushed. "Production is very bare, but the vocals, at that time by someone unknown, mysteriously called 'Bruce, Bruce' are very strong. So you understand, that when he agreed upon participating, I was shouting and jumping in the room. But then distress started. How to get this man into my studio? This has cost me ten thousand phone-calls and in the meantime he traveled all over the world. When I reached him in Paris, where they were recording the new Iron Maiden album, he said, 'Call me in two weeks'. But after five times of, 'Call me in two weeks', I thought, 'Forget it', and I recorded two alternative versions with Damian Wilson and Lana Lane. So the last time he called, saying, 'In two weeks', I said: 'No, it's now or never, no more delays'. And he replied, 'Okay, I'll come over next Sunday.'"

When he arrived at the airport, he carried his home with him in a bag, 'cause he has to live abroad for tax reasons for a year. In the car I played him this song and he really got into it. So, he went directly into the studio, recording three takes. And that was so difficult, because I'm not gonna say, 'That's awful'. I was already impressed when he opened his mouth. But it really was incredible, superb. That night we spent here in the attic, listening to each others' demos and he was really relaxed. And the next morning we had a nice breakfast together and I brought him back to the airport again. A great experience and a wonderful performance."[173]

Air Raid Records, by mid-2001, had run its course, and Bruce accepted an offer from Sanctuary to buy his half of the project; running a label truly is a full-time job if it is to be done successfully, and time was at a premium for the Worksop singer, as he prepared to release his own *Best Of Bruce*

Dickinson, a two-CD retrospective of the best of the solo years, with an added cornucopia of out-takes and extra tracks which were originally intended to be part of the *Catacombs* album. That LP was an idea that did not find much favour with his manager, Rod Smallwood, however.

"He didn't like the word, 'Catacombs,'" laughed Bruce, "And I said, 'What's wrong with Catacombs?' I could not understand. But if it said, 'From The Vault?' then he'd say, 'Yeah, it's great!' and I thought, 'What's the difference?!'

As it turned out, the second CD is a set of acoustic tracks, alternative versions of classics (including the original recording of 'Bring Your Daughter ...') and some surprising material, including a ten-minute audio explanation and overview of all the songs included on the release. It is a splendid insight into the development of the artist not least the inclusion of 'Dracula' which was, of course, the first track Bruce had ever put down to tape. Disc One itself launches manfully through the solo years, and although there will always be some debate amongst fans as to which tracks are and are not included herein, the subsequent 2005 Sanctuary reissues of his solo albums all included enough extra tracks and out-takes to satisfy even the most geeky completist. With Roy Z busy producing Judas Priest's Rob Halford's own solo material, and with plans to begin work on a new Maiden LP during 2002, Bruce commented that he was unlikely to be looking to work on any new solo material for quite some time.

Still bubbling under in 2001 was the idea for the film based on Aleister Crowley's life, *The Chemical Wedding*. Things had moved on by this time to the extent that the script was in the hands of Messiah Pictures, the company owned by Monty Python's Terry Jones, who were seeking funding for a number of projects, of which Bruce's movie was one. By August, 2001, Bruce was able to merely say that, "it's still sitting there with Terry Jones and Messiah Pictures. They're eating their fingernails to the bone for the moment trying to make their cowboy movie, a movie called *Das Cowboy* and they're right on the edge of making this thing. The only two scripts they have is *Das Cowboy* and *The Chemical Wedding* and if they get *Das Cowboy* made *The Chemical Wedding* is the next one." At the time of writing, this remains the case.

Other projects that year included co-writing the track, 'We Are One' for an album by rock band Warrior, having bumbled into a studio session that band were undertaking, whilst visiting Roy Z at his studio. Bruce had some spare lyrics that he thought would fit the track the group were laying down; Warrior decided they fit neatly and so a collaboration was born. Easy as that! Another collaboration that was much-mooted was a three-way vocalist shindig along with Rob Halford and Queensryche's Geoff Tate; after Bruce had joined Halford onstage the previous year to duet on 'The One You Love To Hate', which subsequently appeared on Halford's solo album, *Resurrection*. The original plan was to take the blueprint of the famous Carreres, Domingo and Pavarotti collaboration, *The Three Tenors*, albeit renamed *The Three Tremors* – a name soon changed to *The Unholy Trinity* and then simply, *Trinity*. Although the project was an intriguing one for all concerned, sadly the respective schedules of the protagonists meant that it quickly became a non-starter; Bruce and Roy had even written three songs before realising that with the talent involved, it was hardly the case of merely swapping the lead vocal lines around, chorus by chorus.

"That would be a crap way to do it. But it's a bloody difficult thing to do, to try to make a song with three different voices to get the full benefit out of it. And it takes longer than three weeks, and we didn't have longer than that to do it, so I canned it in the end. It's a great idea, everybody loves the idea; we had marketing people salivating about the idea of the Trinity project." [174] No doubt they were; it's a fine idea should it ever surface.

On November 5, 2001, Bruce jetted over to Stockholm to pick up an award voted by the listeners of radio station *Rockklassiker 106.7* naming him 'Greatest Heavy Metal Singer Of All-Time'. All rather nice, and another one to add to the growing collection as another decade kicked into action with all going peachy for Bruce and all associated with Iron Maiden.

chapter twenty two:
2002

It was whilst bringing together Maiden members past and present to offer their thoughts for the retrospective historical DVD *Iron Maiden – The Early Years* that the band found out that, tragically, ex-drummer Clive Burr, joker and occasional freelance hellraiser for the band in the early 1980s, had been diagnosed with the muscle-wasting disease, multiple sclerosis. And although 2002 had been designated a year off for the group following *Rock In Rio*, they immediately set up the Clive Burr MS Trust Fund to help their mate and his family as much as possible. The band not only performed at three sell-out concerts at Brixton Academy – March 19-21, 2002 – but also auctioned off memorabilia and re-released 'Run To The Hills' with two previously-unreleased live tracks; *Clive Aid*, as it has become known, had not only raised money, but also awareness for the debilitating illness, for which there is no known cure.

* * *

Bruce himself continued his activities outside Maiden by snagging himself a regular DJ spot on the BBC's new flagship digital radio station, 6Music. The station was launched on March 11, 2002, with Bruce presenting – of course – the weekly rock show, which he has continued to enjoy – touring permitting, of course, up until the time of writing. The radio station's site describes Bruce as "the face of British heavy metal ... truly a member of the international metal élite." In the short Q&A on there, Bruce reckons he wishes that he'd written the song 'My Way', made famous by Frank Sinatra, and infamous by Sid Vicious. Sadly some Anka got there first, but you can't have everything.[175]

2002 saw a raft of Maiden reissues and repackages, but an intriguing use of a track by the band was when '2 Minutes To Midnight' was selected as part of the soundtrack for the Playstation game, *Grand Theft Auto: Vice City*, as part of the 'virtual radio station' V-Rock, in the company of the likes of Quiet Riot, Twisted Sister, Loverboy and Ozzy Ozbourne. *Grand Theft Auto*'s plot is based largely round helping old ladies cross the road, being respectful to your elders and betters, eating your greens and never letting a curseword pass your lips, and you win the game by getting to the church on time of a Sunday morning. Possibly.

Maiden's relative inactivity during 2002 enabled Bruce – itchy feet as ever – to set about arranging a return visit to Europe, this time with a solo band, which was mostly those crazy Sack Trick boys, although the drummer this time was to be Robin Guy, who had ended up sharing a house with Chris Dale, and joining Sack Trick, through a series of coincidences and various entertaining events too numerous to recount here, but do ask him if you see him.

"We did a gig at the Kingston Peel," recalls Robin. "Bruce came down with Janick, we rocked out and did our thing and then at the end of the show, I'm packing down my drums in various states of undress and all that jazz, and Chris comes up to me, he'd be talking to Bruce in the corner or whatever, and says 'Just to let you know, Bruce wants to do some European festival headlines, and he wants you to play drums [for him]' and I was like, 'Fuck off mate, that's not even funny, don't joke with me' you know, 'cause that's a matter of the *heart*, Maiden changed my life when I was thirteen, you know, when this one big band basically changes your life, whether it's The Beatles, or Michael Jackson or whatever – and mine was Iron Maiden, the *Killers* record in France on a French [school] exchange. So for me, I literally took it as a joke, but Chris looked me in the eye and said, 'No, no, Rob, I'm serious' and at that point my jaw hit the floor and I went 'You fuckin' what mate?' and he goes, 'Yeah, you know he wants me to play bass, you to play drums and he wants Alex Dickson to play guitar, and we'll find another guitarist' which [eventually was], a good friend who'd also played in Sack Trick, Pete Friesen, who was the Almighty guitarist and also Alice Cooper guitarist. Because Chris and me were in the same house it was fairly easy, Chris would be like, 'I've spoken to Bruce, we might be doing 'Children of the Damned', and I'd run off and check it all out and a coupla days later he'd say, 'Bruce has changed his mind, he wants to do 'Flight of Icarus' … 'No, he wants to do … whatever,' and it was just brilliant. It was great: I knew all the Maiden songs anyway, but when you actually have to really knuckle down and learn them, there are some really specific little bits and obviously with Nicko's drumming there are pushes going on every second, so I really had to lock myself in and work out what he's doing on the bass drum. I'd sit in my car actually with really rubbish stereo speakers, absolutely like cardboard pieces of crap, the kind of ones that are moulded in the dashboard already. Really, really shit, but it was fantastic coz every time the kick drum went, they'd go bbuphhurphhhp, so I'd turn it up really loud, and I'd just get Nicko's kick pattern coming through. Especially on 'Live After Death.'"

It was to prove a surreal experience for Robin, however, although an experience he wouldn't swap for the world. "I was talking to someone about seeing Maiden at Donington on the *Seventh Son Of A Seventh Son* tour and it was like Donington's biggest attendance when Maiden headlined. You know, we're all very proud of that as Maiden fans, and just thinking, what if I went back and tapped myself on the shoulder, and went 'It's alright kid, see that singer up there, you'll be playing 'The Prisoner' to forty thousand people.' That's just too huge to comprehend, and when you do it it's just amazing but you can never really comprehend it, you just get on and do it, and it becomes quite normal."

"Which sounds a very strange statement to say, but I remember checking myself, actually *checking* myself, as I was onstage for Sweden Rocks, [on June 8, 2002, which was] the first gig, thinking, 'Well, how am I feeling?' trying to do the old out of body conversation with myself. I remember drumming away, and going 'There are fifteen thousand Swedes out there, we're headlining, and Motorhead, my other favourite band, were on before us!' and no one really follows Motorhead do they?"

"And I was just drumming away going, 'Yeah, this is very normal really.' And you can't explain that, 'cause it sounds like a throw-away thing, or belittling it, but it's, well, you ask an astronaut how their job is, and they say, 'Oh it's alright'. Cause everybody just does what they do."

Aside from the *Chemical Wedding* tour, Robin and Bruce had actually met a few years before, in the drummer's home village of Chiddingly. "I was sixteen or seventeen, in my little local pub down in a tiny, tiny village," Guy laughs. "It was about a week before they played Donington, and I remember being fairly drunk coming back from the toilet and my mate was pointing at this bloke with long hair, and my initial thoughts were, 'Who's this short-arsed hippy in my way?' And I looked at my mate, and his face looks like he's just seen *The Ring* or whatever, you know he's like freaking out pointing, mouthing something and I'm like looking at him, and I go round the back of this bloke with long hair and my jaw hit the floor as well, 'cause it was Bruce Dickinson, and you don't expect to see Bruce in your pub."

"It turns out, about ten miles away, he's got a fencing buddy and he was having a few drinks down there. And, of course, I was just like, in my drunken voice, 'B-Bruce! Bruce!' And he was a consummate pro, totally cool, and had a little chat, and he obviously didn't want to draw in massive attention which I was sort of flailing around spilling beer at him, but you know, he signed a little tiny scrap of paper for me, which I dare say I've still got. He said to me, which is hilarious, 'I bet you're thinking, why isn't he taller than that?' And it was exactly true, 'cause I was! All sort of big rock stars seem to be tiny."

"So when we were rehearsing for these festival headlines I mentioned all this to Bruce, I said, 'What, don't you remember meeting me Bruce?' you know, the first time you met me. And we had a good old giggle about that. It was quite funny."

"Doing those festival dates was just a phenomenal experience. But also it did all roll into place. I'm surrounded by my best mates, we're playing rocking metal, having a whale of a time doing it. It's all fairly simple. Chris would just be like, jump on this plane, you know, we all travel Ryan Air, and got there and set up the show, and all my drums would arrive from Pearl and I'd unpack them, and an hour before show time Bruce would jump out of his plane and go, 'Alright chaps, everything alright?' and we'd be like, 'Yeah, it's brilliant Bruce!'"

Bruce had also reached the limit of the size of aeroplanes that he could afford to fly on a private licence, and during 2002 had been studying hard for his commercial pilot's licence, which he attained, subsequently being taken on as a first officer for the charter airline company, Astraeus. Which caused some mirth on occasion, as Robin Guy recounts.

"The hilarious thing about the gigs we did, was he'd got himself a job being a professional pilot and he actually had to go and ask his boss for time off so that he could do these shows. Which I thought was marvellous. Can you imagine that? 'Hello, yes, it's Bruce Dickinson here, singer of the biggest metal band in the world, can you spare me a few days? I've got some gigs, you see ...' We'd be rehearsing, we'd sort of get there at eleven or ten or whatever, and in would stroll Bruce at one o' clock going, 'Sorry I'm a bit late' and we'd all be like, 'We've been here for ages, we've been working hard' and try and rub it in, and he'd go, 'Sorry I'm late, I had a pilot's exam in a flight simulator at seven in the morning at Gatwick' and we'd just be like 'Fuckin' hell, we'll shut up then shall we!'"

"We played Greece and had finished this gig so I like, cracked open a beer, and offered one to Bruce, who said 'No, no, no, I've got the flight at six in the morning, I'm flying to Afghanistan,' or something. You know, some big commercial flight. And I was just like, 'Jesus, for God's sake have a drink and take some drugs will ya!' Do what's expected of you. It's really amazing. I don't know how anyone does it." Bruce refrained, naturally.

Robin was to be very grateful for Bruce's constant aversion to sitting still, and the singer's love for the fast pace of life was to prove vital on one occasion. At the time, Robin's main project was with his band Rachel Stamp, whose schedule he was very careful to check before taking on the Bruce gig. Seeing no problems, he signed up for the Dickinson solo tour – until the very eve of matters.

"The worst fuckin' thing in the world happened. Right nearing the time, after we'd done a few rehearsals with Bruce, the Rachel Stamp camp phoned up and said we've got a gig, and it clashed with when we were going to be playing Graspop in Belgium. And Rachel Stamp were booked to headline a smallish festival in Essex called the Thurrock Music Festival (TMF)."

"And you know, I just shat a brick. I was just like, fuckin' hell, I'm done for, what am I gonna do? Then on closer inspection, I realised okay, Rachel Stamp were headlining so a guesstimation [was] we're probably going to be onstage about ten o'clock at night. And as luck would have it, the only one European festival that Bruce Dickinson and clan didn't headline was

Graspop – we were on just after Rob Halford, and before Dream Theatre and Machine Head and Slayer were headlining. I managed to work out our stagetime was five o'clock until six o'clock in Belgium – an hour ahead of the UK, so I figure that gives me five hours to do a James Bond and get from Belgium to Essex. I contacted airlines and there were no flights or they were booked up, and I was beginning to sort of crumble."

"Then I thought, 'Hold on, Bruce is a pilot,' and this is before I'd played any shows with Bruce, so it still could be a bit like, 'Who are you causing problems, fuck off! I'll get someone else.' So I phoned up Bruce at his home, and I got through to one of Bruce's kids and I said, 'It's Robin, I'm doing the drums for the tour' and he knew I was in Rachel Stamp – we had a video on the TV at the time. And he said, 'Are you the guy that's spinning all your sticks and all that?' and I thought, 'This is really good news, the kid digs me!' you know what I mean. And I went, 'Yeah, yeah, that's right, man'. And he was like, 'Cool, man.'"

So Dickinson Jnr went to fetch daddy, during which time Robin Guy freely admits he was, "shitting myself, I could literally hear the steps of Bruce approaching and I just said, 'Bruce, Robin here, I'm doing the drums, got a little bit of a problem. I'm supposed to be in Essex with Rachel Stamp later on and I was just wondering if you'd possibly consider flying me and you in to Belgium, doing the gig and flying me back?' and I just sort of paused thinking, you know, that's it, he's just gonna go, 'Fuck off!'"

He did not; Bruce asked where the Stamps' gig was – and immediately started concocting a typically Dickinsonian plan. "I could hear him flicking through some atlas,' 'Oh yes, there's a little one in dur dur dur' Thurrocksville or wherever he said. And he went, 'Oh we could probably land in the field,' and I'm thinking, 'Fuck, he's considering this.' And then he goes, 'We could go one better. I've got a friend who's got some medieval bombers. Why don't we do it in a bomber?' and I'm going 'fu.. fu… fu…' you know, coz I was expecting him to just boot me out of the camp immediately, let alone go *why don't we do it in a bomber*. And I'm thinking, 'We'll be on the cover of all the mags!' So I said, 'That'll be very nice if you don't mind organising that.' So he said 'I love a challenge. I'll get back to you on that.'"

As it turned out, the bomber idea didn't come to fruition – but impressively Bruce, Sanctuary and the management pulled some major strings regardless for this mini-adventure. "There was a little minivan waiting by the side of the stage in Belgium at Graspop – we literally finished with 'Powerslave', big old ending and walked off the stage. Me and Bruce grabbed our little kit bags and we're still in our sweaty shorts and all that, and Bruce signs a couple of autographs and I sign a couple and Bruce turns around and goes, 'Come on, get in the van!' A swift hour's drive to Brussels airport, with both artists getting changed in the van, ended up with Bruce and Robin boarding a scheduled flight together.

"This is a little last insight into the great man," beams Guy. "Bruce had some first class flight ticket and I was in the old *knees up mother brown* section and he changed his ticket just so he could come and sit and we could chat and all that and hang out and what have you on the flight back. I was like. 'Fucking hell, who do you think would do that?' He actually changed it from first class to come and sit with me. I turned around to thank Bruce, 'Oh, cheers mate, really cool of you to help me out doing all this …' and he's going, 'Just get in the fucking car, go, you've got a gig to do!' and there was a Sanctuary laid-on company car, chauffeur driven, leather seats bloody fast car in a James Bond stylee, and I got in." With his phone red-hot with calls from Rachel Stamp members enquiring as to where he was – which was, obviously, always "just round the corner."

"We pulled up and drove straight through security, right past the crowd [who] of course are stretching to see Rachel Stamp on stage – there was no time for me to go backstage so I just bolted over the crash barrier, jumped onstage, I'd managed to get a mate to set my kit up you know, the crowd sort of recognised me and go 'Whoa! Great! Rachel Stamp!' and I just checked the kit really, a man on a mission, and went back to the side of the stage where the rest of the guys … [three of] their faces were chewing wasps. And I thought, 'There's nothing I can possibly say at this point, I'll just go 'Let's rock!' I walked on and nailed it for an hour and then just passed out. It was fuckin' one for the books. I've done a kind of Phil Collins, playing in two different countries in the same day, and I arrived two minutes before our show. So we did it, and technically, I wasn't late."

chapter twenty three:
Dancing Souls

The second 'comeback' album, 2003's *Dance Of Death* is, if anything, a huge step up from its predecessor, both in terms of production and also with the space allotted for each of the members to shine. Whilst *Brave New World* had been an excellent stab at the occasionally-epic expanded possibilities of a three-guitar line-up, its successor is a beautifully-arranged prog-tinted beast of huge, classic, metal storytelling. Sonically, it is streets ahead of anything that Maiden had put together through their career – even including *Seventh Son's* widescreen approach – and, twenty one years after *Number Of The Beast* caused such a massive stir amongst all lovers of the distorted guitar and the esoteric lyric, all elements of Maiden's outlook had finally come of age.

Bruce's first writing credit is another collaboration with Harris and Murray, the tight and melodic 'Rainmaker', which offers a smoothness of songwriting that underpins the lyrical wordplay (injecting thoughts of Travis Bickle) and wanting the rain to come, to seal cracks in the protagonist's relationship with ... well, with whatever or whoever you choose to make of it, really. It could be another person, missed opportunities, regrets or hope. Again, on the face of it, the song seems straightforward but raises, in fact, more questions than answers. 'Montsegur' – written by Janick, Bruce and 'Arry – is one of Bruce's typical historical tales, this time telling the story of the Cathars, a sect of Christianity who believed in vegetarianism. They felt killing animals for food was cannibalism, as each human soul was essentially reincarnated as an animal. The Cathars' view was that rather than being one, omnipotent God, the Old Testament – vengeful – Lord was a separate being from the New Testament's benign Father. The inferences are clear: the Cathars were subsequently variously hunted down and killed or set free after confirming themselves in the Catholic faith. Its serious source material is perhaps framed a little flippantly with what, somehow, feels like a largely light-hearted backing track. The same writing team come together once more on 'Gates Of Tomorrow', whose intro references The Who and launches into a typically rollocking, rock 'n' roll-based slab of Maiden, which meanders a little round its allusions to the future, where relying on your own wits may still not be enough. In truth, it's one of the weaker points of what is generally a very good Maiden album indeed. Bruce's vocals, for once, are fighting with a multi-tracked and thick assault of rhythm guitars with little counter-melody to bounce off, although its five minutes fly by solidly enough. Following this up immediately by – shock – a Nicko McBrain track (the drummer's first ever on a Maiden album; he'd brought the bassline and drum tracks to the table), 'New Frontier', written also in collaboration with good old Adrian Smith, is a return to melodic darkness for Bruce, who revels in the re-telling, perhaps, of Mary Shelley's *Frankenstein*, for a cloning age. Or, equally, it could all be about *Skunkworks* of course ... Dickinson, Smith and Harris contribute two more tracks as a writing team, the first the desperate, helpless, synth-soaked 'Face In The Sand' which talks of everyone just waiting for death to fall from the sky, or to watch it on the television. It is very tempting to peg this as being firmly about the atmosphere of paranoia and bemusement at the terrorist attack on America on September 9, 2001 – Bruce had been in New York at the time, and experienced the horror first-hand before managing to catch a flight back the day after. On this track, Nicko's double bass drums beat insistently like an accelerated, nervous, relentless heartbeat, pausing not for a second until four minutes in, thus lending the track an utterly hypnotic quality. The other track penned by that trio is the album's tour de force: the acoustic magnificence of 'Journeyman' – a remarkable track with complexity, maturity, a beautiful arrangement and an incredible, controlled vocal performance from Bruce that perfectly delivers as resonant and powerful – and honest – piece of writing that there perhaps ever has been on a Maiden album. Conflict, misunderstanding, sleep, dreams, wakefulness, fitfulness, hope, desolation and finally a clenched-fist affirmation of self; all are here in a track of magisterial, piquant acceptance of humanity. It's an astonishingly grounding, and in many ways exceptionally upbeat, way to complete a long and often complex album. That this is the same set of musicians who made *Number Of The Beast* is, in one sense, difficult to comprehend; and yet, at the same time, the ... *Beast* LP is counterpointed beautifully by *Dance Of Death*, conceptually, musically and historically. *Brave New World* showed that Maiden could still make a very good album, but *Dance Of Death* showed that the band, and their singer, had much left to explore yet.

The group toured, as was their custom, throughout the world over the period of 2003 and 2004; by now, the shows were back to the enormous events of previous years, although this would be the last year that Maiden would embark on relatively punishing schedules. By now, they all had families and the group – who had proved beyond all doubt on *Dance Of Death* that they had nothing whatsoever let to prove – had surely earned the right to spend a little more time with their nearest and dearest. As was becoming the norm, there was to be a live album and DVD associated with the tour, in line with Bruce's idea of the *Alive* albums of the mid-1990s, both designed to stifle bootleggers and offer a real memento of the excellent tours on which Maiden continued to pull up trees left, right and centre. On the

Bruce Dickinson

European leg of the tour, some fans were able to experience an unique moment, by buying special tickets to be flown to and from the gigs by Bruce himself ... Bruce Air was born; a taxi service of some quality, and how many heavy metal legends could offer such a service? It is, in truth, about as far from a preening, cosseted tattooed millionaire as you could possibly imagine.

* * *

Outside Maiden, Bruce contributed his vocals to the mighty Sack Trick, on their Kiss covers album, *Sheep In Kiss Make Up*, lending his vocals to 'Shout It Out Loud'. Somehow seven years had passed, however, since *The Chemical Wedding* tore a hole in the heavy metal scene; returning to Maiden had been a jolt and a half to the system, getting his new job as a commercial pilot a demanding profession, but the fires still burned inside creatiively.

Bruce then spent October recording for a television series, which was to be somewhat inevitably entitled *Flying Heavy Metal*, a look at aviation for the Discovery Channel. "We looked at doing a reality TV show about training airline pilots, and it morphed into this – a five-part series about the development of the airliner since 1945." Over the best part of two weeks, Bruce interviewed engineers, designers and individuals involved in all aspects of the process, something he enjoyed immensely. He spent time at the Boeing factory in Renton, USA, enthusing that he could, "quite happily spend ages poking around and watching. As a pilot, we never see these planes stripped down like this."[176] The series was first aired on Discovery in the spring of 2005, and is regularly repeated; Bruce's enthusiasm and knowledge of the subject, plus a ready wit, make him a natural, and engaging, host. His fixation on heavy engineering then took him to a guest appearance on Discovery Home & Leisure's *Trainspotting* show on Friday, October 22, 2004, on which he was guest of presenter Mark Collins, and Bruce was delighted to spend the day at Bluebell Railway on a steam train driving day. Strange to think now, but driving a train used to be every small boy's dream job. All great fun, but quite frankly it was time Bruce really let rip again with some solo material, and so he turned his hand back to getting the licks licked.

Bruce and Roy had been writing demos – on and off – since 2001, but work began in earnest around November 2003, with both of them firing ideas backwards and forwards to refine the collection of new songs. Initially, this included 'Believil', 'Tyranny Of Souls' and 'Eternal' – 'Broken' and 'Silver Wings' being nicked for Bruce's 2001 *Best Of* release already. The intent was to keep the project manageable alongside all of Bruce's other activities, so the (roughly) twenty demos and sketches were refined down to a slick ten that the pair would be working on for the new album. Once the songs were decided, recording sessions began with Bruce asking Roy Z to lay down the drum tracks with the very talented Dave Moreno in Castle Oaks, Calabasa and Signature Sound in San Diego. Most of the rest of the album that eventually took the title *Tyranny Of Souls* was in fact recorded in Roy Z's living room!

"We never rehearsed," laughed Roy. "The great thing about playing with someone like Bruce live, and being his producer, is that he knows already what's going to work, and the great thing is from playing with him, I can too. So we both can see what those magic things are that the crowd is gonna get off on ... Bruce usually does four takes, and we make one take out of those four. He is very professional, very consistent, right to the point."[177] Roy aside, and with Adrian Smith back of course in the Maiden camp, the *Tyranny Of Souls* line-up was an entirely new band. Bass duties are handled by Z and also Ray 'Geezer' Burke – a moustachioed stylist whose influences and fluidity range from Jack Bruce to, well, Geezer Butler, and a mysterious keyboard player known only as, uh, Mistheria. The keyboard parts on *Tyranny* came together in a very technology-aware manner, with ideas and audio being fired backward and forward over the internet before Bruce would pick the tracks he liked for the album.

Roy Z finds it hard to pick out a weak track from the final LP, commenting that there were, "so many great vocal performances. I mean if you take the vocal performance from, 'Kill Devil Hill', the intro, Bruce just sounds like God! Then you take a song like 'Navigate The Seas Of The Sun' it's so intimate. It shows the delicacy of Bruce's voice. For me, a song like 'Soul intruder' I really like it. I like 'Believil'. I like 'em all!" As well he should. It was even more remarkable given Bruce had recorded a large amount of the vocals in rather a lot of pain, having fallen into the drumkit after a particular Iron Maiden gig where he slipped on some wet steps.

'Navigate The Seas Of The Sun' is one of Bruce's trademark acoustic-based esoteric epics, this time a Bowie-esque effort which looks to the stars for answers, and for possibilities therein, and stands strong against anything he had ever previously written. All in all, *Tyranny Of Souls* is a more-than-worthy addition to his canon; very different from Maiden, it is nonetheless a slab of excellent heavy metal. *Kerrang!* rated it as, "the glorious sound of a heavy metal master in full flight" on its release in March 2005. By which time, of course, the Iron Maiden machine was kicking firmly into action once more.

chapter twenty four:
Survivors

The major retrospective of the early part of Maiden's career, *The History Of Iron Maiden: Part 1 – The Early Years* had been a massive success amongst the fans after its release in November 2004. As 2005 dawned, the band announced their intent to take to the road for the *Eddie Rips Up ... Europe* tour, which would then join the travelling metal festival, Ozzfest, in North America, for most of the rest of the summer before returning to Europe (and missing the last seven dates of the Ozzfest tour) for the late summer festivals. Further, the set-list would concentrate largely on earlier material, in line with the focus of the DVD, intended to be the first in a set of six or so such releases that would tell a comprehensive official history of the group.

When Ozzfest came around, Maiden were sharing the main stage with such luminaries as Mudvayne, Shadows Fall, and headliners, Black Sabbath. It was some reunion for Bruce and Ozzy, who during the 1980s had been, on and off, drinking buddies – on one occasion in 1983, the story has it, ordering fifty beers from their hotel bar before stumbling out on the streets to find and then hopefully steal a taxi, which they singularly failed to do. Sabbath, however, had been one of the bands that Bruce had idolised over the years, one of the reasons he and Steve Harris had both been motivated to get into music in the first place. All this made what happened next all the more bizarre. As has been well-reported in the press, there had been, shall we say, differences of opinion between the Maiden singer and Sharon Osbourne over comments that Bruce had been making onstage during several of the Ozzfest shows, referring to good ol' Ozzy's memory not quite being what it used to be, and that Oz needed lyric sheets written onstage to remember his tracks, and also raging against the reality TV show *The Osbournes*, that was aired with spectacular success that year.

Notably, things came to a head at the show at San Bernadino, on August 20, 2005 – Maiden's last appearance on the tour. The band's set was interrupted several times by someone taking over the PA to shout 'Ozzy, Ozzy'; the band were pelted with eggs, and the stage was invaded twice by a guy dressed in a US flag during 'The Trooper'. The constant deliberate interruptions to Maiden's set looked like an apparently orchestrated campaign to make the band look ridiculous. They, of course, not only completed the set, but ended up with the crowd chanting their name at the tops of their voices despite the problems that had been put in their way. As Bruce said, draped in the Union Flag, whilst all around him was falling apart, 'These Colours Don't Run'. And they did not.

In the aftermath of the incident, both Sharon Osbourne and Rod Smallwood had their own take on matters, the two managers releasing statements to the press. Smallwood had clashed, of course, with Sharon's father, the legendary Don Arden, over the notorious sleeve for 'Women In Uniform', and was simply not a man to be messed with. Sharon released a statement on August 20 that began by saying Maiden had been chosen to play by the Ozzfest committee because they'd not toured America for a while, but from the outset, "Bruce Dickinson started berating Ozzy and belittling the Ozzfest audience. He stated he, 'didn't need a reality show to give him credibility', 'we're not just some f*cking reunion band,' and continuously complained about the sound system, saying that when he comes back to America he'll have a better one." The statement continued to state that because Bruce hadn't toured the States for a long time [Bruce had in fact toured the US with his solo band as well as Maiden], that he didn't grasp how things had changed over the past ten years, and that Bruce felt he had to belittle other artists. Osbourne then made it absolutely clear that it was the singer with whom she had a beef, rather than the rest of the band and crew, who she said were "great" and "professional".

"How sad it was, after ten years, that this little man tried to ruin it for everyone. The bands of Ozzfest don't even look at Ozzfest as touring, but as its heavy metal summer camp. Bruce is in fact a jealous prick and very envious. None of his tirades were directed at Sabbath, only Ozzy ... It also offended me every night how he took out the English flag in America. There are American boys going to war alongside the English boys every day. How dare he forget the American troops on their home turf?" She concluded that Bruce had no respect for his audience."[178] That was her side of the argument then.

In response, Maiden kept their counsel for a few days, aside from apologising that their involvement with Ozzfest had ended on quite such a bizarre note, before the ever-strong Rod Smallwood's release to the press spoke of the Maiden camp's feeling on events. He began by stating that Maiden were preparing for their headlining dates at the Reading and Leeds festivals, "and don't wish to waste time giving Sharon Osbourne's statement the dignity of a reply. Considering the disgraceful nature of the events that occurred, they feel it's a pretty dismal effort at self-justification and they don't think Metal fans are at all gullible and that they will easily see through it. They want no more to do with this sorry incident and are very much looking forward to headlining Reading and Leeds Festivals this weekend." Smallwood, however, had his own personal feelings about matters, musing that after three decades of being in the rock business, he had never seen anything quite so "disgusting and unprofessional as what went on that night. I was standing on our sound desk out front as usual, but ran to the stage as soon as the hail of missiles began and from then on watched from the front of the stage right next to Bruce's walkway. The scale, viciousness and concentration of the throwing made it obvious that this was a premeditated and co-ordinated attack. Assaulting musicians while performing by throwing bottle tops, lighters and eggs at them from just a few yards away is vile, dangerous, criminal and cowardly. It is incredible that Ozzfest security apparently did nothing about it – aren't they there to protect the bands too?" He concluded by saying how proud he was of Maiden, and the singer, for standing their ground for the sake of the fans, and felt that, "the imperturbable attitude and ability of the band shone through and in the end made this a truly remarkable rock and roll event, even if for all the wrong reasons. We will have no more to say on this matter except that I do think the band deserve an apology from a number of people, and you know who you are."[179] Such posturing was akin to a pair of gladiators squaring up to each other, although some of the combatants were perhaps more akin to the Gladiators from the crap TV show from the late 1980s,[180] rather than the Roman version.

And it rumbled on, and on, Sharon Osbourne coming back in "an open letter" to Rod Smallwood's statement thus: "It's shameful that Dickinson felt he had the right to air his issues publicly onstage every night as a way to boost his own ego. Dickinson never once came up to Ozzy and me to voice any concerns. He certainly had the opportunity to do so every night. If he wasn't able to show us that courtesy then why should I give him the respect to air my grievances with him in private? Ozzy's only interaction with Dickinson was on the first night of the tour. Ozzy, being the true gentleman that he is, passed Bruce in the hall and said, 'Good luck and have a great show.' Unfortunately Dickinson felt the need to turn his back to Ozzy and walked away. Frankly, Dickinson got what he deserved. We had to listen to his bullshit for five straight weeks. He only had to suffer a couple of eggs on the head."

Sharon Osbourne went on to conclude that perhaps "Dickinson doesn't have the manners to realize that when you are invited into someone's home, are seated at their dinner table, are eating their food and drinking their wine, you shouldn't talk disrespectfully about them [Ozzy, Black Sabbath and Ozzfest], otherwise you just might get your ass handed to you. Every action has a reaction. Was Dickinson so naïve to think that I was going to let him get away with talking shit about my family night after night? I don't think he realises who he's dealing with. I will not endure behaviour like this from anyone."[181] And after speculating that this had created the most press interest in the band for twenty years, she signed it 'The Real Iron Maiden'.

Bruce's only response was in an interview with *The Sun* newspaper, during which he made it clear that he believed it had been an orchestrated attack, re-iterating his pride that Maiden had been so stolid, and commented that "Everyone knows it's Sharon Osbourne. It's certainly not Ozzy or Sabbath – they have too much class to condone stunts like that. She hates me for making remarks about reality TV. I hate reality TV. People should get off their arses and do stuff and not be so voyeuristic."[182] He ended by stating that it was lucky that the audience had been happy with Maiden's set despite it all, otherwise there could well have been a rather serious situation develop as a consequence. No matter, Bruce and Maiden came out of it with dignity enhanced rather than damaged, and anyone who was lucky enough to catch the band at those Reading and Leeds performances would have seen an act fired-up even more than usual.[183]

On September 2, Maiden played another Clive Aid set, this time at Hammersmith Odeon, raising profile and cash once more for their erstwhile drummer, with tickets sold mostly to fan club members with a small amount set aside for the general public. The remainder of 2005 saw Bruce and the band have some time off before intending to hit 2006 running by writing and recording sessions for another new album. Bruce spent most of the rest of his time in the sky, concentrating on his day job, although he did manage to find some time to contribute to another interesting musical project which also involved Chris Dale, Roy Z and the legendary Brazilian metal artist, Renato Tribuzy. The pair had met some four years earlier, but it took some time for them to pin down a recording session. Bruce lent his singing to the very metallic 'Beast In The Light', one of the many highlights on an excellent album that also features Michael Kiske of Helloween, Mat Sinner of Sinner and Andreas Kisser of the legendary Sepultura. Bruce performed two concerts with Renato and his band at Sao Paolo and Belo Horizonte on November 12 and 13, 2005. It had been another year of creativity, triumph, lots of flying and general mischief for Bruce, proving that things were never likely to truly settle down for the mercurial vocalist.

chapter twenty five:
A Matter Of Life And Death

Iron Maiden's fourteenth studio album, *A Matter Of Life And Death*, was written in early 2006 and the band set to recording sessions during spring that year. With tour dates being arranged at a rate of knots, the Maiden machine was lurching into familiar action once more. By mid-May, 2006, the band was ready to master the new long player. The remarkable thing about the band's third record as a six-piece is the ease with which they scale musical, lyrical, production and mood heights turn after turn. It is a sprawling, enormous, challenging but at the same time listener-friendly piece of work that could only have been written and recorded by a set of musicians – of people – who had lived, as they say, in interesting times. Listening to *A Matter Of Life And Death* is like listening to Iron Maiden's life stories, their hopes, dreams and musical influences. In a sense, it goes even further than its predecessor, *Dance Of Death*, in laying bare the personalities of its creators. In that all art has an essentially naked, autobiographical element if it is truly successful, *A Matter Of Life And Death* stands up as a documentation of the band's development over the years. Although it is not a concept album in the sense that *Seventh Son ...* is, or come to that, *The Chemical Wedding* is, the themes running through the LP are heavily set in those of war, conflict, the place of the common soldier in a greater and more overpowering system, and the common man seeking to reconcile the often dichotomic demands of duty and moral consistency. There's paranoia, sleeplessness and resolution, fire-eyed defiance and retribution. Though the tracks are not overtly political, the album nevertheless exudes questions with which the listener is presented. And although these are stories, tales and epic imaginative filmic scenarios, the common theme running through the album is an ultimately human one that often demands an interaction with the fan that is frequently missed in the bellicose cacophony of the genre. Like the previous Maiden LP – and elements of *Tyranny Of Souls* – it serves to recontext the band's previous work. Listening, for example to 'These Colours Don't Run' back to back with 'The Trooper' – or even 'Tail Gunner' – swipes away the linearity of time and reveals the tracks to be part of a greater whole that is bound not by chronology but by wider themes at work, and themes that are universal. Some thirty years – give or take – since Bruce first began writing songs in earnest, there is a sense that, not only is there still fuel in the tank, but he – and Maiden – are entering an adventurous and vibrant period of their careers.

Oh, and it fucking *rocks*.

The band, and producer Kevin Shirley, were rightly enthused about the quality of the work they had produced. Said Bruce, "There is such a wide scope of musicianship on this album, and in parts [it is] truly epic. I thought with the likes of 'Paschendale' from the last studio album that we could only hope to surpass that but having now heard the album back as well as sitting with a few select people and hearing their reactions as well, I truly believe we have managed it. Every one of us has put everything into this record and it's really paid off. However, we've had such fun making it that it's almost difficult to believe what we've managed to achieve in the time it took."[184] Old 'Arry 'Arris made reference to the fact that it was the most natural-feeling writing and recording process of their entire career, praising the power of the record, whilst expressing his excitement about playing the new tracks in the live arena. The album – which was largely recorded live, and features very little in the way of additional sonic manipulation – was not mastered, on the insistence of Steve Harris. Kevin Shirley explained that it "means that you will get to hear the new album exactly as it sounded in the studio, no added EQ, compression, analog widening, etc, and I must say, I am pretty happy with the end result. I think some tracks could use a smidge more top end, and others a bump of bottom — but I know 'Arry well enough now to know how wary of outsiders he is, and I fully expected he may have done that, so I made sure I was happy with the results when I printed the mixes in the studio."[185] Which says much about Steve's traditionalist approach; despite the increasing complexity of the material, there is still a huge streak in the bass player and driving force seeking to retain the unpolished aggression inherent in the music he loves so much. There are very, very few albums these days that are unmastered; to most bands it is an aspect of the process that is as familiar as setting up a SM57 and setting it live with its own designated tape machine to record their farts all day.

Bruce's first writing credit on the new record is the near seven-minute beast, 'These Colours Don't Run' – a phrase with many connotations but in this context a discussion of the role of the ordinary soldier in conflict. Bruce explained to *Revolver Magazine* that it was about what, "motivates soldiers and what they fight for. Some of them have a big flag tattooed on their ass and genuinely believe all the patriotic stuff, and they'll get their heads blown off for Uncle Sam. But I think most of them fight because if they didn't, their buddies would get killed." The team of Smith/Harris/Dickinson also collaborated on the mighty 'Brighter Than A Thousand Suns', which, echoing the singer's historical leanings, and – again, coming full circle – compares the Cold War to the very hot war *du jour*, the arguably more horrific, vague and inhuman aspects of the current, post-9/11, war on terror.

"I spent most of my adolescence under the shadow of the atomic bomb," he said. "I was brought up in a generation that was led to believe that a klaxon siren would go off, and you'd just have four minutes to kiss your ass goodbye. This generation has a different paranoia. Today, it's all about terrorism. We just thought we were going to get wiped off the face of the earth. So the song looks at how you reconcile building something as destructive as the bomb with sleeping at night." Given Harris' well-documented insomnia and/or nightmares, it is a powerful metaphor.

The three constructed another one of Bruce's soldier epics, 'The Longest Day' together, which talks about the D-Day landings and the extreme circumstances and acts that the mostly eighteen-year-old soldiers were put through. In a sense, its lyrics that refer to both God and Valhalla present an interesting collision of mythology, reality and desperation. 'Lord Of Light' is the trio's extended discussion of – essentially – the Cathars' concept of there being a benign spirit and an Old Testament-type, vengeful Lord; except this time, and in a move that would no doubt 'cause outcry in the moral majority, it seeks to present an alternative view. That the Lord Of Light – or, to put it another way, Lucifer, the bringer of light – has basically had some bad press. Somewhat tongue-in-cheek, Bruce explained his thought process thus: "Just imagine there was a whole range of places between Heaven and Hell and that you got to pick, and ... all this stuff about the vengeful, eternal God wagging his finger and punishing you is all just a load of PR nonsense."[186]

Which says a great deal about the mischievous frontman; many people – having been labelled as Satanists, puppy-killers and generally the sort of person you wouldn't trust to water your potplants whilst you were away without performing some kind of voodo-esque ceremony on them – would shy away from writing a track like that, let alone talking about it in such apparently flippant terms. The singer collaborated also with his bassist on 'Out Of The Shadows', at five-and-a-half minutes one of the shorter tracks on *A Matter Of Life And Death*, which speaks loudly of rebirth, karma and essentially the idea that what doesn't kill us will make us only stronger. And, again, should you choose to, there is obvious resonance there about the pair's sometime fractious relationship.

Maiden could do no wrong in the eyes of the press. On the album's release, *Kerrang!* said it was, "another Maiden classic"; *Metal Hammer* gave it full marks and felt that the band had "utterly surpassed themselves" and *Classic Rock* enthused that Maiden were all-time greats, both living up to their reputation, as well as having released what that magazine thought was "possibly the album of the year". Not bad for a bunch of old grunts in or approaching their fifties. For Bruce's part, when asked about the plans the band had for the next decade, he referred to the fact that he now considered his airline work his bread and butter, having spent eight hundred hours in the air (the maximum is nine hundred) over the previous twelve months. "I'm one of these guys who always has the glass half-full," he said. "I'm looking ahead going, 'Okay, I'm almost fifty. What am I going to be doing when I get to sixty?' Well, I might be running around with Iron Maiden. But probably not. So what am I going to be doing? Shit, I'll be flying airliners – that's cool!"[187] It is indeed.

The extensive tour took in much of the world as usual, the band playing to huge crowds night after night alongside support acts Lauren Harris (daughter of Steve) and metal upstarts Trivium, who had just released their third album, which in another of those satisfyingly circular moments, is called *The Crusade*. Tom Parker was one of the P.A. engineers for the shows. He gave me an insight into the Maiden camp on the album tour.

"Their travelling and stuff isn't done together at all," says the audio technician, giving an invaluable insight into the slickness and tightness of the Maiden touring machine – as well as the intense, professional trust they band and their crew have between each other. "Everyone turns up about an hour before the actual show, maybe two hours. It's Steve that turns up before everybody else, unless something's gone wrong the night before and then they'll come and iron it out, but they [rarely] do their own soundcheck; it's always the roadies that'll do that. Now and again, like when it's coming to the end of a tour, they'll come and chat with the crew and everything, but it's only the actual guitar techs for each member that'll really have a chat. They're quite anonymous otherwise. Cause they all travel separately, they drive to all the venues, or fly to them, especially in Bruce's case." Behind the scenes of Iron Maiden on the road, then, it is a rock 'n' roll beast at its most consummate and professional.

Parker feels that Maiden's continued longevity is down to the fact that the band have been able to not only keep their own fanbase intact, but to add to it with every passing generation of music and metal fans. "The things that surprised me the most," he muses, "are the actual facts that they could sell out a sixteen thousand capacity arena every night, and also the *diversity* of the crowd was absolutely ridiculous – from the age of eight to eighty eight. Seeing as though they are the forefathers of British heavy metal, I think that every single band that's been in that genre has been influenced by them in some way it's fair to say really." Not least Trivium, whose driving force and singer Matt Heafy was widely-quoted as saying what a massive part Maiden's music has had in their own nascent career; and although Trivium's most obvious reference point is Metallica, that band were firmly inspired by the New Wave Of British Heavy Metal themselves.[188] To each its turn. There other more 'revealing' insights: "One thing Bruce isn't scared to do is be naked, he'll just stand there and talk to anyone or anybody who comes in after a shower an everything."[189]

2006 was, then, a year wherein Bruce's band retained their dignity under pressure, whilst wowing audiences across the globe; the singer had also appeared alongside many other metal legends in the documentary *Metal: A Headbanger's Journey*, presented a satellite television investigation into the phenomenon of spontaneous human combustion (a show cunningly-entitled *Inside Spontaneous Human Combustion With Bruce Dickinson*), been one of many people paying tribute to DJ Tommy Vance, who had recently passed away (as legend has it, Vance was the only person to advise Bruce *not* to take the job as singer in Iron Maiden), and even been banned from watching the gigs of his son Austin's rock band (perhaps even the vocalist in the greatest heavy metal act of all-time comes under the heading of 'embarrassing dad' sometimes). Incredibly, he even undertook a mercy mission to Cyprus on July 20, airlifting two hundred Brits fleeing war-torn Lebanon and bringing them safely back to the United Kingdom. Bruce also flew the Glasgow Rangers football team to their UEFA Cup game against Halpoel Tel Aviv on February 11, 2007.

The pace of life and work stopped not for a second, nor is it likely to in the near future, with Maiden still looking to territories that have not had the opportunity to see the band live, including India. The year 2007, for Bruce and the band, saw more of the same with Iron Maiden once more headlining Donington Park for *Download*, the rock festival that replaced *Monsters Of Rock*.

* * *

Dickinson is a man driven by more than success; indeed one gets the impression that despite his many triumphs, once he achieves something of note, rather than rest on his laurels he merely seeks the next challenge. It is undeniable that there have been some dark days over the years, days where he questioned his place in the world of music. But each time, this remarkable artist has come out all the stronger for it. From radio and television presenting to solo work and Maiden, from fencing to flying, Paul Bruce Dickinson seeks to throw himself into his work and be the very best he can be. And for a man of his considerable talents, that is – almost without fail – exceptional.

"I literally do not know how he does it," laughs Robin Guy. "When I come off tour, I have a brief relationship with the washing machine, all my dirty linen. And then I want to lie down for quite a long time and do bugger all. Let alone go, 'Oh, I've just got to kick-start my other job!' His own radio show on Radio 6, that requires keeping a fresh show every week, not playing the same crap, interviewing other bands, keeping guests coming in, it's something you can't let stagnate, you can't just roll in and do it. That takes time, and it's amazing. It's testament to how a lot of people should be. Do as much as you can, and do them all as good as you can." Sage advice.

Chris Paolo Dale, bassist extrordinaire and one of the driving forces behind Sack Trick, has rather a more prosaic view on Bruce. "He's just not lazy like the rest of us," laughs the Welsh-speaking, Kiss-fixated funkatron. "I like a good lie-in in the mornings. On tour, I'd get up late and find he'd already been for a walk around the city, done some press interviews, had lunch with the record company to talk about the next video and written some new lyric ideas. I'd be sitting there bleary eyed, going, 'Oh, really?' and thinking about having breakfast before soundcheck and then he'd go off to the gym! Honestly, he just doesn't stop." And as Bernie Torme rightly says, "He's a clever bloke Bruce, he really is." Producer Chris Tsangarides recalls his part in one of Bruce's parallel careers. "We had the flight simulators on the Atari computers in the studio," he laughs. "It was when he went to America to do the Keith Olsen thing that he started taking the flying lessons, so while he was making a record he was flying everywhere. Maybe it was a good thing that he learnt to fly, given what happened with the music at that time. Always have a backup plan!" The man speaks wise and godly truths.

"He was always a very interesting person, very intelligent, good sense of humour," offers Stuart Smith, a man who could have easily played a part in changing musical history. "You know there are certain people in your life that you run into – Bruce was a great shining light and I knew something would happen with him, either together or whatever he decided to do. He just had this amazing voice, this amazing power and this amazing energy as well. He was very conscious of being a showman [too] which was very refreshing at the time, because most singers just stood there. There's always the 'Lead Singer Syndrome' that you have to deal with in bands but Bruce always got it that it's the singer and the song that are going to sell the act and the singer has to put on some kind of show as well as, sing really well. And Bruce had it all." It's a statement echoed by Jennie Halsall, who was instrumental in Bruce's decision to join Iron Maiden. "He has so many things he wanted to do and he's quite a workaholic," she beams. "Any rock band person that stops working and goes off flying planes for a couple of weeks … he's a 'life grabber'. He wants to do different things, and try different things, and that's why he's so good at his job."

Tony Newton: "I remember Steve saying to me once, 'I'll get on a plane and read a book, and Bruce gets on and plane a writes one.' He is amazing. He's just got so much energy about him, you can see that when he performs and even in his face when you talk about stuff. He's got a lot of interests, and that just makes him an interesting person, that's the thing. I just don't know how the guy finds the time to do it all, I think he's amazing."

"He's a phenomenally talented guy," says NWOBHM expert John Tucker. "You have to hold your hand up to the fact that, every time there's a disaster everyone's there – [famous people] having a photo call – they turn up and do their little bit, but you don't find out that Bruce Dickinson's been *flying planes* in and out of the area until a week later. Cause he doesn't take a photo call, he just does his job. Some people pick on some of the rants he comes out with onstage sometimes, but why not get it off your chest if somebody's pissed you off? He seems to be an honest bloke."

"Jeez, fifteen/sixteen years later," enthuses Keith Olsen, producer and raconteur, "and Maiden's as strong now as they ever were. And Bruce's voice and Bruce as a lead singer is known world-wide. Probably even more now than they were in the 1980s."

As ever, Neal Kay has something interesting to contribute. "The facts are," says the DJ, "that Iron Maiden through the years, with this basic line-up and the addition of the extra guitarist again, they've outlasted everyone else. They are an *astonishing* story. Yeah, they're a 'dinosaur', yeah, it's thirty years – who gives a shit? They're still the greatest; they outlived the years Zeppelin spent together, they outlived the years Sabbath spent together: *together*, note. Iron Maiden have lasted thirty years. *A Matter Of Life And Death* for me is sophisticated, darker, powerful. I saw them at Earl's Court a couple of years back – they just seem to get better and better as they get older and older. There's no stopping them."

"He is an enigma in rock 'n' roll as well because he can step outside rock 'n' roll and place himself almost anywhere. He's virtually unique. I've never known Bruce to be flippant about bloody anything. He is, in the way of a public schoolboy, incredibly outspoken and if he doesn't like something, he says it. And if he likes something, he [also] says it. He pushed the boundaries over the fence and beyond."

Long may he continue to do so; Christ knows the world needs mavericks more than ever before. In the Noughties, we are beset by the culture of celebrity; people are famous for being famous, and reality television 'stars' can cause furores on a political level for oinking their half-baked semi-racist ignorance on similarly half-baked and ignorant reality television shows. A world where the disenfranchised generations would rather interact through 3D graphics than with each other; a world where wars are undertaken on flimsy 'evidence' in direct contravention of United Nations law. There is a generation who are yet to find their voices as political and musical beings; the two are often inseparable. Characters like Bruce Dickinson defy convention, deride the naysayers and get the fuck on with making a difference by their *deeds* rather than mere words. Not bad for a boy from a small mining town, who didn't quite fit in at school; who got expelled for some juvenile pranks and subsequently became the singer in the biggest heavy metal group of all-time.

postscript

On January 13, 2007, Samson bass player Chris Aylmer lost his own fight with cancer, passing away to chase giggling lady angels round their clouds, and to jam with Paul Samson, Hendrix and Moony at the great gig in the sky.

One of the bassist's greatest wishes was that Bruce and the Samson camp would soon come together and talk through their misunderstandings. And at the time of writing, this appears to be the case; it would be a fitting tribute indeed.

selected discography

Albums

Samson

Survivors: *Easy As It Seems / I Wish I Was The Saddle Of A Schoolgirls Bike
/ Big Brother / Tomorrow Or Yesterday / Koz / Six Feet Under / Inside Out
/ Wrong Side of Time*
LP – Laser 1979
NOTE: Bruce credited with harmonica, vocals and guitar but doesn't appear on it;
Chris Aylmer credited similarly with bass
Reissued LP – Thunderbolt 1983 with different sleeve: 'Goat's Head'
Reissued LP – Repertoire 1990 with five bonus tracks of Bruce's re-recorded vocals

Survivors: *Easy As It Seems / I Wish I Was The Saddle Of A Schoolgirls Bike
/ Big Brother / Tomorrow Or Yesterday / Koz / Six Feet Under / Inside Out
/ Wrong Side of Time*
CD – Air Raid 2000

Survivors: *Easy As It Seems / I Wish I Was The Saddle Of A Schoolgirls Bike
/ Big Brother / Tomorrow Or Yesterday / Koz / Six Feet Under / Inside Out
/ Wrong Side of Time / Mr Rock N Roll / The Shuffle / Its Not As Easy As It Seems
/ I Wish I Was / Big Brother / Tomorrow Or Yesterday / Six Foot Under /Inside Out
/ Wrong Side Of Time*
Reissued CD – Sanctuary/Essential 2001 with nine bonus tracks, some unreleased

Head On: *Hard Times / Take It Like A Man / Vice Versa / Manwatcher
/ Too Close Too Rock / Thunderburst / Hammerhead / Hunted
/ Take Me To Your Leader / Walking Out On You*
LP – Gem 1980
Reissued LP – Repertoire 1989

Head On: *Hard Times / Take It Like A Man / Vice Versa / Manwatcher
/ Too Close Too Rock / Thunderburst / Hammerhead / Hunted
/ Take Me To Your Leader / Walking Out On You*
CD – Grand Slamm 1990
Reissued CD – Air Raid 2000

Head On: *Hard Times / Take It Like A Man / Vice Versa / Manwatcher / Too Close Too Rock / Thunderburst / Hammerhead / Hunted / Take Me To Your Leader / Walking Out On You / Angel With A Machine Gun / Kingsway Jam*
Reissued CD – Sanctuary/Essential 2001 with two bonus tracks, one unreleased

Shock Tactics: *Riding With The Angels / Earth Mother / Nice Girl / Bloodlust / Go To Hell / Bright Lights / Once Bitten / Grime Crime / Communion*
LP – RCA 1981
Reissued LP – Repertoire 1989

Shock Tactics: *Riding With The Angels / Earth Mother / Nice Girl / Bloodlust / Go To Hell / Bright Lights / Once Bitten / Grime Crime / Communion*
CD – Grand Slam 1990
Reissued CD – Air Raid 2000

Shock Tactics: *Riding With The Angels / Earth Mother / Nice Girl / Bloodlust / Go To Hell / Bright Lights / Once Bitten / Grime Crime / Communion / Little Big Man / Pyramid To The Stars / Losing My Grip*
Reissued CD – Sanctuary/Essential 2001 with three bonus tracks

Live At Reading '81: *Big Brother / Take It Like A Man / Nice Girl / Earth Mother / Vice Versa / Bright Lights / Walking Out On You / Hammerhead / Riding With The Angels / Gravy Train*
LP – Raw Fruit 1990
Reissued LP – Repertoire 1990

Live At Reading '81: *Big Brother / Take It Like A Man / Nice Girl / Earth Mother / Vice Versa / Bright Lights / Walking Out On You / Hammerhead / Riding With The Angels / Gravy Train*
CD – Grand Slam 1990
Reissued CD – Air Raid 2000

Live At Reading '81: *Big Brother / Take It Like A Man / Nice Girl / Earth Mother / Vice Versa / Bright Lights / Walking Out On You / Hammerhead / Riding With The Angels / Gravy Train / Red Skies / Turn Out The Lights / Firing Line*
Reissued CD – Sanctuary/Essential 2001 with three unreleased bonus tracks

Iron Maiden

The Number Of The Beast: *Invaders / Children Of The Damned / The Prisoner
/ 22 Acacia Avenue / The Number Of The Beast / Run To The Hills / Gangland
/ Total Eclipse / Hallowed Be Thy Name*
LP/CD – EMI 1982
Reissued CD – FAME 1987
Reissued vinyl replica CD – Sanctuary 2002

The Number Of The Beast: *Invaders / Children Of The Damned / The Prisoner
/ 22 Acacia Avenue / The Number Of The Beast / Run To The Hills / Gangland
/ Total Eclipse / Hallowed Be Thy Name / Total Eclipse / Remember Tomorrow (live)*
Reissued CD – EMI 1995 with two bonus tracks

Piece of Mind: *Where Eagles Dare / Revelations / Flight of Icarus
/ Die With Your Boots On / The Trooper / Still Life / Quest For Fire / Sun And Steel
/ To Tame A Land*
LP/CD EMI 1983
NOTE: Also US pressing picture disc including *Cross Eyed Mary*
Reissued vinyl replica CD – Sanctuary 2002

Piece of Mind: *Where Eagles Dare / Revelations / Flight of Icarus
/ Die With Your Boots On / The Trooper / Still Life / Quest For Fire / Sun And Steel
/ To Tame A Land / I've Got The Fire / Cross Eyed Mary*
Reissued CD – EMI 1995 with two bonus tracks

Powerslave: *Aces High / 2 Minutes To Midnight / Losfer Words / Flash Of The Blade
/ The Duellists / Back In The Village / Powerslave / Rime Of The Ancient Mariner*
LP/CD – EMI 1984
NOTE: Also on picture disc
Reissued CD – FAME 1986
Reissued vinyl replica CD – Sanctuary 2002

Powerslave: *Aces High / 2 Minutes To Midnight / Losfer Words / Flash Of The Blade
/ The Duellists / Back In The Village / Powerslave / Rime Of The Ancient Mariner
/ Rainbow's Gold / Mission From 'Arry / King Of Twilight
/ The Number Of The Beast (Live)*
Reissued CD – EMI 1995 with four bonus tracks

Powerslave: *Aces High / 2 Minutes To Midnight / Losfer Words / Flash Of The Blade / The Duellists / Back In The Village / Powerslave / Rime Of The Ancient Mariner / Rainbow's Gold / Mission From 'Arry / King Of Twilight / Number Of The Beast (live)*
Reissued double CD – EMI 1998

Live After Death: *Aces High / 2 Minutes To Midnight / The Trooper / Revelations / Flight Of Icarus / Rime Of The Ancient Mariner / Powerslave / The Number Of The Beast / Hallowed Be Thy Name / Iron Maiden / Run To The Hills / Running Free / Wrathchild / Children Of The Damned / 22 Acacia Avenue /Die With Your Boots On / The Phantom Of The Opera*
LP/CD – EMI 1985
Reissued vinyl replica CD – Sanctuary 2002

Live After Death: *Aces High / 2 Minutes To Midnight / The Trooper / Revelations / Flight Of Icarus / Rime Of The Ancient Mariner / Powerslave / The Number Of The Beast / Hallowed Be Thy Name / Iron Maiden / Run To The Hills / Running Free / Wrathchild / Children Of The Damned / 22 Acacia Avenue /Die With Your Boots On / The Phantom Of The Opera / Losfer Words (Big 'Orra) / Sanctuary / Murders In The Rue Morgue*
Reissued CD – EMI 1995 with three bonus tracks

Somewhere In Time: *Caught Somewhere In Time / Wasted Years / Sea Of Madness / Heaven Can Wait / The Loneliness Of The Long Distance Runner / Stranger In A Strange Land / Deja Vu / Alexander The Great*
LP/CD – EMI 1986
Reissued vinyl replica CD – Sanctuary 2002

Somewhere In Time: *Caught Somewhere In Time / Wasted Years / Sea Of Madness / Heaven Can Wait / The Loneliness Of The Long Distance Runner / Stranger In A Strange Land / Deja Vu / Alexander The Great / Reach Out / Juanita / Sheriff Of Huddersfield / That Girl*
Reissued double CD – EMI 1995

Somewhere In Time: *Caught Somewhere In Time / Wasted Years / Sea Of Madness / Heaven Can Wait / The Loneliness Of The Long Distance Runner / Stranger In A Strange Land / Deja Vu / Alexander The Great / Reach Out / Sheriff Of Huddersfield / That Girl / Juanita*
Reissued double CD – EMI 1998

Seventh Son Of A Seventh Son: *Moonchild / Infinite Dreams*
/ Can I Play With Madness / The Evil That Men Do / Seventh Son Of A Seventh Son
/ The Prophecy / The Clairvoyant / Only The Good Die Young
LP/CD EMI 1988
NOTE: Also on picture disc with a free banner
Reissued vinyl replica CD – Sanctuary 2002

Seventh Son Of A Seventh Son: *Moonchild / Infinite Dreams*
/ Can I Play With Madness / The Evil That Men Do / Seventh Son Of A Seventh Son
/ The Prophecy / The Clairvoyant / Only The Good Die Young / Black Bart Blues
/ Massacre / Prowler '88 / Charlotte The Harlot '88 / Infinite Dreams (Live)
/ The Clairvoyant(Live) / The Prisoner (Live) /Killers (Live) / Still Life (Live)
Reissued double CD – EMI 1995

Seventh Son Of A Seventh Son: *Moonchild / Infinite Dreams / Can I Play With*
Madness / The Evil That Men Do / Seventh Son Of A Seventh Son / The Prophecy
/ The Clairvoyant / Only The Good Die Young / Black Bart Blues /Massacre
/ Prowler '88 / Charlotte The Harlot / The Clairvoyant (live) / The Prisoner (live)
/ Infinite Dreams (live) Killers (live) Still Life (live)
Reissued double CD – EMI 1998

No Prayer For The Dying : *Tail Gunner / Holy Smoke / No Prayer For The Dying*
/ Public Enema Number One / Fates Warning / The Assassin / Run Silent Run Deep
/ Hooks In You / Bring Your Daughter ... To The Slaughter / Mother Russia
LP/CD – EMI 1990
NOTE: Limited Edition on blood red vinyl, also on picture disc
Reissued vinyl replica CD – Sanctuary 2002

No Prayer For The Dying : *Tail Gunner / Holy Smoke / No Prayer For The Dying*
/ Public Enema Number One / Fates Warning / The Assassin / Run Silent Run Deep
/ Hooks In You / Bring Your Daughter ... To The Slaughter / Mother Russia
/ All In Your Mind / Kill Me Ce Soir / I'm A Mover / Communication Breakdown
Reissued double CD – EMI 1995
Reissued double CD – EMI 1998

Fear Of The Dark: *Be Quick Or Be Dead / From Here To Eternity*
/ Afraid To Shoot Strangers / Fear Is The Key / Childhood's End / Wasting Love
/ The Fugitive / Chains of Misery / The Apparition / Judas Be My Guide
/ Weekend Warrior / Fear Of The Dark
LP/CD – EMI 1992
Reissued vinyl replica CD – Sanctuary 2002

Fear Of The Dark: *Be Quick Or Be Dead / From Here To Eternity / Afraid To Shoot Strangers / Fear Is The Key / Childhood's End / Wasting Love / The Fugitive / Chains of Misery / The Apparition / Judas Be My Guide / Weekend Warrior / Fear Of The Dark / Tailgunner /Holy Smoke / The Assassin*
CD – EMI 1992
NOTE: Australasian tour edition CD with three bonus tracks

Fear Of The Dark: *Be Quick Or Be Dead / From Here To Eternity / Afraid To Shoot Strangers / Fear Is The Key / Childhood's End / Wasting Love / The Fugitive / Chains of Misery / The Apparition / Judas Be My Guide / Weekend Warrior / Fear Of The Dark / Nodding Donkey Blues / Space Station No. 5 / I Can't See My Feeling / Roll Over Vic Vella / No Prayer For The Dying (live) / Public Enema #1 (live) / Hooks In You (live)*
Reissued double CD – EMI 1995
Reissued double CD – EMI 1998

A Real Live One: *Be Quick or Be Dead / From Here to Eternity / Can I Play With Madness / Wasting Love / Tailgunner / The Evil that Men Do / Afraid to Shoot Strangers / Bring Your Daughter ... To The Slaughter / Heaven Can Wait / The Clairvoyant / Fear of the Dark*
LP/CD – EMI 1993
NOTE: Also with gatefold sleeve
Reissued vinyl replica CD – Sanctuary 2002

A Real Dead One: *The Number Of The Beast / The Trooper / Prowler / Transylvania / Remember Tomorrow / Where Eagles Dare / Sanctuary / Running Free / Run To The Hills / 2 Minutes To Midnight / Iron Maiden / Hallowed Be Thy Name*
LP/CD – EMI 1993
NOTE: Also with gatefold sleeve
Reissued vinyl replica CD – Sanctuary 2002

Live At Donnington: *Be Quick Or Be Dead / The Number Of The Beast / Wrathchild / From Here To Eternity / Can I Play With Madness / Wasting Love / Tailgunner / The Evil That Men Do / Afraid To Shoot Strangers / Fear Of The Dark / Bring Your Daughter ... To The Slaughter / The Clairvoyant / Heaven Can Wait / Run To The Hills / 2 Minutes To Midnight / Iron Maiden / Hallowed Be Thy Name / The Trooper / Sanctuary / Running Free*
3 LP/ 2 CD – EMI 1993
NOTE: LP was limited edition, 5,000 copies.
Reissued vinyl replica CD – Sanctuary 2002 (Maiden's own spelling of 'Donington')

207

A Real Live Dead One: *The Number Of The Beast / The Trooper / Prowler / Transylvania / Remember Tomorrow / Where Eagles Dare / Sanctuary / Running Free / Run To The Hills / 2 Minutes To Midnight / Iron Maiden / Hallowed Be Thy Name / Be Quick Or Be Dead / From Here To Eternity / Can I Play With Madness / Wasting Love / Tail Gunner / The Evil That Men Do / Afraid To Shoot Strangers / Bring Your Daughter ... To The Slaughter / Heaven Can Wait / The Clairvoyant / Fear Of The Dark*
LP/CD – EMI 1998
NOTE: A new format, 2 CD compilation of **A Real Live One** and **A Real Dead One**.

Brave New World: *The Wicker Man / Ghost Of The Navigator / Brave New World / Blood Brothers / The Mercenary / Dream Of Mirrors / The Fallen Angel / The Nomad / Out Of The Silent Planet / The Thin Line Between Love & Hate*
CD – EMI 2000

Rock In Rio: *Intro / The Wicker Man / Ghost of the Navigator / Brave New World / Wrathchild / 2 Minutes to Midnight / Blood Brothers / Sign of the Cross / The Mercenary / The Trooper / Brave New World (Enhanced Video) / Dream of Mirrors / The Clansman / The Evil That Men Do / Fear of the Dark / Iron Maiden / The Number of the Beast / Hallowed Be Thy Name / Sanctuary / Run to the Hills / A Day In The Life (enhanced video)*
CD – EMI 2002

Beast Over Hammersmith: *Murders In The Rue Morgue / Wrathchild / Run To The Hills / Children Of The Damned / The Number Of The Beast / Another Life / Killers / 22 Acacia Avenue / Total Eclipse / Transylvania / The Prisoner / Hallowed Be Thy Name / Phantom Of The Opera / Iron Maiden / Sanctuary / Drifter / Running Free / Prowler*
CD – EMI 2002
NOTE: Double CD documenting the band's live show at Hammersmith Odeon in 1982, part of the 'Beast On The Road' tour. The accompanying inlay booklet is a complete recreation of the 'Beast On The Road' tour programme and lists all the world tour dates and includes notes from the band written at that time.

Dance Of Death: *Wildest Dreams / Rainmaker / No More Lies / Montsegur / Dance Of Death / Gates Of Tomorrow / New Frontier / Paschendale / Face In The Sand / Age Of Innocence / Journeyman*
CD – EMI 2003

Death On The Road: *Wildest Dreams/ Wrathchild / Can I Play With Madness / The Trooper / Dance Of Death / Rainmaker / Brave New World / Paschendale / Lord Of The Flies / No More Lies / Hallowed Be Thy Name / Fear Of The Dark / Iron Maiden / Journeyman / Number Of The Beast / Run To The Hills*
CD – EMI 2005

A Matter Of Life And Death: *Different World / These Colours Don't Run / Brighter Than a Thousand Suns / The Pilgrim / The Longest Day / Out Of the Shadows / The Reincarnation Of Benjamin Breeg / For The Greater Good Of God / Lord Of Light / The Legacy*
CD – EMI 2006

Solo

Tattooed Millionaire: *Son Of A Gun / Tattooed Millionaire / Born In '58 / Hell On Wheels / Gypsy Road / Dive! Dive! Dive! / All The Young Dudes / Lickin' The Gun / Zulu Lulu / No Lies*
LP/CD – EMI 1990

Tattooed Millionaire: *Son Of A Gun / Tattooed Millionaire / Born In '58 / Hell On Wheels / Gypsy Road / Dive! Dive! Dive! / All The Young Dudes / Lickin' The Gun / Zulu Lulu / No Lies / Bring your Daughter ... To The Slaughter (original soundtrack version) / Ballad Of Mutt / Winds Of Change / Darkness Be My Friend / Sin City / Dive! Dive! Dive! (live) / Riding With Angels (live) Sin City (live) Black Night (live) Son Of A Gun (live) Tattooed Millionaire (live)*
Reissued double CD – EMI 2005

Balls To Picasso: *Cyclops / Hell No / Gods Of War / 1000 Points Of Light / Laughing In The Hiding Bush / Change Of Heart / Shoot All the Clowns / Fire / Sacred Cowboys / Tears Of The Dragon*
LP/CD – EMI 1994

Balls To Picasso: *Cyclops / Hell No / Gods Of War / 1000 Points Of Light / Laughing In The Hiding Bush / Change Of Heart / Shoot All the Clowns / Fire / Sacred Cowboys / Tears Of The Dragon / Fire Child / <u>Elvis</u> Has Left The Building / The Breeding House / No Way Out ... To Be Continued / Tears Of The Dragon / Winds Of Change / Spirit Of Joy / Over And Out / Shoot All The Clowns (12" extended remix) Laughing In The Hiding Bush (live) / The Post Alternative Seattle Fall Out (live) / Shoot All the Clowns (7" Remix) Tibet / Tears Of The Dragon (First Bit, Long Bit, Last Bit) / Cadillac Gas Mask / No Way Out ... To Be Continued*
Reissued double CD – EMI 2005

Alive In Studio A: *Cyclops / Shoot All The Clowns / Son Of A Gun / Tears Of The Dragon / 1000 Points Of Light / Sacred Cowboys / Tattooed Millionaire / Born In '58 / Fire / Change Of Heart / Hell No / Laughing In The Hiding Bush / Cyclops / 1000 Points Of Light / Born in '58 / Gods Of War / Change Of Heart / Laughing In The Hiding Bush / Hell No / Tears Of The Dragon / Shoot All The Clowns / Sacred Cowboys / Son Of A Gun / Tattooed Millionaire*
LP/CD – Raw Power 1995

Skunkworks: *Space Race / Back From The Edge / Inertia / Faith / Solar Confinement / Dreamstate / I Will Not Accept The Truth / Inside The Machine / Headswitch / Meltdown / Octavia / Innerspace / Strange Death In Paradise*
LP/CD – Raw Power 1996

Skunkworks: *Space Race / Back From The Edge / Inertia / Faith / Solar Confinement / Dreamstate / I Will Not Accept The Truth / Inside The Machine / Headswitch / Meltdown / Octavia / Innerspace / Strange Death In Paradise / R 101 / Re-Entry*
CD – Victor 1996
NOTE: Japan only

Skunkworks: *Space Race / Back From The Edge / Inertia / Faith / Solar Confinement / Dreamstate / I Will Not Accept The Truth / Inside The Machine / Headswitch / Meltdown / Octavia / Innerspace / Strange Death In Paradise / I'm In A Band With An Italian Drummer / Rescue Day / God's Not Coming Back / Armchair Hero / R 101 / Re-Entry / Americans Are Behind / Inertia (live) / Faith (live) / Innerspace (live) / The Prisoner (live)*
Reissued double CD – Castle 2005

Accident Of Birth: *Freak / Toltec 7 Arrival / Starchildren / Taking The Queen / Darkside of Aquarius / Road To Hell / Man Of Sorrows / Accident Of Birth / The Magician / Welcome To The Pit / The Ghost Of Cain / Omega / Arc Of Space*
LP/CD – CMC International 1997
NOTE: *The Ghost Of Cain* only appears on the Japanese and American releases and is on the second disc of the 2005 reissue. The cover featured a puppet bursting out of a man's stomach. This was deemed too explicit for the U.S. market, where the album was released with was a more frontal view of the puppet, not showing the stomach. The 2005 re-release has another different cover, with the puppet nailed to a cross.

210

Accident Of Birth: *Freak / Toltec 7 Arrival / Starchildren / Taking The Queen / Darkside Of Aquarius / Road To Hell / Man Of Sorrows / Accident Of Birth / The Magician / Welcome To The Pit / The Ghost of Cain / Omega / Arc Of Space / Ghost Of Cain / Accident Of Birth (demo) / Starchildren (demo) / Taking The Queen (demo) / Man Of Sorrows (radio edit) / Man Of Sorrows (orchestral version) / Man Of Sorrows (Spanish version) / Darkside Of Aquarius (demo) / Arc Of Space (demo)*
Reissued double CD – CMC International 2005

The Chemical Wedding: *King In Crimson / Chemical Wedding / The Tower / Killing Floor / Book Of Thel / Gates Of Urizen / Jerusalem / Trumpets Of Jericho / Machine Men / The Alchemist*
CD – Sanctuary 1998

The Chemical Wedding: *King In Crimson / Chemical Wedding / The Tower / Killing Floor / Book Of Thel / Gates Of Urizen / Jerusalem / Trumpets Of Jericho / Machine Men / The Alchemist / Return Of The King*
CD – Victor 1998
NOTE: Japan only

The Chemical Wedding: *King In Crimson / Chemical Wedding / The Tower / Killing Floor / Book Of Thel / Gates Of Urizen / Jerusalem / Trumpets Of Jericho / Machine Men / The Alchemist / Real World*
CD – Paradoxx 1998
NOTE: Brazil only

The Chemical Wedding: *King In Crimson / Chemical Wedding / The Tower / Killing Floor / Book Of Thel / Gates Of Urizen / Jerusalem / Trumpets Of Jericho / Machine Men / The Alchemist / Return Of The King / Real World / Confeos*
Reissued CD – Sanctuary 2005

Scream For Me Brazil: *Trumpets Of Jericho / King In Crimson / Chemical Wedding / Gates of Urizen / Killing Floor / Book Of Thel / Tears Of The Dragon / Laughing In The Hiding Bush / Accident Of Birth / The Tower / Darkside Of Aquarius / The Road To Hell*
CD – Sanctuary 1999

Tyranny Of Souls: *Mars Within / Abduction / Soul Intruders / Kill Devil Hill / Navigate The Seas Of The Sun / River Of No Return / Power Of The Sun / Devil On A Hog / Believil / A Tyranny Of Souls*
CD – Sanctuary 2005

Compilations and Box Sets

Samson

Head Tactics: *Vice Versa / Earth Mother / Losing My Grip / Take It Like A Man / Once Bitten / Go To Hell / Hard Times / Nice Girl / Too Close To Rock / Walking Out On You*
LP – Capitol 1986
NOTE: Compilation featuring Bruce Vox, all tracks re-mixed

Riding With The Angels – The Anthology: *Mr Rock And Roll / Driving Music / Big Brother / Tomorrow Or Yesterday / Hard Times / Take It Like A Man / Vice Versa / Angel With A Machine Gun / Hammerhead / Hunted / Riding With The Angels / Earth Mother / Blood Lust / Bright Light / Pyramid To The Stars / Communion / Leaving Love (Behind) (alternative studio version) / Losing My Grip / Love Hungry / Don't Get Mad, Get Even / Test Of Time / Are You Ready / Red Skies / Chosen Few / Tell Me / I Must Be Crazy / Too Late / Good To See You / Can't Live Without Your Love / Hey You / Room 109 / Brand New Day*
CD – Essential 2002

Iron Maiden

The First Ten Years: *Running Free / Burning Ambition / Sanctuary / Drifter (live) / I've Got The Fire (live) / Listen With Nicko! Part I / Women In Uniform / Invasion / Phantom Of The Opera (live) / Twilight Zone / Wrathchild / Listen With Nicko! Part II / Purgatory / Genghis Khan / Running Free (live) / Remember Tomorrow" (live) / Killers (live) / Innocent Exile" (live) / Listen With Nicko! Part III / Run To The Hills /Total Eclipse / The Number Of The Beast / Remember Tomorrow (live) / Listen With Nicko! Part IV / Flight of Icarus / I've Got The Fire / The Trooper / Cross-Eyed Mary / Listen With Nicko! Part V / 2 Minutes To Midnight / Rainbow's Gold / Mission From 'Arry /Aces High / King Of Twilight / The Number Of The Beast (live) /Listen With Nicko! Part VI / Running Free (live) / Sanctuary (live) / Murders In The Rue Morgue (live) Run to the Hills (live) /Phantom Of The Opera (live) / Losfer Words (Big 'Orra) (live) / Listen With Nicko! Part VII / Wasted Years / Reach Out / Sheriff Of Huddersfield / Stranger In A Strange Land / That Girl / Juanita / Listen With Nicko! Part VIII / Can I Play With Madness / Black Bart Blues / Massacre / The Evil That Men Do / Prowler 88 / Charlotte The Harlot 88 / Listen With Nicko! Part IX / The Clairvoyant (live) / The Prisoner (live) / Heaven Can Wait*

/ *Infinite Dreams (live)* / *Killers* / *Still Life* / *Listen With Nicko! Part X*
CD/12" – EMI 1990
NOTE: A Series of 10 CDs and double 12" singles released to commemorate 10
years of Iron Maiden. Each CD/12" contains two of Iron Maiden's singles,
including the b-sides. In addition, each contained a bonus track, a part in the 'Listen
With Nicko' series, in which drummer <u>Nicko McBrain</u> talks about the songs on the
discs. Each part in the series included a special <u>voucher</u>. If you collected all ten
vouchers, you could order a special box in which you could store the CDs or vinyl
records.

The Story So Far (Part One): Limited and numbered box set containing the five
remastered albums from 1980 to 1984 [**Iron Maiden, Killers, The Number Of
The Beast, Piece Of Mind, Powerslave**] Each with the relevant era's b-sides on a
bonus disc
CD – EMI 1995

The Story So Far (Part Two) : Limited and numbered box set containing the five
remastered albums from 1985 to 1992 [**Live After Death, Somewhere In Time,
Seventh Son Of A Seventh Son, No Prayer For The Dying, Fear Of The Dark**]
Each with the relevant era's b-sides on a bonus disc
CD – EMI 1995

The Best Of The Beast: *Virus* / *Sign Of The Cross* / *Afraid To Shoot Strangers (live)*
/ *Man On The Edge* / *Be Quick Or Be Dead* / *Fear Of The Dark (live)* / *Holy Smoke*
/ *Bring Your Daughter ... To The Slaughter* / *Seventh Son Of A Seventh Son*
/ *Can I Play With Madness* / *The Evil That Men Do* / *The Clairvoyant*
/ *Heaven Can Wait* / *Wasted Years* / *2 Minutes To Midnight* / *Running Free (live)*
/ *Rime Of The Ancient Mariner (live)* / *Aces High* / *Where Eagles Dare*
/ *The Trooper* / *The Number Of The Beast* / *Revelations (live)* / *The Prisoner*
/ *Run To The Hills* / *Hallowed Be Thy Name* / *Wrathchild* / *Killers*
/ *Remember Tomorrow* / *Phantom Of The Opera* / *Sanctuary* / *Prowler* / *Invasion*
/ *Strange World* / *Iron Maiden*
CD/LP – EMI 1996 NOTE: Available in three different packaging:
one CD, double-CD or four-LPs

Eddie's Head: A large box in the shape of Eddie's head. Containing the first 12
albums remastered, from **Iron Maiden** to **Live at Donnington**, each with bonus
multimedia material, plus a limited edition **In Profile** CD
CD – EMI 1998

Ed Hunter: *Iron Maiden (live) / The Trooper / The Number of the Beast / Wrathchild / Futureal / Fear of the Dark / Be Quick Or Be Dead / 2 Minutes to Midnight / Man on the Edge / Aces High / The Evil That Men Do / Wasted Years / Powerslave / Hallowed Be Thy Name / Run to the Hills / The Clansman / Phantom of the Opera / Killers / Stranger In A Strange Land / Tailgunner*
CD ROM – EMI 1999
NOTE: A first-person shooter video game, 'Ed Hunter', was released in 1999, and is based on and accompanied by Iron Maiden's music. The package included 3 CDs. The first CD contained 14 songs, the second CD contained 6 songs and the installation program for the game and the third CD contained the game data. The soundtrack allegedly consists of the top 20 songs voted for by Iron Maiden fans on Maiden's official website. The US version has a hidden bonus track of a new recording of *Wrathchild* with Bruce Dickinson on lead vocals. This was also released as a limited edition single at the same time as 'Wrathchild with Bruce Dickinson'.

The BBC Archives: *Iron Maiden / Running Free / Transylvania / Sanctuary* Reading Festival 1982 */ Wrathchild / Run To The Hills / Children Of The Damned / The Number of The Beast / 22 Acacia Avenue / Transylvania / The Prisoner / Hallowed Be Thy Name / Phantom Of The Opera / Iron Maiden* Reading Festival 1980 *Prowler / Remember Tomorrow / Killers / Running Free / Transylvania / Iron Maiden* Monsters Of Rock Festival Donington 1988 *Moonchild / Wrathchild / Infinite Dreams / The Trooper / Seventh Son of a Seventh Son / The Number Of The Beast / Hallowed Be Thy Name / Iron Maiden*
CD – EMI 2002

Edward The Great: *Run To The Hills / The Number of the Beast / Flight Of Icarus / The Trooper / 2 Minutes To Midnight / Wasted Years / Can I Play With Madness / The Evil That Men Do / The Clairvoyant / Infinite Dreams / Holy Smoke / Bring Your Daughter ... To the Slaughter / Man on the Edge /* <u>*Futureal*</u> */* <u>*The Wicker Man*</u> */Fear Of The Dark (live)*
CD – EMI 2002

Edward The Great: *Run To The Hills / The Number of the Beast / The Trooper / Flight of Icarus / 2 Minutes To Midnight / Wasted Years / Can I Play with Madness / The Evil That Men Do / Bring Your Daughter ... To the Slaughter/ Man on the Edge / Futureal / The Wicker Man / Brave New World / Wildest Dreams / Rainmaker /Fear of the Dark (live)*
Reissued CD – EMI 2005
NOTE: A revised edition of **Edward The Great** was released in Europe, Asia and South America, with a slightly different tracklist. This 'updated' version was to

coincide with the release of **The Essential Iron Maiden** compilation that was released in North America. The revised edition features some songs from the **Dance Of Death** album, and a different live version of *Fear of the Dark*. The new version also adds the song *Brave New World* from the album of the same name. The booklet includes a new foreword by Iron Maiden manager Rod Smallwood, whereas the original version has a foreword by founding member Steve Harris. The album cover does not differentiate between the two other than the tracklisting – some shops still sell old stock of the original.

Best Of The B-Sides: *Murders In The Rue Morgue / Wrathchild / Run To The Hills / Children Of The Damned / The Number Of The Beast / Another Life / Killers / 22 Acacia Avenue / Total Eclipse / Transylvania / The Prisoner / Hallowed Be Thy Name / Phantom Of The Opera / Iron Maiden / Sanctuary / Drifter / Running Free / Prowler*
CD – EMI 2004

Eddie's Archive: Limited and numbered box set, later re-released without the numbering limitation. Contains 3 double-albums [**Best of the B-Sides, BBC Archives, Beast Over Hammersmith**] plus a numbered scroll of the Iron Maiden timeline, and an 'Eddie' crystal shot glass.
CD – EMI 2004

The Essential Iron Maiden: *Paschendale / Rainmaker / The Wicker Man / Brave New World / Futureal / The Clansman / Sign Of The Cross / Man On The Edge / Be Quick Or Be Dead / Fear Of The Dark (live) / Holy Smoke / Bring Your Daughter ... To the Slaughter / The Clairvoyant / The Evil That Men Do / Wasted Years / Heaven Can Wait / Minutes To Midnight / Aces High / Flight of Icarus / The Trooper / The Number Of The Beast / Run To The Hills / Wrathchild / Killers / Phantom Of The Opera / Running Free (live) / Iron Maiden (live)*
CD – Sanctuary/Columbia 2005
NOTE: USA Only

Solo

The Best Of Bruce Dickinson: *Broken / Tattooed Millionaire / Laughing In The Hiding Bush (live) / Tears Of The Dragon / The Tower / Born in '58 / Accident Of Birth / Silver Wings / Darkside Of Aquarius / Chemical Wedding / Back From The Edge / Road To Hell / Book Of Thel (live) / Bring Your Daughter ... To The Slaughter (original soundtrack version) / Darkness Be My Friend / Wicker Man / Real World / Acoustic Song / No Way Out ... To Be Continued / Midnight Jam / Man Of Sorrows / Ballad Of Mutt / Re-Entry / I'm In A Band With An Italian Drummer / Jerusalem (live) / The Voice Of Crube / Dracula*
CD – Metal-Is 2001

Singles

Samson

Vice Versa (edit) / Hammerhead
7" – Gem/RCA 1980

Hard Times (remix) / Angel With A Machine Gun
7" – Gem/RCA 1980

Riding With The Angels (edit) / Little Big Man
7" – Gem/RCA 1981
NOTE: Also picture disc

Iron Maiden

Run To The Hills / Total Eclipse
7" – EMI 1982

The Number Of The Beast / Remember Tomorrow (live version)
7" – EMI 1982

The Number Of The Beast / Hallowed Be Thy Name (video clip) / The Number Of The Beast (video clip)
CD – EMI 2005

Flight Of Icarus / I've Got The Fire
7" – EMI 1983

The Trooper / Cross Eyed Mary
7" – EMI 1983

The Trooper (live from 'Death on the Road' tour)
/ The Trooper (original studio version) / Prowler (live from Iceland)
/ The Trooper (live video of main track) / The Trooper (original promo video)
CD – EMI 2005

2 Minutes To Midnight / Rainbow's Gold / Mission From 'Arry
12" EMI 1984

Aces High / King Of Twilight / The Number Of The Beast (live version)
7" – EMI 1984

Aces High / King Of Twilight / The Number Of The Beast (live version)
/ Rainbow's Gold / Cross-Eyed Mary / 2 Minutes To Midnight
12" – EMI 1984

Running Free (live version) / Sanctuary (live version)
/ Murders In The Rue Morgue (live version)
7" – EMI 1985

Run To The Hills (live version) / Phantom Of The Opera (live version)
/ Losfer Words (Big 'Orra) (live version)
7" – EMI 1985

Stranger In A Strange Land / That Girl / Juanita
7" – EMI 1986

Can I Play With Madness / Black Bart Blues / Massacre
CD/7" – EMI 1988

The Evil That Men Do / Prowler '88 / Charlotte The Harlot '88
CD/7" – EMI 1988

The Clairvoyant (live version) / The Prisoner (live version)
/ Heaven Can Wait (live version)
CD/7" – EMI 1988

Infinite Dreams (live version) / Killers (live version) / Still Life (live version)
CD/7" – EMI 1989

Holy Smoke / All In Your Mind / Kill Me Ce Soir
CD – EMI 1990

Bring Your Daughter ... To The Slaughter / I'm A Mover
/ Communication Breakdown
CD/7" – EMI 1990

Be Quick Or Be Dead / Nodding Donkey Blues / Space Station No. 5
CD – EMI 1992

From Here To Eternity (triumph mix) / Roll Over Vic Vella
/ Public Enema #1 (live version / No Prayer For The Dying (live version)
/ I Can't See My Feeling
CD – EMI 1992

Wasting Love / Tailgunner (live version) / Holy Smoke (live version)
/ The Assassin (live version)
CD – EMI 1992

Fear Of The Dark (live version) / Be Quick Or Be Dead (live version)
/ Hooks In You (live version) Tailgunner (live version)
/ No Prayer For The Dying (live version)
CD – EMI 1993

Hallowed Be Thy Name ((live) The Trooper (live) / Wasted Years (live)
/ Wrathchild (live)
CD – EMI 1993

The Wicker Man (radio version) / The Wicker Man (radio edit)
CD – Columbia/Sony 2000
NOTE: US only

The Wicker Man / Man On The Edge (live version) / Powerslave (live version)
/ The Wicker Man (video clip)
CD – EMI 2000

The Wicker Man / Futureal (live version) / Killers (live version)
/ Futureal (video clip, live version)
CD – EMI 2000

Out Of The Silent Planet / Wasted Years (live version) / Aces High (live version)
/ Out Of The Silent Planet (video clip)
CD – EMI 2000

Run To The Hills (live) / *22, Acacia Avenue (live)* / *The Prisoner (live)*
/ *Run to the Hills (Camp Chaos video)*
CD – EMI 2002

Run To The Hills (live) / *Children of the Damned (live)* / *Total Eclipse (live)*
/ *Run to the Hills (video)*
CD – EMI 2002

Wildest Dreams / *Pass The Jam* / *Blood Brothers (orchestral mix)*
CD – EMI 2003

Rainmaker / *Dance of Death (orchestral version)* / *More Tea Vicar*
CD – EMI 2003

The Reincarnation Of Benjamin Breeg
/ *Hallowed Be Thy Name (Radio 1 'Legends' session)*
CD – EMI 2006

The Reincarnation of Benjamin Breeg / *The Trooper (Radio 1 'Legends' Session)*
/ *Run to the Hills (Radio 1 'Legends' session)*
10" clear vinyl – EMI 2006

Different World / *Hallowed Be Thy Name (Radio 1 'Legends' Session)*
/ *The Trooper (Radio 1 'Legends' session)*
CD – Sanctuary 2006
NOTE: US only

Different World / *Iron Maiden (live from Copenhagen)*
CD – EMI 2006

Different World / *The Reincarnation Of Benjamin Breeg (live from Copenhagen)*
/ *Hocus Pocus (Focus cover)*
DVD – EMI 2006

Different World / *Fear Of The Dark (live from Copenhagen)*
7" picture disc – EMI 2006

Solo

Tattooed Millionaire / Ballad Of Mutt
7" – EMI 1990

Tattooed Millionaire / Ballad of Mutt / Winds Of Change
CD – EMI 1990

Tattooed Millionaire / Tattooed Millionaire (radio remix) / Interview
CD – Columbia 1990
NOTE: US only

All The Young Dudes (Mott The Hoople cover) / Darkness Be My Friend
7" – EMI 1990

All The Young Dudes / Darkness Be My Friend / Sin City
CD/12" – EMI 1990

Dive! Dive! Dive! / Riding With The Angels (live)
7" – EMI 1990

Dive! Dive! Dive! / Riding With The Angels (live)
/ Sin City (live) Black Knight (live)
CD/12"/12" picture disc – EMI 1990
NOTE: Also came with free poster

Born in '58 / Son Of A Gun (live)
7" – EMI 1990

Born in '58 / Son Of A Gun (live) / Tattooed Millionaire
CD/12" – EMI 1990

Tears Of The Dragon / Firechild
7" clear vinyl – EMI 1994

Tears Of The Dragon / Elvis Has Left The Building
7" picture disc – EMI 1994

Tears Of The Dragon / The Breeding House / No Way Out ... To Be Continued
CD – EMI 1994

Tears Of The Dragon / Spirit Of Joy / Winds Of Change
CD – EMI 1994

Tears Of The Dragon / The Breeding House / No Way Out...To Be Continued
/ Tears Of The Dragon (acoustic chill out)
CD – EMI Holland 1994
NOTE: Holland only

Shoot All The Clowns / Over And Out
7" clear vinyl – EMI 1994

Shoot All The Clowns / Laughing In The Hiding Bush (live)
/ The Post Alternative Seattle Fall-Out (live)
12" – EMI 1994
NOTE: With free poster

Shoot All The Clowns / Tibet / Tears Of The Dragon (I,II,III)
/ Shoot All The Clowns (remix)
CD – EMI 1994

Shoot All The Clowns / Cadillac Gas Mask / No Way Out (continued)
CD – EMI 1994

Shoot All The Clowns (remix) / Tibet / No Way Out...To Be Continued
/ Tears Of The Dragon (I,II,III)
CD – EMI Holland 1994
NOTE: Holland only

Back From The Edge / I'm In A Band With An Italian Drummer
7" picture disc – Raw Power 1996

Back From The Edge/ Rescue Day / Armchair Hero / God's Not Coming Back
CD – Raw Power 1996

Back From The Edge / R 101 / Re-Entry / Americans Are Behind
CD – Raw Power 1996

Back From The Edge / Rescue Day / Armchair Hero / God's Not Coming Back
R 101 / Re-Entry / Americans Are Behind
CD – Victor 1996
NOTE: Japan only

Accident Of Birth / Accident Of Birth (demo) / Ghost Of Cain
CD/12" red vinyl – Raw Power 1997
NOTE: Has red cover

Accident Of Birth / Star Children (demo) / Taking The Queen (demo)
CD – Raw Power 1997
NOTE: Has green cover

Man Of Sorrows (radio edit) / Man Of Sorrows (orchestral version)
/ Man Of Sorrows (Spanish version) / Darkside Of Aquarius (demo)
/ Arc Of Space (demo)
CD – Victor 1997
NOTE: Japan only

Killing Floor / Confeos / Real World
CD – Victor 1998
NOTE: Japan only

Broken / Silver Wings / Bring Your Daughter...To The Slaughter (original version)
CD – Metal-Is 2001

Broken / Silver Wings
CD – Metal-Is 2001

Abduction
CD – Mayan/Sanctuary 2005

EPs

Iron Maiden

No More Lies – Dance Of Death Souvenir EP: *No More Lies*
/ Paschendale (orchestral version) / Journeyman (electric version)
/ Age of Innocence ... How Old?
CD – EMI 2004

Solo

Skunkworks Live EP: *Inertia / Faith / Innerspace / The Prisoner*
CD – Victor 1996
NOTE: Japan only

Miscellaneous

Speed

Down The Road/Man On The Street
7" – Speed Records 1980
NOTE: Bruce appears on 'Man On The Street', credited as 'Bruce Bruce'

Xero

Oh Baby / Hold On / Lone Wolf
7" – Brickyard 1983
NOTE: Bruce vocals on *Lone Wolf'*

Oh Baby EP: *Oh Baby / Hold On / Lone Wolf*
EP – Brick Yard Records 1983
NOTE: Bruce vocals on *Lone Wolf* only, secret track

A Nightmare On Elm Street 5: Dream Child. Original soundtrack album:
Bring Your Daughter...To The Slaughter
LP/CD – 1989 Zomba
NOTE: Original version by Bruce Dickinson and Janick Gers

Rock Aid Armenia:
Smoke On The Water
LP/CD – Life Aid Armenia Records 1990

Smear Campaign:
(I Want To Be) Elected
7" – London Records 1992
NOTE: Comic Relief charity single

Nativity in Black: A Tribute to Black Sabbath:
Sabbath Bloody Sabbath
CD – Sony 1994
NOTE: Bruce appears with Godspeed.

Friends For Life:
Bohemian Rhapsody
CD – BMG 1997
NOTE: Montserrat Caballé duets album

Extreme Championship Wrestling Compilation – Extreme Music:
The Zoo
CD – Earache 1998
NOTE: Compilation of extreme music tracks chosen to musically represent Extreme Championship Wrestling.

The Bride Of Chucky Original Soundtrack Album:
Trumpets of Jericho
CD – Sanctuary 1998

Humanary Stew: A Tribute To Alice Cooper:
Black Widow
CD – Columbia 1998

Universal Migrator Part 2: Flight Of The Migrator:
Into the Black Hole
NOTE: A musical album composed by Arjen Anthony Lucassen and released under his project name Ayeron. **Fight of the Migrator** is a metal opera, which is narrated across several eras which precede the existence of the known universe, with each era being interpreted by a different singer. Bruce is on *Into the Black Hole*
CD – Transmission 2000

Halford

Resurrection
The One You Love To Hate
CD/LP – Sanctuary 2000

Live Insurrection
The One You Love To Hate
Double CD – Sanctuary 2001

Sack Trick

Sheep In Kiss Make Up
Shout it Out Loud
CD – Sacktrick 2004
NOTE: Kiss tribute album by eccentric music collective Sack Trick – who of course featured as the *Skunkworks* band
www.sacktrick.com

Tribuzy

Execution
Beast In The Light
CD – Locomotive 2005

Bootlegs

There are innumerable bootlegs in circulation from across Bruce's career, from late 1970s pub gigs to today's stadium events. Here's a short list of websites that indicate what might be available. Remember that Home Taping Is Killing Music.

http://hem.passagen.se/essarf/bootlegs.html – Bootleg trading website

http://maidenshows.ryasrealm.com/masterlist.htm – Near complete gig list with details as to whether audio or video footage exists

http://maidenbootlegs.com/index.cfm – Very well designed and extensive Maiden bootleg trading site

http://hometown.aol.com/acshigh/ – Large list of bootlegs up for trade

http://www.ead666.com/ – Bootleg trading site

http://maidenshows.ryasrealm.com/ – Bootleg listing and trading site

http://www.geocities.com/Zdenius666/ – Large list of bootlegs for trade

http://home.wanadoo.nl/maurice.straatman/– Good list of audio and video bootlegs for trade

http://www.maidenboots.de.vu/ – Bootleg trading site

http://www.geocities.com/ironsoul_2000/ – Metal bootleg trading site, large selection of Iron Maiden bootlegs

http://www.mirdaroh.dolsat.pl/list-video.html – Large and well designed Maiden video and audio bootleg trading site

Videos and DVDs

Samson

Biceps Of Steel: *Hard Times / Vice Versa*
VHS – Synergie Logistics 2002
DVD – Navarre Corporation 2003

Iron Maiden

Video Pieces: *Run To The Hills / The Number of the Beast / Flight of Icarus / The Trooper*
VHS/BETA/Laserdisc/VHD – EMI 1983

Behind The Iron Curtain: *2 Minutes to Midnight / Aces High / Hallowed Be Thy Name (live) / Run To The Hills (live)*
VHS/BETA/Laserdisc/VHD – EMI 1985

Live After Death: *Aces High / 2 Minutes To Midnight / The Trooper / Revelations / Flight of Icarus / The Rime Of The Ancient Mariner / Powerslave / The Number Of The Beast / Hallowed Be Thy Name / Iron Maiden / Run To The Hills / Running Free / Sanctuary*
VHS/BETA/Laserdisc/VHD/Hi-8 – EMI 1985

12 Wasted Years: *Stranger In A Strange Land (promotional video) / Charlotte The Harlot (live) / Running Free (live) / Women In Uniform (promotional video) / Murders In The Rue Morgue (live) / Children Of The Damned" (live) / The Number of the Beast (live) / Total Eclipse (live) / Iron Maiden (live) / Sanctuary (live) / The Prisoner (live) / 22 Acacia Avenue (live) / Wasted Years (live) / The Trooper (live)*
VHS/Laserdisc – EMI 1987

Maiden England: *Moonchild / The Evil That Men Do / Prisoner / Still Life / Die With Your Boots On / Infinite Dreams / Killers / Can I Play With Madness / Heaven Can Wait / Wasted Years / The Clairvoyant / Seventh Son Of A Seventh Son / The Number Of The Beast / Hallowed Be Thy Name / Iron Maiden*
VHS – EMI 1989

Maiden England: *Moonchild / The Evil That Men Do / The Prisoner / Still Life / Die With Your Boots On / Infinite Dreams / Killers / Can I Play With Madness / Heaven Can Wait / Wasted Years / The Clairvoyant / Seventh Son Of A Seventh Son / The Number Of The Beast / Hallowed Be Thy Name / Iron Maiden*

Bonus CD listing: *Moonchild / The Evil That Men Do / The Prisoner / Still Life / Die With Your Boots On / Infinite Dreams / Killers / Heaven Can Wait / Wasted Years / The Clairvoyant / Seventh Son Of A Seventh Son / The Number Of The Beast / Iron Maiden*
Reissued VHS – EMI 1994 with a bonus CD that contained several songs that were missing on the video due to space constraints

The First Ten Years: *Women In Uniform / Wrathchild (live) / Run To The Hills / The Number Of The Beast / Flight of Icarus / The Trooper / 2 Minutes To Midnight / Aces High / Running Free (live) / Wasted Years / Stranger In A Strange Land / Can I Play With Madness / The Evil That Men Do / The Clairvoyant / Infinite Dreams (live) / Holy Smoke*
VHS/Laserdisc – EMI 1990

From Here To Eternity: *Women In Uniform / Wrathchild (live) / Run To The Hills / The Number Of The Beast / Flight Of Icarus / The Trooper / 2 Minutes To Midnight / Aces High / Running Free (live) / Wasted Years / Stranger In A Strange Land / Can I Play With Madness / The Evil That Men Do / The Clairvoyant (live) / Infinite Dreams (live) / Holy Smoke / Tailgunner / Bring Your Daughter...To The Slaughter / Be Quick Or Be Dead / From Here To Eternity / Wasting Love*
VHS – EMI 1992

Donnington Live 1992: *Be Quick Or Be Dead / The Number Of The Beast / Wrathchild / From Here to Eternity / Can I Play with Madness / Wasting Love / Tailgunner / The Evil That Men Do / Afraid To Shoot Strangers / Fear Of The Dark / Bring Your Daughter ... To the Slaughter / The Clairvoyant / Heaven Can Wait / Run to the Hills / 2 Minutes To Midnight / Iron Maiden / Hallowed By The Name / The Trooper / Sanctuary / Running Free (with Adrian Smith)*
VHS – EMI 1993

Raising Hell: *Be Quick Or Be Dead / The Trooper / The Evil That Men Do / The Clairvoyant / Hallowed Be Thy Name / Wrathchild / Transylvanisa / From Here To Eternity / Fear Of The Dark / The Number Of the Beast / Bring Your Daughter ... To The Slaughter / 2 Minutes To Midnight / Afraid To Shoot Strangers / Heaven Can Wait / Sanctuary / Run To The Hills / Iron Maiden*
VHS – EMI 1993
DVD – EMI 2000

Classic Albums: **The Number Of The Beast**: *Invaders / Children O fThe Damned / The Prisoner / 22 Acacia Avenue / The Number Of The Beast / Run To The Hills / Gangland / Total Eclipse / Hallowed Be Thy Name*
VHS/DVD – EMI 2001

Rock In Rio: *Intro: Arthur's Farewell / The Wicker Man / Ghost Of The Navigator / Brave New World / Wrathchild / 2 Minutes To Midnight / Blood Brothers / Sign Of The Cross / The Mercenary / The Trooper / Dream Of Mirrors / The Clansman / The Evil That Men Do / Fear Of The Dark / Iron Maiden / The Number Of The Beast / Hallowed Be Thy Name / Sanctuary / Run To The Hills / Candid interviews with the band members / A 'Day in the Life' of Iron Maiden / Ross Halfin Photo Diary – 50 exclusive photos from Iron Maiden's South American Tour*
DVD/VHS – EMI 2002

Visions Of The Beast: *Women In Uniform / Wrathchild (live) / Run To The Hills / The Number Of The Beast / Flight Of Icarus / The Trooper / 2 Minutes To Midnight / Aces High / Wasted Years / Stranger In A Strange Land / Can I Play With Madness / The Evil That Men Do / The Clairvoyant (live) / Infinite Dreams (live) / Holy Smoke / Tailgunner / Aces High (Camp Chaos version) / The Number Of The Beast (Camp Chaos version) / Futureal (Football version) / Fear Of The Dark (live) / Bring Your Daughter ... To The Slaughter / Be Quick Or Be Dead / From Here To Eternity / Wasting Love / Fear Of The Dark (live) / Hallowed Be Thy Name (live) / Man On The Edge / Afraid to Shoot Strangers / Lord Of The Flies / Virus / The Angel And The Gambler / Futureal / The Wicker Man / Out Of The Silent Planet / Brave New World (live) / The Wicker Man (Camp Chaos version) / Flight Of Icarus (Camp Chaos version) / Run To The Hills (Camp Chaos version)*
DVD/VHS – EMI 2003

The History Of Iron Maiden Part One: The Early Days: **Live at the Rainbow**: *The Ides Of March / Wrathchild / Killers / Remember Tomorrow / Transylvania / Phantom Of the Opera / Iron Maiden* / **Beast Over Hammersmith**: *Murders In The Rue Morgue / Run To The Hills / Children Of The Damned / The Number Of The Beast / 22 Acacia Avenue / Total Eclipse / The Prisoner / Hallowed Be Thy Name / Iron Maiden* / **Live In Dortmund**: *Sanctuary / The Trooper / Revelations / Flight Of Icarus / 22 Acacia Avenue / The Number Of The Beast /Run To The Hills* / **Live At The Ruskin Arms**: *Sanctuary / Wrathchild / Prowler / Remember Tomorrow / Running Free / Transylvania / Another Life / Phantom Of The Opera / Charlotte The Harlot* / **Promo Videos**: *Women In Uniform / Run To The Hills / The Number Of The Beast / Flight Of Icarus / The Trooper* / **Extras**: *Running Free (Live on Top of the Pops) / Women In Uniform (Live on Top of the Pops) / Running Free (Live on Rock and Pop, Germany / Also photo gallery featuring more than 150 pictures, images and artwork, full tour listings, discography and tour programmes*
DVD – EMI 2004

Death On The Road: *Wildest Dreams / Wrathchild / Can I Play With Madness / The Trooper / Dance Of Death / Rainmaker / Brave New World / Paschendale / Lord Of The Flies / No More Lies / Hallowed Be Thy Name / Fear Of The Dark / Iron Maiden / Journeyman / The Number Of The Beast / Run To The Hills*
DVD – EMI 2006

Solo

Dive! Dive! Live!: *Riding With The Angels / Born In '58 / Lickin' The Gun / Gypsy Road / Dive! Dive! Dive! / Drum Solo / Zulu Zulu / The Ballad Of Mutt / Son Of A Gun / Hell On Wheels / All The Young Dudes / Tattooed Millionaire / No Lies / Fog On The Tyne / Winds Of Change / Sin City / Bring Your Daughter...To The Slaughter / Black Night*
VHS – Picture Music International 1991

Skunkworks Live: *Space Race / Back From the Edge / Tattooed Millionaire / Inertia / Faith / Meltdown / I Will Not Accept The Truth / Laughing In The Hiding Bush / Tears of The Dragon / God's Not Coming Back / Dreamstate / The Prisoner*
VHS – Victor 1996
NOTE: Japan only

Bruce Dickinson – Anthology: Additional Release Material: *Tattooed Millionaire / All The Young Dudes / Dive! Dive! Dive! / Born In '58 / Tears Of The Dragon / Shoot All The Clowns / Back From The Edge / Inertia / Accident Of Birth / Road To Hell / Man Of Sorrows / Killing Floor / The Tower / Abduction*
Dive! Dive! Live!: *Riding With The Angels / Born In '58 / Lickin' The Gun / Gypsy Road / Dive! Dive! Dive! / Drum Solo / Zulu Zulu / The Ballad Of Mutt / Son Of A Gun / Hell On Wheels / All The Young Dudes / Tattooed Millionaire / No Lies / Fog On The Tyne / Winds Of Change / Sin City / Bring Your Daughter...To The Slaughter / Black Night*
Skunkworks Live: *Space Race / Back From The Edge / Tattooed Millionaire / Inertia / Faith / Meltdown / I Will Not Accept The Truth / Laughing In The Hiding Bush / Tears Of The Dragon / God's Not Coming Back / Dreamstate /The Prisoner*
Scream For Me Brazil: *King In Crimson / Gates Of Urizen / Killing Floor / Book Of Thel / Tears Of The Dragon / Laughing In The Hiding Bush / Accident Of Birth / The Tower / Darkside Of Aquarius /The Road To Hell*
DVD – Sony 2006

Books

The Adventures Of Lord Iffy Boatrace by Bruce Dickinson
First published: Sidgwick & Jackson: London: 1990.
ISBN 0-283-06043-3

The Missionary Position by Bruce Dickinson
First published: Sidgwick & Jackson: London: 1992
ISBN 0-283-06092-1

Websites

Quite possibly the only one you need is www.google.com and some imagination ... but as I have none of that these places were most helpful as a starting point for many lost days and nights of what is laughingly called 'research' but should probably be actually called 'drinking whisky and surfing about on the web'.

http://www.paulsamson.co.uk
http://www.bookofhours.net/samson
http://www.ironmaiden.com
http://en.wikipedia.org/wiki/Iron_Maiden

http://www.metalhammer.co.uk/bands/band/?searchstring=Iron%20Maiden&filterse
ctionname=all&filtersubsectionname=all&articleid=42835

http://metalglory.tripod.com/imaiden/imaiden.htm
http://www.maidenfans.com/
http://www.ironmaidenheaven.com
http://maiden-world.com/
http://www.bbc.co.uk/music/artist/6pmq/
http://www.brucedickinson.co.uk/
http://www.brucefans.com/
http://www.screamforme.com/
http://www.geocities.com/sunsetstrip/club/5619/
http://en.wikipedia.org/wiki/Bruce_Dickinson
http://www.bookofhours.net/bdwbn/

www.gmtrocks.com – to see what John McCoy, Robin Guy and Bernie Torme sound like when they rock it up

and ... one more time please may I offer the enormitude of mystical wonder, sex, sheep, guts and gribble that is www.sackrtrick.com

Footnotes and Index Of Articles Referenced

Unless otherwise stated, all quotes are taken from original interviews with the author. Publications that were useful for reference were numerous, but the magazines *Kerrang!*, *Metal Hammer, Raw, Enfer, Rock Sound* were particularly useful, as were websites such as www.wikipedia.com, www.bookofhours.net, www.google.com and www.citizens-choice.co.uk/contents.

[1] Some of the unprintable ones are, '   ', '   ', '   ' and even '   '.

[2] See endnote 13 in *Whose Space Is It Anyway: An Unofficial Guide To The Sites That Changed The World* – Shooman, J. (Independent Music Press, March 2007) ISBN: 0955282217

[3] England were knocked out after the first group stage, weakened as they were by the terrible Munich air disaster.

[4] "In 1801, Worksop's population had been 3,263, but by 1901 it had risen to more than 16,000." – http://www.nottsnet.co.uk/Worksop/worksop_facts.htm retrieved December 2006

[5] The Everly Brothers were at Number One with the single 'All I Have To Do Is Dream / Claudette'. Bruce shares a birthday with comedian Alexei Sayle and Free bass player, Andy Fraser (both born six years earlier).

[6] *Iron Maiden: Run To The Hills – The Authorised Biography* – Wall, M.

[7] The gangs in the film: The Beetles, who ride in to challenge Brando's outfit, and Black Rebel Motorcycle Club. Now there's a band name!

[8] *The Story Of A Great Schoolmaster* - Wells, H.G.

[9] Oundle graduate Richard Dawkins expands on his own personal relationship with this man's legacy here: http://education.guardian.co.uk/schools/story/0,5500,750270,00.html retrieved December 2006

[10] *Iron Maiden: 30 Years Of Metal Mayhem* – Metal Hammer Presents Collectors Edition, 2005

[11] *Infinite Dreams: Iron Maiden* – Bowler, D. & Dray, B

[12] *Enfer* Magazine Interview – Phillip Touchard, December 1983

[13] http://www.hardradio.com/shockwaves/dickinson2-8.html – retrieved February 2007

[14] On December 1, 1976 a boozed-up Pistols appeared on an equally boozed-up Bill Grundy's *Tonight* show, the latter goading first a rather sheepish Johnny Rotten, then guitarist Steve Jones into swearing live on air; Jones all-too-gleefully obliged with a torrent. Outrage followed; newspaper headlines screamed, and the downfall of Western civilization was surely only around the corner.

[15] http://www.hardradio.com/shockwaves/dickinson2-8.html – retrieved February 2007

[16] '60 Second Interview' – James Ellis, Metro Newspaper

[17] *Iron Maiden: Running Free* – Bushell, G. & Halfin, R.

[18] '60 Second Interview' – James Ellis, *Metro* Newspaper

[19] *Enfer* Magazine Interview – Phillip Touchard, December 1983

[20] ibid.

[21] Rob could in fact be sitting on something of a pension scheme had he not lost a certain tape: "I used to have The Shots demo tape from that time; Graham who was running the Prince Of Wales used to

get all the demo tapes in and we used to swipe them from behind the bar. I had The Shots demo and you lend them out and they don't come back, and it isn't the end of the world at the time. Go forward thirty years... I know some serious Maiden collectors and they've never seen any Shots stuff, anywhere." Oops! Have you checked behind the sofa?

[22] Possibly the lyrics – if not the music – of the Speed track?

[23] As legend has it, this is the track over which one John Lydon sneered and gyrated in an audition for his own band during 1975, the Sex Pistols.

[24] To translate, this is American for the perfectly reasonable Anglo-Saxon word, 'arse'.

[25] www.battlehelm.com/interviews/Samson.html – retrieved December 2006

[26] www.battlehelm.com/interviews/Samson.html – retrieved December 2006

[27] After that intro Neal, you owe me a curry. Nice one.

[28] Dome has a suitably rich show on Total Rock Radio, which Kay regularly appears on to equally suitably entertaining effect.

[29] A term coined by Alan Lewis, editor of *Sounds*, according to that magazine's journalist Geoff Barton, who first had this byline under the phrase in an article of May 19, 1979. There is rather a good book about NWOBHM called *Suzie Smiled: The New Wave Of British Heavy Metal*. It is by a chap called John Tucker, and it is published by Independent Music Press. ISBN: 0-9549701-7-0

[30] Exclusive unpublished extract taken from the forthcoming Paul Samson biog *Burning Emotion*, courtesy Rob Grain, copyright The Paul Samson Estate and reproduced with respectful thanks.

[31] *Metal Hammer* Interview, Date unknown

[32] Spencer Leigh interview, BBC Radio Merseyside 1990

[33] 'My Life Story' – *Metal Hammer*, Date Unknown

[34] www.battlehelm.com/interviews/Samson.html – retrieved December 2006

[35] Rob Grain: "What frustrates me is the whole media thing about the NWOBHM is that it's under the belief that it was Iron Maiden and nobody else. Which wasn't the case! I was there. It's frustrating for me, as a crew member and road manager of Paul's over the years, every rock magazine is like the Iron Maiden weekly and they tend to forget about everybody else at the time. The Crusade thing was always three band bills, rotating. Samson did every show but then the other bands rotated; Angel Witch, Saxon, Maiden, I've got handouts and tickets floating about of Samson & Angel Witch... then in little letters at the bottom 'with Iron Maiden'."

[36] Spencer Leigh interview, BBC Radio Merseyside 1990

[37] www.battlehelm.com/interviews/Samson.html – retrieved December 2006

[38] Exclusive unpublished extract taken from the forthcoming Paul Samson biog *Burning Emotion*, courtesy Rob Grain, copyright The Paul Samson Estate and reproduced with respectful thanks.

[39] Ibid.

[40] Ibid.

[41] Thunderstick remembers it a little differently, however: That was at Guildford – they ate half of our rider and what happened after that I don't know. Whether Ramkup got hold of [other people] ... to throw them off the tour, 'cause Iron Maiden had eaten our peanut butter sandwiches or whatever? It's *Spinal Tap* isn't it? What can you say?! I remember it but I can't remember what the repercussions were, they ate half our rider – well, there you go. Such is life."

[42] Or, at least, some of them; the EMI compilation was based round bands who were in negotiations with, or already signed, to that label; hence no Def Leppard, Witchfynde, or even Saxon.

[43] Sorry. Truly. I'm really not that much of a geek. It could be a Mexican one.

[44] Probably also female, although the image is cropped in the exact place that makes it very difficult to confirm which gender it is.

[45] Exclusive unpublished extract taken from the forthcoming Paul Samson biog *Burning Emotion*, courtesy Rob Grain, copyright The Paul Samson Estate and reproduced with respectful thanks.

[46] Ibid.

[47] *Sounds* Interview, August 16, 1980

[48] Sorry Barry, nobody can forgive that one; go and stand in the corner and think about what you've done.

[49] Also see *Earth Girls Are Easy*, *Absolute Beginners* and more.

[50] i.e. what punk had morphed into; no OBHMs in this case.

[51] Thatcher had just been dubbed 'The Iron Maiden' by the British media in reference to her tough negotiation style in dealing with the U.S.S.R. that year

[52] Bruce later told interviewer Matthias of the Bruce Dickinson Wellbeing Network that "A piece of it with 'Vice Versa' appeared in the horror movie *Incubus*. If you look in *Incubus* and there is a big chunk of *Biceps Of Steel* in it with our heads going; 'She was a real two timer ...' just before some woman gets cut into pieces in a bathroom. I haven't seen *Incubus* but loads of [people] came up to me after, when I was in Maiden, saying, 'Wow, you're in *Incubus*.' And I'd go, 'I am?'

[53] As told to Henrik Johansson of http://www.bookofhours.net and reproduced with thanks

[54] All quotes from *Sounds* album review, June 1980

[55] *Head On* reissue sleevenotes, 2001

[56] *Sounds* Interview, August 16, 1980

[57] *Ready And Willing*, released June 30, 1980, EMI Intl.

[58] *Iron Maiden: Run To The Hills – The Authorised Biography* – Wall, M.

[59] Thunderstick: "Tony Platt took us for two weeks pre-production during which the songs changed dramatically. I've still got copies of the originals of all the Little Big Man and what have you, 'Nice Girl' originally was called 'Much The Miller', from Robin Hood, and 'Grime Crime' was originally called, 'Where Did All The Money Go?' which was a nice ditty. All the different versions, I still have the originals. He whittled them down and they became what they are now on *Shock Tactics*."

[60] Somewhat inevitably known as, 'Jane Jane'...

[61] *Sounds* interview – Robbi Millar, June 13 1981

[62] Ibid,

[63] *Record Mirror* Interview – Dante Bonutto, July 18, 1981

[64] As told to Henrik Johansson of http://www.bookofhours.net and reproduced with thanks, plus elements of interview with the author during February 2007

[65] I hate that term too but someone bet me a bottle of Jack Daniels to put it in, so apologies all round.

[66] http://www.classicrockrevisited.com/Interviews05/pauldianno05.htm – retrieved December 2006

[67] http://www.battlehelm.com/interviews/Pauldianno.html retrieved December 2006

[68] Later in the same Battlehelm interview he commented on his Maiden experience that, "It was kind of like joining the army in peace time and having a great time seeing the world and fucking all the women. But then, when it started to take off, it was like being in that same lovely army but now a fucking world war had just broken out. I hadn't signed up for that in the first place." The two Pauls – Di'Anno and D'Icko – perhaps have a lot more in common than at first glance.

[69] 'Classic Albums' – Number Of The Beast, Eagle Vision DVD

[70] Depending largely on who's telling the tale this sum ranges from £500,000 to a whopping £2.5 million. Either way, we're talking Krug and Caviar, not Frosty Jack and Sardines here.

[71] Andy Taylor, a college mate and accountant, the 'silent and steady' half of Sanctuary Management

[72] http://www.praying-mantis.com/mantis/dennis99.shtml Interview – retrieved January 2007

[73] This was a powerful avatar for Bruce's change of direction; his own sense of style was based round individuality rather than adherence to any heavy metal, or other, uniform that was expected of him. Having donned the leather was a powerful statement in itself if not also an affirmation that he had now moved on and reconciled the decision within himself. There are certain people around the scene at the time who refer to the Maiden 'uniform' rather disparagingly, and certainly too rude to repeat here.

[74] www.battlehelm.com/interviews/Samson.html – retrieved December 2006

[75] Chris Welch Interview, October 5, 1989.

[76] Bruce later told Henrik Johannson: "I had a very big moral contribution on 'Gangland' too. But 'Gangland' kind of sucks. 'Gangland' and 'Invaders' are my two least favourite songs on that record."

[77] Classic Albums – Number Of The Beast, Eagle Vision DVD

[78] 'The Village' was shot in Sir Bertram William Clough-Ellis' Italianate folly, Portmeirion, built in the Lleyn Peninsula of north Wales and refined between 1926 and 1976 to showcase the possibilities of developing an aesthetically pleasing architecture even in an area of such outstanding natural beauty.

[79] Classic Albums – Number Of The Beast, Eagle Vision DVD

[80] Bruce: "As a kid, I was always banging on the walls so I thought I would end up playing drums. The first bands that I really got into, in my opinion, all had fabulous drummers ... Ian Paice of Deep Purple, Bill Ward out of Sabbath, John Bonham, Keith Moon ... I loved Mooney's personality, in fact, he was a front-man who played the drums. But I also loved Ian Paice's ability and his technique, so I often fanaticised about being Ian Paice and Keith Moon all rolled into one. But it was an absolutely hopeless case because there was no way I was ever gonna get a drum kit. I mean, I couldn't even drive a car so how would I transport the kit?" – Fredrijk Helm interview, 2005

[81] Thunderstick: "It's always occurred to me that every Maiden song had that [galloping bass] – I always expected them to break into the Bonanza theme. We used to joke in Samson about it being, 'The Flight Of The Bumblebee on 78' – instant Iron Maiden!"

[82] BBC Radio Interview, 1990

[83] There's actually an alternative translation of the famous passage in the Book Of Revelation (Chapter13: Verse18) from a recently-discovered ancient Greek papyrus fragment – the oldest in existence – that offers 616, rather than 666, as the number in question; there is also a theory that the book itself is a political document, with numerical clues said to represent contemporary political figures including the Emperor Nero.

[84] Classic Albums' – Number Of The Beast, Eagle Vision DVD

[85] Rod Smallwood told me, when I interviewed him for Metal Hammer's Iron Maiden special issue: "I asked Derek to do a specific artwork of Eddie in hell, as a puppet of the Devil, but with Eddie having the Devil as a puppet. So it's like, 'Who's pulling whose strings?' And Derek did a wonderful interpretation of it, it has a very Bosch-like look to it. And when he brought it, I thought, 'Well, it's just too good, it should be an album sleeve.' We did a new one for [the single] 'Purgatory', which is the one where Eddie's head's rotting, and you've got half the devil's head coming from behind it. So

we had the artwork before we even started writing the album. But then when Steve had a song called 'Number Of The Beast', it obviously made sense. So that was sort of accidental in a way."

[86] As heard on the bootleg of that concert

[87] It was on this tour, so the story goes, that one particular reporter – not exactly enamoured of Dickinson's delivery – dubbed him as sounding like an out of control 'air raid siren'. Subsequently this became something of a badge of honour, of course.

[88] *Classic Albums' – Number Of The Beast*, Eagle Vision DVD

[89] *Enfer* Magazine Interview – Philippe Touchard, 1983

[90] Neal Kay: "Clive was a nice guy, very funny, and an absolute practical joker and a half. I roomed with him on one of the tours. Did some very bizarre things that I can't go into – to protect the innocent."

[91] Rob Grain: "There was some bad feeling in the Samson camp when they all first heard *Number Of The Beast*."

[92] *Enfer* Magazine Interview – Philippe Touchard, 1983

[93] Spencer Leigh interview, BBC Radio Merseyside 1990

[94] http://www.thebulletin.org/minutes-to-midnight/timeline.html – retrieved February 2007

[95] As quoted in *Infinite Dreams: Iron Maiden* – Bowler, D. & Dray, B

[96] Enfer Magazine Interview, Phillipe Touchard – October 1984

[97] '60 Second Interview' – James Ellis, *Metro* Newspaper

[98] *Sports Illustrated* Interview, Jack Mason, January 10, 1990

[99] *Metal Attack* Magazine Interview by Ace, September 1984

[100] *Iron Maiden: Run To The Hills – The Authorised Biography* – Wall, M.

[101] http://www.hardradio.com/shockwaves/dickinson2-6.html – Fredrik Hjelm retrieved November 2006

[102] *Sports Illustrated* Interview, Jack Mason, January 10, 1990

[103] *Hard Rock* Magazine Interview, Nelly Saupiquet, May 1986

[104] *Sports Illustrated* Interview, Jack Mason, January 10, 1990

[105] Spencer Leigh interview, BBC Radio Merseyside 1990

[106] http://www.nando.myacen.com/brucefans/index.php?option=
com_content&task=section&id=4&Itemid=26 – retrieved March 2007

[107] *Associated Press* Interview, July 1996

[108] http://www.moshville.co.uk/MusicPage/bruce.html – retrieved November 2006

[109] Spencer Leigh interview, BBC Radio Merseyside 1990

[110] *Hard Force* Magazine Interview, Sylvie Simmons – April 1988

[111] Ibid.

[112] http://www.hardradio.com/shockwaves/dickinson2-6.html – Fredrik Hjelm retrieved November 2006

[113] *Hard Force* Magazine Interview, 'Marc' – September 1987

[114] *Hard Force* Magazine Interview, Sylvie Simmons – April 1988

[115] According to liner notes in his 1985 LP, *Dream Of The Blue Turtles* Sting's track, 'Moon Over Bourbon Street' was inspired by this book; and The Damned's song, 'The Dog', from their 1982 Strawberries album also references the novel.

[116] *Kerrang!* Interview, October 1988

[117] Spencer Leigh interview, BBC Radio Merseyside 1990

[118] ibid.

[119] *Hard Force* Magazine Interview, Sylvie Simmons – April 1988

[120] *Kerrang!* Interview, October 1988

[121] Typically self-effacing, Bruce told *Metro* that it may be better to, "use caution on that one. It was the year the Olympic team were on holiday. In truth, I would probably have been about tenth."

[122] Spencer Leigh interview, BBC Radio Merseyside 1990

[123] From www.duellist.com: "Bruce started the company with the intention to provide the UK fencing population with products as good as that available on the continent but at an affordable cost. Enthusiastic reports about the quality of the equipment soon spread to far corners of the earth." So there you have it.

[124] http://www.stormbringerwebzine.co.uk/Interviews/ BruceDickinsonInterview.htm – retrieved December 2006

[125] Spencer Leigh interview, BBC Radio Merseyside 1990

[126] http://www.metaluk.com/interviews/viewInterview.cfm?iInterviewID=3 – retrieved November 2006

[127] *Hard Force* Magazine Interview, Henry Dumatray – September 1990

[128] Hartlepool natives are often warmly known as 'monkey hangers' after a – possibly apocryphal – tale where once, in the mists of the past, a monkey had washed up ashore after falling from a passing ship on which he was mascot. The Hartlepudians, not understanding the mad jabbering of said strange individual, tried the simian in a court of law, decreed that he was a French spy, and sentenced the ape to be hanged by the neck until he was dead. Fast forward a hundred years or two, and Hartlepool FC's mascot, H'Angus The Monkey, was elected mayor of the town. Twice. I am making none of this up, I swear it.

[129] http://www.screamforme.com/index.html – retrieved November 2006

[130] Spencer Leigh interview, BBC Radio Merseyside 1990

[131] The multitude of formats may also have helped a little, of course.

[132] *The Missionary Position*, Dickinson, B, – Sedgwick & Jackson, 1992. Bruce goes on to dedicate the book to his wife, son and imminent addition to the family. I can only agree with his wish for the UK to expand the bloody train timetables again; ever tried getting home from certain North Western cities after midnight on a weeknight? It's idiotic.

[133] *Hard Force* Magazine Interview – Henri Dumatrey. 1992

[134] NWOBHM expert, John Tucker: "I started losing interest a little when they were putting out albums that sounded like they were recorded in Steve Harris' barn – which they were."

[135] *Hard Force* Magazine Interview – Henri Dumatrey. 1992

[136] As told to Henrik Johansson and Matthias Rheinholdsson of http://www.bookofhours.net and reproduced with many thanks

[137] Olsen explains how to get a song sounding hi-hat-less: "Did you know that about the song? When you listen you'll be amazed, 'My God, there's no cymbal. How do you have a drummer to play with out any cymbals?'" – Dunno Keith, how do you do it? His answer: "You take them away." Oh yeah.

[138] He expands: "Back then, how you programmed this stuff was you entered in individual notes … This whole thing was done entering notes individually, my lord, talk about due diligence. It was boring, you know. Anal retentiveness, either one kind of fills the explanation of how programming was done back then. It was either that, or one of those MC1000 digital workstations. A midi input recorder. And that's how you did it. And at the time TOTO was over there in their studio, about five miles away. Putting together their record, I think it was TOTO 4, the same way. Putting it together note by note by note by note. But using that micro composer, that MC. It was unbelievable that it could work

that way. I don't know if that was TOTO 4 – it must have been TOTO 10 by then."

[139] Olsen: "We had two really good songs, and had two Number 1 hits in twenty six countries. Klaus wrote a really good melody and that's what he wrote. And there you go, they are The Scorpions and there is a guy whistling in the intro. That part of it wasn't my idea – I want you to know! That's about as German as you can get, *'Ve are die Scorpions and ve vill Vhistle!'*"

[140] *Kerrang!* Magazine Interview, April 1993

[141] *Hard Rock* Interview, Ravin' Pestos – November 1993

[142] *Kerrang!* Magazine Interview, April 1993

[143] *Hard Rock* Interview, Ravin' Pestos – November 1993

[144] Ibid.

[145] As told to Matthias Rheinholdsson of http://www.bookofhours.net and reproduced with many thanks

[146] ibid.

[147] http://www.geocities.com/sunsetstrip/club/5619/interviews/ shay_baby.htm – retrieved February 2007

[148] ibid,

[149] The title's taken from a rather yawnsome student-joke referring to that artist's cubist periods of 1907-1912 and later works from 1937 onwards,

[150] http://www.geocities.com/sunsetstrip/club/5619/interviews/bd1094.html – retrieved November 2006

[151] *Balls To Picasso* Sleevenotes – Ling, D, 2005

[152] http://www.screamforme.com/index.html – retrieved November 2006

[153] http://www.screamforme.com/index.html – retrieved November 2006

[154] Chris expands: "I can't remember where the mistakes were now, can anybody else spot them? If you can, email me through www.myspace.com/chrispaulodale and let me know."

[155] Never mind 'Jesus Juice', this super-strength lager is 'Jesus Never Again Juice'

[156] As told to Henrik Johansson of http://www.bookofhours.net and reproduced with many thanks

[157] www.moshville.co.uk/MusicPage/bruce.html – retrieved February 2007

[158] And it was not only musically that Jack Endino had an influence on Bruce: "I was the one who convinced him to try cutting his hair for the first time. I was half-joking, but then he blew our minds by showing up at the studio one day with short hair! So apparently he didn't need much convincing … and his wife Paddy thanked me and told me she LOVED it! And I will duly credit Bruce with turning me on to the original *Prisoner* TV series, which I will carry with me in my heart for the rest of my days. To conclude: Bruce is a very funny and delightful fellow. And I remain a huge Sack Trick fan."

[159] As told to Henrik Johansson of http://www.bookofhours.net and reproduced with many thanks

[160] As told to Henrik Johansson and Matthias Reinholdsson of http://www.bookofhours.net and reproduced with many thanks

[161] http://www.geocities.com/sunsetstrip/club/5619/interviews/bd1097.html – retrieved November 2006

[162] As told to Henrik Johansson and Matthias Reinholdsson of http://www.bookofhours.net and reproduced with many thanks

[163] http://www.geocities.com/sunsetstrip/club/5619/interviews/as1097.html – retrieved November 2006

[164] http://www.geocities.com/sunsetstrip/club/5619/interviews/081998.html – retrieved November 2006

[165] As told to Henrik Johansson and Matthias Reinholdsson of http://www.bookofhours.net and reproduced with many thanks

[166] http://www.geocities.com/sunsetstrip/club/5619/interviews/as1097.html – retrieved November 2006

[167] http://www.geocities.com/sunsetstrip/club/5619/interviews/bd1097.html – retrieved November 2006

[168] As told to Henrik Johansson and Matthias Reinholdsson of http://www.bookofhours.net and reproduced with many thanks

[169] *Iron Maiden: Run To The Hills – The Authorised Biography* – Wall, M.

[170] In the same interview, Bruce actually anticipated musical events of some seven years later, commenting that, "As the internet develops, it may very well be possible to do a couple of shows and have people download them. I could almost stay at home, you know, play some concerts with some friends and then people can download them subsequently." Step forward Sandi Thom, and give credit where it's due …

[171] http://www.hardradio.com/shockwaves/dickinson2-2.html – retrieved February 2007

[172] The skull went on to win Brazilian *Big Brother*, being by far the most charismatic and engaging member in the house. The Brazilian *Daily Star* commending the skull as a "fellow of infinite jest, of most excellent fancy."

[173] http://www.dprp.net/specials/ayreon/ayreon.html – retrieved December 2006

[174] http://www.hardradio.com/shockwaves/dickinson2-2.html – retrieved February 2007

[175] To be 100% accurate, Paul Anka wrote the English words to the 1967 French single, 'Comme d'habitude' by Jacques Revaux, Claude François and Gilles Thibault.

[176] http://www.heraldnet.com/stories/04/10/14/bus_maiden001.cfm – retrieved November 2006

[177] http://www.bookofhours.net/bdwbn/royint2005.htm – retrieved February 2007

[178] As posted on www.ozzfest.com August 2005

[179] Sanctuary release to the press, August 25, 2005

[180] Characters on that show including The Evil Wolf, Warm Jet, Pie, Helicopter-Face and Scrappy-Doo

[181] http://www.metalunderground.com/news/details.cfm?newsid=15199 as reported on August 25, 2005

[182] *The Sun* Newspaper Interview, August 28, 2005

[183] The author was lucky enough to be at Leeds and it was an incendiary performance from start to finish. Later he also lost all his mates and slept under an abandoned gazebo, with only chewing gum for sustenance.

[184] http://www.metalunderground.com/news/details.cfm?newsid=19752 – retrieved March 2007

[185] www.cavemanproductions.com – retrieved August 2006

[186] As quoted on http://www.brucefans.com/ – retrieved March 2007

[187] Toronto Star Interview, October 2006

[188] Matt's views on Maiden are discussed in *Trivium – The Mark Of Perseverance*, Shooman. J – Independent Music Press, September 2006, ISBN: 0955282209

[189] Tom expanded on the technical aspect: "I can tell you some very interesting things about the monitors he uses if you want. Basically they're these Belgian built absolute beasts and they're probably about 25-30 years old and the reason that he has them is so that he can stand on them, and that's about that … He only requests real ale in his dressing room every night, that's one of the only things that's on his rider."

There you have it.